Latin American Political Economy

Latin American Political Economy publishes new, relevant, and empirically-grounded scholarship that deepens our understanding of contemporary Latin American political economy and contributes to the formulation and evaluation of new theories that are both context-sensitive and subject to broader comparisons. Inspired by the need to provide new analytical perspectives for understanding the massive social, political, and economic transformations underway in Latin America, the series is directed at researchers and practitioners interested in resurrecting political economy as a primary research area in the developing world. In thematic terms, the series seeks to promote vital debate on the interactions between economic, political, and social processes; it is especially concerned with how findings may further our understanding of development models, the socio-political institutions that sustain them, and the practical problems they confront. In methodological terms, the series showcases cross-disciplinary research that is empirically rich and sensitive to context and that leads to new forms of description, concept formation, causal inference, and theoretical innovation. The series editors welcome submissions that address patterns of democratic politics, dependency and development, state formation and the rule of law, inequality and identity, and global linkages.

More information about this series at
https://link.springer.com/bookseries/14825

Ignacio Puente

Private Equity and Financial Development in Latin America

palgrave
macmillan

Ignacio Puente
Boston, MA, USA

Latin American Political Economy
ISBN 978-3-030-88982-1 ISBN 978-3-030-88983-8 (eBook)
https://doi.org/10.1007/978-3-030-88983-8

This Palgrave Macmillan imprint is published by the registered company Springer Nature Switzerland AG
The registered company address is: Gewerbestrasse 11, 6330 Cham, Switzerland

Acknowledgments

This book is based on my doctoral dissertation. Publishing it gives me an opportunity to reflect and be grateful for everyone who helped me through graduate school.

I would like to express my deepest appreciation to my dissertation committee. A wholeheartedly thank you to Ben Schneider. I am truly grateful for his mentorship throughout all the stages of the Ph.D. He is an inspiration and a model of advisor, who supported my professional development in innumerable ways. Suzanne Berger consistently push me toward harder and more consequential questions; I am honored she was part of my committee. I am also very grateful that Aldo Musacchio joined the committee and for the generosity of his feedback and advice. Danny Hidalgo certainly made this dissertation better. It was a real privilege to work and research with all of them.

I would also like to extend my thanks to those who inspired me to pursue a Ph.D. and made it possible to come to MIT. Sebastian Etchemendy sparked my interest for the political economy of development. I also cherish Alejandro Bonvecchi's advice through all stages of the Ph.D. Thank you to the Economics Department at UDESA who welcomed me; to colleagues at Hermes who nourished my curiosity for finance; and to Luis Schiumerini and Eddie Camp who guided me through the application process.

I have been fortunate to complete my doctoral studies at MIT's Political Science Department. Grad School would not have been such a memorable experience if it were not for so many remarkable and welcoming students, faculty, and staff. I was very lucky to be part of a graduate cohort of friends: Nicholas Intscher, Guillermo Toral, Marsin Alshamary, Kacie Miura, Nicolas Dumas, Rachel Esplin Odell, and Olivia Bergman. I am also grateful I had the chance to meet new colleagues that provided support and friendship throughout these years: Martin Liby Troein, Tesalia Rizzo, Loreto Cox, Danilo Limoeiro, Renato Lima de Oliveira, Emilia Simison, Isadora Cruxên, Matias Giannoni, Weihuang Wong, Rori Lekalake, Lukas Wolters, Minh Trinh, Remi Cura, Elisha Cohen, Peter Cummings, Belen Fernandez Milmanda, Pablo Balan, Juan Dodyk, Martin Gonzalez, Jimena Valdez, and Tom Bril. I learnt a lot from Matt Amengual during an awesome summer of fieldwork in Peru. And I am thankful for the time shared with Michael Piore.

I am deeply indebted to all the "anonymous" interviewees who shared their time, experiences, and networks and ultimately made this book possible. Special thanks to Lourdes Melgar and to the Jujnovsky family, a second home in Mexico. Rodrigo Bandeira Mello helped me land in Brazil, and Ignacio Garrido and Guillermo Toral hosted me. Loreto Cox and Erica Salvaj opened multiple doors in Chile, where I also counted with the help of Jeff Swiryn from Luksic Scholars and Lee Ullman; also, thanks to Roberto Rigobon for the introductions. I am also grateful for the time spent with IDB Invest's ESG team, in particular with Marta Viegas. I would also like to acknowledge the support from the Luksic Foundation, MIT Sloan Latin American Office, and the Center for International Studies.

I also wanted to thank the editorial team of Palgrave's Latin American Political Economy series, as well as to an anonymous reviewer for the insightful comments.

I am extremely privileged to be part of a beautiful family, whose encouragement and love bridged distance. I am grateful for my parents, my late grandfather, in-laws, sisters, brothers-in-law, nephews, and a group of friends who are already part of my family.

Grad school—and this book—was a shared journey. I would certainly not have been able to complete it without Mapu. On top of her dearest support, she is a true intellectual partner. We did fieldwork together, brainstormed arguments, and edited countless drafts. I very much look forward to continue our adventures together, and now with Oli!

To all of them, thank you!

Contents

Abbreviations

ABVCAP	Associação Brasileira de Private Equity e Venture Capital (Brazil)
ACAFI	Asociación Chilena de Administradores de Fondos de Inversión (Chile)
ACVC	Asociación Chilena de Venture Capital (Chile)
AFORE	Administradora de Fondos Para el Retiro (Mexico)
AFP	Administradora de Fondos de Pensión (Chile and Colombia)
AMEXCAP	Asociación Mexicana de Capital Privado (Mexico)
ANSES-FGS	Administración Nacional de la Seguridad Social—Fondo de Garantía de Sustentabilidad (Argentina)
ARCAP	Asociación Argentina de Capital Privado (Argentina)
BANCOLDEX	Banco de Comercio Exterior de Colombia
BNDES	Banco Nacional de Desenvolvimento Econômico e Social (Brazil)
BNDESPAR	BNDES Participações (Brazil)
CAF	Corporación Andina de Fomento
CKD	Certificado de Capital de Desarrollo
COLCAPITAL	Colombia Capital
CORFO	Corporación de Fomento de la Producción (Chile)
CVM	Comissão de Valores Mobiliários (Brazil)
DFI	Development Financial Institution
EMPEA	Emerging Markets Private Equity Association
ESG	Environmental, Social and Governance
FdF	Fondo de Fondos (Mexico)
FDN	Financiera de Desarrollo Nacional (Colombia)
FINEP	Financiadora de Estudos e Projectos (Brazil)

FIP	Fundo de Investimiento en Participacões
FONADIN	Fondo Nacional de Infraestructura (Mexico)
FONDCE	Fondo Fiduciario Para el Desarrollo del Capital Emprendedor (Argentina)
GP	General Partner
IDB	Inter-American Development Bank
IFC	International Financial Corporation
IPO	Initial Public Offering
LAVCA	Latin American Venture Capital Association
LP	Limited Partner
MDFI	Multilateral Development Financial Institution
MIF	Multilateral Investment Fund (IDB)
MNC	Multinational Company
NAFIN	Nacional Financiera (Mexico)
PE	Private Equity
PPP	Public-Private Partnership
SME	Small-Medium Enterprises
SOE	State-Owned Enterprise
VC	Venture Capital

List of Figures

List of Tables

CHAPTER 1

Introduction

This book is motivated by two observations. The first one is that three decades after democratization and liberalization reforms, Latin American capital markets remain underdeveloped. The second one is the amount of government-related funding behind private equity (PE) investors. Putting together these two observations and studying the emergence of private equity markets in Latin America, it proposes a shift in arguments about financial development and corporate governance reform: it emphasizes the role of institutional investors as an alternative to just focusing on the institutional—political and economic—determinants of investment.

Financial markets play a nodal role in capitalist economies. Well-functioning financial systems attract savings and channel them to productive investments. They encourage firm creation and competition, foster investment, and enhance productivity and innovation. There is strong evidence that a country's financial development is causally associated with its long-term economic growth and the material well-being of its population (Levine 2005; Levine et al. 2000; Rajan and Zingales 1998; Samila and Sorenson 2011). While there is broad consensus on the importance of finance for economic development, there is less agreement on the political economy dynamics behind the high degree of variation in financial development observed across countries.

I. Puente, *Private Equity and Financial Development in Latin America*, Latin American Political Economy, https://doi.org/10.1007/978-3-030-88983-8_1

Most of the political economy literature on financial development highlights the relevance of inclusive political and economic institutions. Open political systems, competitive markets, and secure property rights curb incumbents power and inhibit expropriation, unleashing capital markets (Girma and Shortland 2007; Haber et al. 2008; Menaldo and Yoo 2015; Rajan and Zingales 2003). Latin America made substantial advances in the key variables identified by this literature. In the last three decades, by consolidating democracy, Latin American political institutions have become more inclusive and executive-powers more constrained. Macroeconomies have mostly stabilized, privatization programs were implemented, and trade was liberalized. The regulatory frameworks of most Latin American financial systems also came closer to those of advanced economies: interest rates were deregulated, capital controls lifted, and legal reforms were passed to protect investor rights (Abiad et al. 2010). Still, in terms of outcomes, progress has been limited, in particular with respect to equity markets.

The market capitalization and liquidity of Latin American stock markets are significantly lower than what would be expected given the region's level of development (Heng et al. 2016; Schmukler et al. 2007). Firm ownership structures remain markedly concentrated and institutional investors are mostly absent, even among listed companies (De La Cruz et al. 2019). Corporate governance remains organized around families, multinational companies, or the state, making Latin American capitalism more hierarchical and arguably hurting its competitiveness and productivity (Caselli 2014; Schneider 2013).

Beyond Latin America, and at least over the last two decades, inclusive political and economic institutions do not seem to have great explanatory power either. Figure 1.1 displays the cross-sectional relationship between capital raised through initial public offerings (IPOs) at the country level and average scores for investor protections and democracy.[1] Shareholder legal protections do not appear to be associated with IPO activity (Guillén and Capron 2016). And democratic institutions have a weak but negative relationship with the amount of capital raised in stock markets (Huang 2010; Yang 2011). While far from conclusive, these correlations suggest

[1] IPOs are the process through which a private company goes public by selling its stocks to the general public. IPO proceeds is arguably a better indicator of stock market development than market capitalization figures (see, for example, discussion in Rajan and Zingales [2003]).

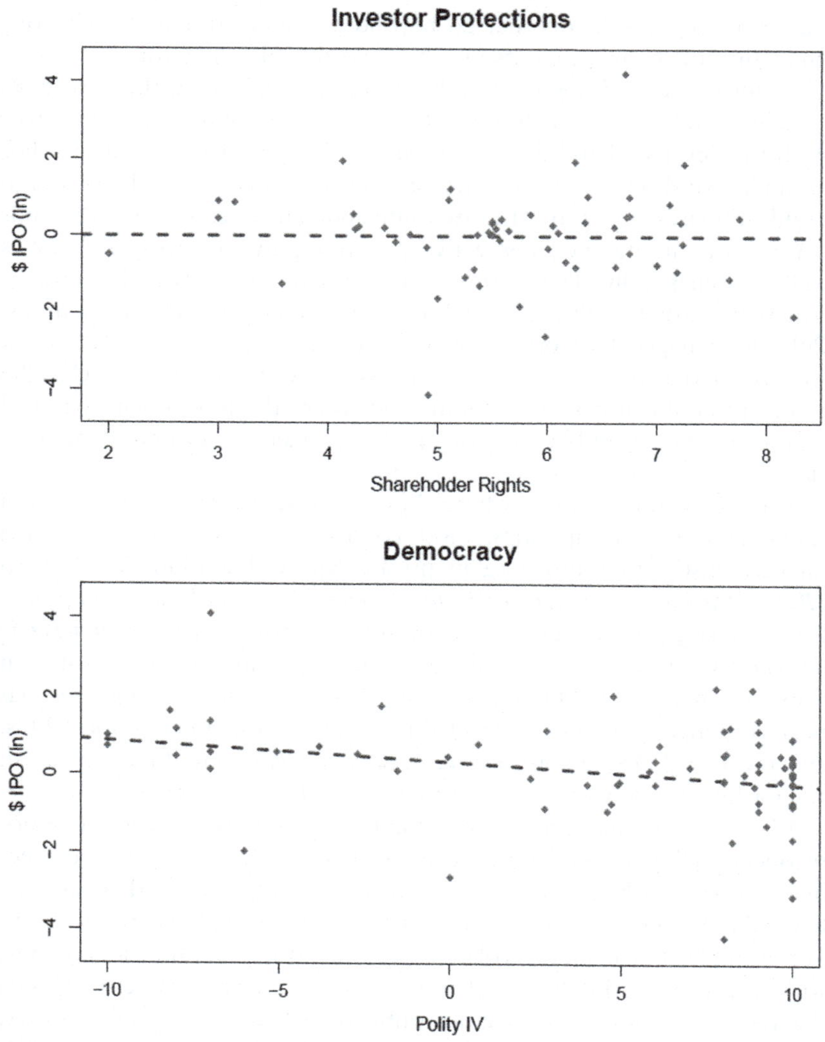

Fig. 1.1 Investor protections, democracy, and IPOs (*Note* Data from IPOs was obtained from Capital IQ and covers the 2002–2017 period for all countries with an active stock market. The y-axis plots the residuals after regressing the IPO proceeds ($) on country's GDP and GDP per capita. Data for shareholder protections comes from Guillén and Capron [2016]; democracy and executive constraints' scores are from Polity IV; controls are from the World Bank. Results are directionally unchanged when including GDP growth as a covariate, using executive constraints' scores instead of democracy, and excluding Hong Kong as an independent observation)

that exploring arguments that go beyond a framework based exclusively on institutional environments may be a worthwhile endeavor.

As for the second observation that motivated this book, there is significant government-related funding behind private equity investors across both the developed and the developing world (Brander et al. 2015). For example, Saudi money is behind the $100B mammoth SoftBank Vision Fund. Temasek and GIC, the two Singaporean sovereign wealth funds (SWF), are among the most active private equity investors, globally as well as domestically. The European Investment Fund (EIF) is Europe's largest investor in venture capital and mid-market private equity funds. Publicly-managed Canadian pension funds are one of the world's most sophisticated investors in alternative assets. And even in the US, the archetypical liberal market economy and where the private equity model is most extended, public pension funds are major investors in the asset class.

Even in Latin America, where these markets are less developed and states have weaker capacities, most countries have government-owned financial institutions investing in private equity. For example, BNDES *(Banco Nacional de Desenvolvimento Econômico e Social)*, a development bank, is a large private equity investor in Brazil; government-owned *Fondo de Fondos* pushed for the emergence of a private capital industry in Mexico; Chile's CORFO *(Corporación de Fomento de la Producción)* has been running a government-funded risk capital program since the 1990s, and the new FDN *(Financiera de Desarrollo Nacional)* functions as an anchor investor supporting infrastructure funds in Colombia.

Within Latin America, the development of equity markets does not reconcile well with rule-based arguments based only on constrained executives, open markets, and minority investor protections either, at least beyond the more extreme Argentinean (and, of course, Venezuelan) cases. For example, Brazil's more volatile, closed, and interventionist economy, with recurring fiscal deficits and an underfunded pension system, exhibits the region's largest and most institutionalized private capital industry, as well as the most active stock market. Chile, the richer, more stable, and market-oriented country in the region, with the largest privately-managed pension funds, exhibits a relatively smaller presence of private equity investors. And Chile's stock market, even though large in terms of market capitalization, is illiquid and has limited IPO activity. Then, what explains the emergence and institutionalization of PE and the development of stock markets in Latin America? And what can we learn from these experiences about more general questions on financial development and corporate governance reform?

This book makes three main arguments. First, it argues that private equity investors contribute to the development of financial systems by providing firms with a distinctive source of financing that has no bank-based substitutes. PE investors drive more institutional ownership and corporate governance structures, helping modernize business.

Second, it shows government-related investors play a relevant role during the emergence of domestic PE markets. In particular, multilateral and domestic development financial institutions appear to "incubate" the early stages of the PE industry, followed by the involvement of pension funds.

Third, and regarding the politics behind the emergence of this new market, it advances a "quiet politics" explanation. It emphasizes the role of asset-specific business associations created through the collaboration between industry participants and public agencies. These associations, in turn, help "co-create" the industry's regulatory framework. Operating at the margins of partisan politics and Congress, they push for regulations that allow fund managers to tap into pension funds resources, obtain tax benefits, create new investment vehicles, and help legitimize their investment model.

It is important to clarify upfront that while these agency-based arguments forefront policymaking, the outcome of interest is private sector development. The argument is not that development financial institutions are always effective, that bureaucrats have better capabilities to allocate capital than market participants, or that property rights are not important for development. Government programs aimed at enhancing private capital markets certainly face many trade-offs, non-trivial organizational capabilities are a pre-requisite for their effective implementation, and many of them fail and waste taxpayers' money (Lerner 2009). Recurrent state expropriation definitely inhibits financial development. And the book does not challenge the vast evidence that suggests well-defined and strongly protected property rights foster long-term development (Stephan Haggard et al. 2008). Instead, the argument is that it is hard to develop a private capital industry without a more active role of government than the one implied by most of the literature on financial development.

By providing evidence for these three arguments, this book hopefully makes several broader contributions, beyond its narrower interest in the development of private capital markets in Latin America.

First, it updates the typology of business actors in emerging economies and introduces a novel investor to the development debate. Private equity financing provides firms with a distinctive source of ***institutional***, ***risk***, and ***patient*** capital that has no bank-based substitute. Private equity firms can be described as hybrid organizations in at least three ways: (1) they broker international finance with local management, (2) they manage external—mostly institutional—capital but act as owners, and (3) even though they are financial investors, their role goes beyond solving capital constraints and include an active involvement in firm governance and management (Fuller 2016; Taylor 2016). The book highlights the centrality of finance, firm ownership structures, and corporate governance when thinking about productive development.

Second, it proposes a shift in the literature on financial development and corporate governance reform by presenting an actor-based approach that emphasizes the role of institutional investors—in particular development banks and pension funds—as an alternative to rule-based explanations centered just on investor protections and inclusive political institutions. Investor property rights, while most certainly relevant, are insufficient to explain the emergence of more dynamic private equity markets. The book suggests that these markets also have to be nurtured by government-related investors. Moreover, the regulatory reforms that encourage the emergence of private equity investors are made mostly outside of Congress and partisan politics and are not consistent with arguments that emphasize the relationship between democracy and financial development. Equity markets do not simply unleash with more constrained rulers. And reforms do not appear to be pushed by popular support. Instead, the case studies provide visibility to the "quiet" public–private collaboration behind the institutionalization of private capital markets. Private sector organizational capabilities appear to be a prerequisite for successful policy design and implementation. Public agencies often play a role facilitating collective action and shaping interest representation in order to have an organized business counterpart. Consistently across cases, fund manager industry associations emerge with strong support from domestic and multilateral agencies. In turn, these associations serve as the private sector counterparts of their sponsors and other public agencies, and help build the industry's regulatory framework. Overall, the book's findings introduce some skepticism to the literature's linear relationship between democracy, property rights protection, and financial development.

And third, the book introduces a novel model of "financial" productive policymaking. States promote private equity with the "horizontal" purpose of completing capital markets and making equity financing more accessible, and also channel public resources through privately-managed investment funds in a more targeted way, focusing on specific sectors and industries. This new policy model seems to be part of a paradigm shift in market interventions. It has finance at its core, intends to "crowd-in" other private investors, and has the private sector as the main provider of developmental solutions. At the expense of losing some control, states "outsource" productive development policymaking to PE firms. Doing so, they arguably achieve better governance schemes, improve their screening and monitoring capacities, and discourage rent-seeking (Inoue et al. 2013; Musacchio et al. 2015).

The rest of this chapter is organized as follows: first, it introduces private equity. It describes private equity's investment model, discusses evidence about its performance, and contrasts it with other corporate governance arrangements prevalent in the region. Second, it makes the case for why Latin America is an interesting, though unexpected, region to study this topic. Third, it comments on data sources and presents the methodological approach. And fourth, it gives an overview of the rest of the book.

1.1 What is Private Equity?[2]

I define the book's object of study as those investors who share three characteristics. First, they are financially oriented, in contrast to corporate—strategic—investors. Second, they have an active approach to management and, up to different extents, get involved in firm-level decision-making.[3] And third, they exhibit a medium to long-term investment horizon, in contrast, for example, to standard mutual funds. Regarding the *private* component of private equity, PE encompasses a group of "alternative"

[2] For a general introduction to private equity, see Cendrowski et al. (2011). For an introduction to private equity in emerging markets, see Leeds (2015).

[3] By investors that have an active approach to management I refer to those that participate in the operational and strategic decision-making of their portfolio companies. I am not referring here to hedge-funds "raiders" that buy public shares, obtain a seat in the company's board, and try to effect major changes in the company, usually described as "activist investors.".

and mostly illiquid assets defined in opposition to traditional public securities such as stocks and bonds that trade in open and more liquid markets. And PE investors mostly do *equity* investments rather than loans, which grants them ownership rights and enables them to have a more active approach to governance.

It is worth clarifying two concepts upfront. First, "public" securities refer to those financial instruments—typically stocks and bonds—that are listed on exchanges markets (e.g. New York Stock Exchange or B3 in São Paolo) and accessible to the general investor public. The "public" characterization does not refer to these instruments being state owned, but that they are traded in public markets. Second, throughout the text, private equity and private capital are used interchangeably, taking a broader definition that can include quasi-equity instruments such as convertible debt or mezzanine financing,[4] among others.

I group an "alternative" asset class that includes venture capital (VC), private equity (growth and buyout), as well as infrastructure investments.[5] Private equity and private capital more broadly serve as umbrella terms. The distinction between these sub-classes is fuzzy and context-specific: it can be based on industry (e.g. tech vs. infrastructure), risk profile (e.g. early stage vs. mature), or transaction size. Beyond the blurry definitions, the main reason to group these sub-classes is that they follow a similar business model and share similar regulatory requirements, and therefore are often part of the same industry associations.

Private equity allows the flow of institutional capital into firms outside of public markets. Institutional investors such as pension funds invest in private equity to complement their portfolio with more illiquid and risky assets, with the goal of enhancing their returns. They usually outsource the management of their PE investments to independent professional fund managers, typically organized into partnerships, who pool capital from various sources. Fund managers can specialize in a particular geography and/or market segment. This allows them to better screen

[4] Hybrid of debt and equity financing, typically senior only to common shares.

[5] The specific meaning of these different sub-classes is context-dependent and may induce some confusion. In its origin, private equity was mostly referred as venture capital, which was less associated with tech investments as it may be now. Then, the term private equity was more associated with leveraged buyouts. Given the industry's disparate reputations, different terms are also used strategically to legitimize the activity (e.g. risk and venture capital over private equity or buyouts).

investment opportunities, structure transactions, and provide oversight and guidance to their portfolio companies. They invest in concentrated stakes in a few companies, instead of having a well-diversified portfolio of public securities, as traditional asset managers do.[6]

PE managers are distinguished by their financial expertise (Ivashina and Kovner 2011). But they also have a hands-on approach with regard to their portfolio companies. What makes the private equity phenomenon more interesting is this dual role: they are not only external capital providers but also may provide strategic guidance to the firms they invest in. As opposed to portfolio investors who just "exit," private equity investors more often use their voice (Hirschman 1970).

PE fund managers exhibit a multi-level embeddedness as they are both closely related to international and local business communities. In order to secure financing, they have distinctive ties with international investors, acting as brokers of external funds into the countries they operate in. Many of them also participate in international networks of technology, entrepreneurship, and management. Global ties are fostered by career paths that include studying and working experiences outside of their home countries, mostly in the US. At the same time, these managers are also tightly integrated into local business communities. They usually form dense working networks with local entrepreneurs as well as with multiple intermediaries and service providers such as law, accounting, and consulting firms, pension funds, investment banks, business associations, and policymakers, among others.

In the US, the private equity model first emerged associated with venture capital and small business financing. But the industry grew in the eighties through the—typically highly leveraged—buyouts of larger and more established firms. The consolidation of the industry followed changes in pension system regulations, laxer regulations facilitating takeovers, and a paradigm shift in theories of financial economics centered on shareholder value (G. F. Davis 2009; Gompers 1994; Lazonick and O'Sullivan 2000). The growth of the PE model was part of a reaction to the agency costs of public markets and contributed to undermine the traditional model of a dispersed shareholder corporation with a clear separation between ownership and control. Jensen's (1989) seminal article argued that private equity firms would eventually become the dominant

[6] For a critical assessment of the LP-GP (i.e. investors-managers) relationship, see Phalippou (2020).

form of corporate organization, "eclipsing" the publicly held corporation with dispersed shareholders, low levels of debt, and managerial autonomy (Jensen and Meckling 1976). As an alternative to Berle and Means' (1932) model of the firm and to Chandler's (1977) multi-division business conglomerates, leveraged buyout organizations emerged as a governance technology that would provide superior results for shareholders based on concentrated ownership stakes usually involving some level of control, intensive use of debt-financing, high-powered incentives both at the partnership and at the portfolio company level, concentration in core competencies, and minimal overhead costs.

In this vein, PE is viewed as the ultimate expression of financial capitalism and the shareholder-value model. A controversial player, it is often portrayed as extracting rather than creating value (e.g. Eaton et al. 2019). Below I discuss the existing evidence of its impact over different dimensions. More importantly, I compare the model as it operates in the US, where it first emerged and is far more developed, with its functioning in less developed contexts such as Latin America. The sharp contrast between these two contexts suggests differences in both the political economy dynamics behind PE and on its implications. In Latin America, the overall low levels of external finance are arguably a preceding—and more fundamental—problem than its possible excesses.

PE was introduced to Latin America after the liberalization reforms of the 1990s, having the American model as a blueprint. But in this region, as well as in other emerging economies, private equity does not substitute a governance model of publicly-listed companies with dispersed shareholders. Instead, it has to emerge from an environment characterized by scant external finance from both banks and capital markets, traditional ownership structures and no market for corporate control. In contrast to its role in more developed capital markets, where private equity concentrates ownership as a way to check managers' autonomy, in underdeveloped economies, private equity is an alternative to traditional governance models organized around families and individuals. In a context where stock markets with dispersed ownership and unchecked managers are notably absent, PE plays a different role. It helps develop public capital markets, modernize firm ownership, and professionalize corporate governance models.

Notwithstanding these key contextual differences, PE in Latin America, as elsewhere, is certainly a force favoring the extension of markets and, for some, "financialization" (G. F. Davis and Kim 2015;

Philippon 2015; Storm 2018). Private equity investors are often portrayed as the forefront of financial globalization. And indeed fund managers often raise capital internationally, source deals in multiple countries, and operate through off-shore vehicles. Still, the private capital industry is also anchored by national-level institutions. And behind the expansion of markets—following a Polanyian logic (Polanyi 1944)—there are novel forms of policy interventions. As described throughout the book, states promote this new corporate player by investing in nascent private equity ventures, encouraging local institutional investors to follow their lead, and helping managers organize into business associations to co-create the industry's regulatory framework. But before engaging in the question about the industry's origin, the section below further describes some key elements of the private equity model and compares it to other ownership and governance models prevalent in the emerging world.

1.1.1 The PE Model: Finance, Governance, and Operations

The main novelties of this organizational model can be noted by analyzing its distinctive approach to financial management, governance, and operations (Kaplan and Strömberg 2001, 2009).

On the financial side, a central characteristic of private equity investors, particularly in the case of buyouts, is their intensive use of debt finance. Debt usually enjoys an advantageous tax treatment given the deductibility of interest payments, and leverage boosts returns and helps concentrate control. Moreover, the pressure to meet debt repayments disciplines management, avoiding slack and "empire building" practices. This aspect of the business model is often highlighted by its critics (e.g. Appelbaum and Batt 2014) as the heavy use of debt and the resulting high leverage ratios also increase firm's risk profiles, can induce moral hazard, and ultimately jeopardize the business sustainability.

Given the more volatile macroeconomic context and less developed debt markets, highly-leveraged strategies do not seem to be a great fit with the Latin American environment. During the nineties in Latin America, there were some cases of highly-leveraged buyouts (e.g. in Argentina, see Lerner et al. 1997). But generally, buyout transactions exhibit less leverage than in the US: the proportion of debt with respect to equity is lower, generating less risky capital structures. As shown later on, in Latin America, leverage is actually more associated with family control. There are no mega-buyouts such as the ones in the US and in Europe, which are usually the focus of critics to the industry. Instead, most transactions are in the equivalent of mid-and-small-market categories in the US. Transactions are usually growth-oriented and in almost all cases take place with the cooperation of management and shareholders (Leeds 2015).[7]

Regarding the sources of capital, PE funds tap into large pools of institutional financing. The main sponsors of this business model are public and private pension funds, insurance companies, university endowments, sovereign wealth funds, as well as wealthy individuals and their family offices. Retail investors are notably absent, except indirectly as pensioners.

Some of the larger international partnerships investing in Latin America have access to large "global capital allocators." Domestic and regional-focused fund managers also secure capital commitments from national and multilateral development financial institutions, local pension funds, as well as from wealthy individuals and families. But as discussed throughout the book, developing a domestic base of institutional fundraising sources is one of the key challenges for the Latin American industry.

Private equity firms exhibit a distinctive approach to compensation based on performance, in an attempt to make managers act more like owners. PE fund managers have compensation structures that make them participate in the upside of their investments.[8] They are also heavy users of high-powered incentives when approaching the governance of their portfolio firms (Leslie and Oyer 2008). In order to align the interests of

[7] A stark difference between the US and the Latin American more recent experience is the commonness of hostile takeovers. As opposed to what happens in the US, given Latin American shallow capital markets and concentrated ownership structures, most (if not all) deals are "friendly," meaning that they are executed with the active cooperation of existing management and founders/shareholders. Notably, in the US as elsewhere, private equity firms often invest in companies that are suffering from financial distress. Their financial and legal expertise makes PE investors particularly skilled to deal with debt refinancing and overall corporate restructuring (e.g. see, Hotchkiss et al. 2010; Johnston-Ross et al. 2020).

[8] Fund managers usually receive two types of compensation: they charge management fees (annual payments of around 2% of the capital committed). But they also receive a carried interest of typically 20% of the gains above a pre-established hurdle annual rate of return (often around 8%). To further align their incentives with their outside investors, they usually invest a substantial part of their wealth in the same funds they manage. They may also charge management fees to their portfolio companies (e.g. see Phalippou et al. 2018).

management and shareholders, for example, they often grant aggressive stock option schemes to senior executives.

Moreover, private equity firms have a hands-on approach to operations, in contrast to other financial investors who are limited to the passive buying and selling of securities (Acharya et al. 2013). After an investment, they may appoint some new managers recruited from their professional networks into key positions. And they also build more engaged board of directors that usually include partners of the fund together with industry experts.[9]

Firm-level evidence shows PE's more aggressive financial, governance, and operational model tends to improve firm performance. PE-owned firms are better managed (Bernstein and Sheen 2016; Bloom et al. 2015), grow faster (Bernstein et al. 2017; Boucly et al. 2011; J. Cohn and Towery 2013; Fracassi et al. 2020), innovate more (Lerner et al. 2011), and increase their overall productivity more (S. J. Davis et al. 2014, 2019; Kaplan 1989; Kaplan and Strömberg 2009) than non-PE-backed firms. These results apply not only for buyouts, but also to the less controversial cases of PE/VC firms investing in high-growth firms (Puri and Zarutskie 2012; Rin et al. 2013).

The PE model raises critical questions regarding labor relations. The strategies followed by new financial owners often entail layoffs and more flexible labor relations (Appelbaum and Batt 2014). Large-scale evidence from the US indeed shows buyouts increase the rates of job reallocation, i.e. greater job destruction and creation (S. J. Davis et al. 2014). For the case of public-to-private buyout transactions, where PE often plays a restructuring role, layoffs appear to be larger than new jobs, lowering net employment levels. In contrast, after private-to-private buyouts, firm-level net employment tends to rise relative to control firms (S. J. Davis et al. 2019). Studies on the labor effects of buyouts also suggest they tend to augment inequality at the micro-level by increasing the gap between

[9] When it comes to deal sourcing, there are also differences between the US well-institutionalized market and more informal Latin American practices. Instead of investment-bank brokered deals and competitive bids, which are the norm in the more formal and institutionalized US environment, self-sourced proprietary deals appear to be much more common in Latin America (Leeds 2015). This reinforces the importance of having a local presence with managers well embedded in the local business communities (Klonowski 2013).

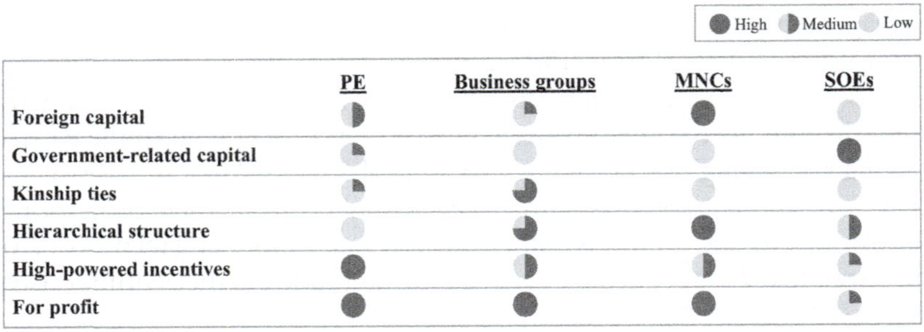

Fig. 1.2 PE in comparative perspective

productivity and earnings per worker (S. J. Davis et al. 2014, 2019; Kochan 2013).[10]

For venture capital and growth equity type of investments, there are fewer concerns around their effect on employment levels. These types of transactions are probably more comparable to the ones observed in Latin America. The empirical literature on private equity's impact on labor is mostly US-based. I am not aware of any systematic work done in Latin America beyond some reports from multilateral institutions on the employment generated by the funds they invest in. Still, given the type of transactions more prevalent in the region, PE investments are more likely to have an effect on Latin America's workforce productivity and formalization, rather than in overall employment levels.

1.1.2 *How are they Different? Groups, Multinationals, and State-Owned Enterprises*

Private equity investors propose a different governance arrangement than those traditionally prevalent in Latin America: business groups, multinational companies (MNCs), and state-owned enterprises (SOEs). Figure 1.2 compares these models on some key dimensions that are further developed below.

[10] There is an emergent empirical literature on the effects of private equity on labor. See, for example, Agrawal and Tambe (2016) work on private equity's effect on workers skills and their long-term career paths, or Cohn et al. (2019) on PE and workplace safety.

Business Groups

Schematically, private equity shares three characteristics with business groups: both exhibit a diversified portfolio across various and possibly unrelated industries, they invest in concentrated—majority or minority—positions and they are domestically embedded, although in different ways.

Many business groups have professionalized their management and integrated into global financial markets by developing ties to international investors. Similarly to private equity firms, business groups can function as brokers of international financing and domestic ventures. And "modern" business groups, who leverage their reputation in international financial markets and a distinctive pool of domestic managerial talent, have been characterized as a longer-term version of the private equity fund model (Colpan and Hikino 2018; Khanna and Yafeh 2007). Moreover, it is common for PE investors to co-invest and partner with groups. And business group owners are also investors in PE funds, usually through their family offices.

Still, there are some key differences between business groups and private equity.[11] In sharp contrast to the kinship relationships that often underlie business groups, members of PE partnerships and portfolio companies are professional managers who are not usually related through family ties. In contrast to business groups, PE firms are ultimately financial intermediaries, and the vast majority of the capital they control is provided externally (although to align incentives managers normally invest part of their personal wealth in the funds they manage). Therefore, business groups are possibly less accountable to their financiers. Also, business groups usually have "buy-and-hold" investment strategies with longer investment horizons relative to the typical 5–7 year timeframe of private equity investors. Business groups often have a more defined sectoral affiliation, in contrast to the sector-agnostic approach of PE. Moreover, it is common for business groups to cross-subsidize their different business units and to use pyramid schemes rather than keeping portfolio companies independent, which is the norm for PE firms.

[11] For an analysis of the origin, evolution, structure, and strategy of business groups, see Schneider (2009).

Multinational Companies and "Financial" FDI

While both PE and multinational companies can channel money from external sources, the contrast between them is starker.[12] There is a well-defined hierarchical relationship between MNCs parent company and their local subsidiaries, in contrast to PE portfolio companies' stand-alone status. Crucially, private equity firms have much greater autonomy in their capital allocation strategies and management than multinationals do. MNCs' more bureaucratic management style is at odds with PE's financial conception of the firm and the heavy use of high-powered incentives. And rather than focusing on small-high-growth ventures and the mid-market, multinationals usually control some of the largest companies in Latin America. Nevertheless, multinationals can enable private equity firms to complete their investment cycle. Multinationals may sell some of their operating units to PE funds and often provide an exit strategy to private equity firms, who sell their portfolio companies to MNCs.

Beyond its impact on corporate governance, the significance of PE investors also stems from the perspective of financial flows into emerging economies. As mentioned, private equity partnerships raise capital from various sources. Even though the share of domestic investors can be substantial, PE partnerships are vehicles of external funds into emerging economies, similar to MNCs.[13]

Both PE and MNC channel FDI into emerging markets. PE investors are financial players, as opposed to multinationals who have a more "strategic" and industry-specific approach. Still, the capital that PE investors mobilize would generally be categorized as FDI rather than as portfolio flows.[14] In line with the definition of FDI, private equity

[12] For an insightful comparison of the upgrading potential of MNC and VC-backed companies, see Fuller (2016).

[13] In Brazil, for example, around half of the PE capital is reported to come from foreign sources (KPMG-ABVCAP 2016).

[14] PE investment is arguably less pro-cyclical than portfolio flows but more volatile than traditional FDI. As mentioned, investments in private companies are fundamentally illiquid and cannot be easily cashed-out during an economic downturn. Fundraising volumes do follow international interest rates and global appetite for risk and exposure to emerging markets, but from the moment the capital is committed until it is deployed there can be a significant period of time, arguably making the deployment of capital somewhat less volatile. Moreover, once the capital is deployed, it is expected to remain locked-in for at

firms are usually foreign entities that through investment establish effective control or at least have a substantial influence over a local business, above the often used 10% voting-power threshold (OECD 2008).[15]

Private equity investors suggest a novel "financial" dimension to the typology of foreign direct investments that combine local management with foreign funding. Inquiring into the origins and impact of this new type of financial flow can contribute to "heterogeneities" arguments usually made about FDI (Alfaro 2017; Cohen 2007). PE investors can be present in a wide range of sectors, including commodities, infrastructure, services, and manufacturing, and can have market-seeking as well as export-oriented strategies. In the M&A vs. greenfield distinction, private equity—broadly defined—can fit both.[16] But PE investments are different from traditional FDI channeled through integrated MNC. As mentioned, PE investors often enjoy substantial autonomy from its international investors and keep their portfolio companies independent. Since they do not necessarily have industry expertise nor integrated operations, they are not likely to serve a role in transferring (non-managerial) technology. And they do not have a clear home country or "nationality" (e.g. Wellhausen 2014), at least in what refers to the origin of capital since they pool money from diverse sources and investment decisions are made by fund managers and not by investors.

least 5 to 7 years. Bernstein, Lerner, and Mezzanotti (2019) show evidence of PE's less pro-cyclical behavior during 2008's financial crisis.

[15] It is conceptually clear cross-border PE investments are under the FDI umbrella (OECD 2008); still, in terms of measurement, this categorization is more challenging. If the interest on FDI does not come from its macroeconomic impact on the balance of payments, usual metrics of FDI flows are probably flawed (Kerner 2014). For example, deals done by private equity firms are commonly conducted using offshore vehicles, by both the sell and the buy sides of the transaction, and debt from both international and domestic sources is used to finance the deals. These features obscure the way private equity investments are captured in cross-border accounting. Alternatively, when FDI accounting is approached using a survey or census microdata, it is not entirely clear whether portfolio companies managed by locals but ultimately "owned"—at least partially—by foreign capital would be considered as FDI. In any case, besides its empirical relevance, this measurement discussion helps distinguish conceptually whether the external origin of capital or the identity of the control/management is the relevant feature of FDI. Fuller (2016) argues the identity of firms' management, and not the origin of the capital, has a bigger influence on the type of operational strategy they pursue, which in turn has the greatest impact on technology upgrading and development.

[16] While traditional buyout operations are classified as M&A, VC funding or investment in new infrastructure projects would be considered as greenfield investments.

State-Owned Enterprises

Finally, even if PE's approach to management is at odds with how we think about "bureaucratic" state-owned enterprises that combine for-profit with social goals, there are some connections that can be drawn between the two models.

State-related investors are important sources of capital for private equity firms. PE funds raise a large portion of their funding from the pension system, partly from pension funds in developed countries, and also from local pension funds. Many of these pension funds are publicly managed. Development financial institutions also invest in PE, in both advanced and emerging economies. And sovereign wealth funds are also large private equity direct and indirect investors (Bernstein et al. 2013; Braunstein 2019), particularly in emerging economies. Interestingly, PE/VC funds are utilized by states as vehicles to "outsource" productive policymaking, arguably replacing the majority-owned SOE as a policy instrument.

Beyond financing, there are other interesting connections between SOEs and private equity. PE investors often enter new markets by participating in the privatization of state-owned enterprises. And many private equity investments are also made in companies "surrounding" SOEs as well as in public concessions (e.g. in Latin America Petrobras' pre-salt exploration and production activities, PPP programs, etc.).

1.2 Why Latin America?

At first glance, Latin America is not the most obvious region to study the development of private equity markets. Its private capital industry is recent and does not show high levels of penetration, in line with the region's overall under-developed capital markets. Still, there are good methodological and substantive reasons that make it a worthwhile object of study.

The region exhibits common macro-trends that "fix" some variables and enhance the comparability of the cases. The literature on financial development highlights the origin of a country's legal system (e.g. civil vs. common law) as one of the key long-term determinants of the depth of its capital markets (Aminadav and Papaioannou 2020; La Porta et al. 1998). Similarly, cultural arguments emphasize norms related to religion and the strength of kinship ties as important determinants of external finance (Bertrand and Schoar 2006; Stulz and Williamson 2003). Latin American countries share common colonial origins and therefore are comparable in terms of the origin of their legal systems and broader cultural characteristics (e.g. Catholicism, strength of family values, etc.). Latin American countries also followed similar patterns in terms of the timing of their democratization and liberalization. Countries are at roughly similar levels of development and are exposed to common international shocks (e.g. commodity cycle, capital flows to emerging markets, etc.). Still, there is variation in the development of the private equity markets—across countries but also within cases—that can help test the book's arguments.

Analyzing all the largest countries in a region instead of identifying lessons from successful cases also avoids biasing results by selecting on the dependent variable. Moreover, Latin American states are comparatively weaker—less capable and autonomous—than, for example, those in East Asia (Fukuyama 2014; Stephan Haggard and Kaufman 2008; Schrank 2007), in particular, with regard to their financial bureaucracies. Latin America is therefore a hard testing ground—a "least likely" region—for an argument based on the role of government-related investors and their capacity to shape business.

Corporate governance reform is a fairly novel topic for political economy academic work in Latin America. It is well documented how Latin America's extensive deregulation and liberalization in capital flows have tightened government budget constraints and limited the autonomy of macroeconomic policymaking (Campello 2015; Stephen Haggard and Maxfield 1996; Mosley 2003). But there is less understanding of how this increased financial integration affected corporate governance models nor of the politics behind it. This research contributes to closing this gap.

Most political economy work on corporate governance models in Latin America stresses either the stability (Aguilera and Crespi-Cladera 2016; Schneider 2008, 2013) or the adaptation of previous models (Musacchio and Lazzarini 2014). Schneider (2008, 2013) points to the continuities across countries and through time, given the complementarities between MNC, business groups, the political system, and other characteristics of "hierarchical" Latin American political economies. In contrast, this project inquires on the emergence of a new model of firm financing and governance. In particular, it focuses on the role public policies have fostering these changes.

Beyond scholarly novelty, other substantive reasons make the topic relevant. As already noted, the institutional environment in Latin America is different from the one in the US, where this model originally emerged and is more developed. This different context calls for a different argument about the emergence of private equity. It also suggests that private equity can have different implications. In Latin America, the sources of medium and long-term financing are scarce. Beyond a few large groups, firms are usually atomized, productivity levels are low, informality is high, and traditional governance structures and management practices centered on families prevail (Caselli 2014; Herrera and Lora 2005; Lemos and Scur 2012; Pagés 2010; Remes et al. 2019). This context urges the need for scale, enhanced productivity, and professionalization in order for firms to be competitive. These are all outcomes that can arguably be driven by PE investors.

The link between external finance and economic growth is well established. More recently, a compelling literature emphasizes the impact of management on productivity and overall firm performance and growth (Bloom et al. 2013; Bloom and Van Reenen 2007; Bruhn et al. 2010). In this realm, too, Latin America seems to lag behind (Bloom and Van Reenen 2010; Lemos and Scur 2012). As mentioned, PE investors not only provide capital but also get involved in management and the strategic guidance of their portfolio companies. PE-owned firms are closer to international best practices and the managerial frontier (Bloom et al. 2015).[17] In Latin America, private equity firms are not necessarily agents driving cutting-edge technical innovation, although maybe this is the case for some venture capital investors. The main role of PE firms is more mundane but perhaps even more important: to generate financial returns and create value by increasing productivity and modernizing the business. PE firms can increase productivity by allocating capital more efficiently, funding new business models, professionalizing management, modernizing governance and management practices, reducing operating costs, achieving scale, consolidating markets, cracking down on informality, and eventually helping firms upgrade functionally.

Overall, there are good methodological and substantive reasons to focus on the comparative study of Latin America countries, even if in this

[17] For further evidence of the role of PE/VC investors on firm-level outcomes, see, for example, Bernstein et al. (2017), Bernstein and Sheen (2016), Chemmanur et al. (2011), S. J. Davis et al. (2019), and Lerner et al. (2011).

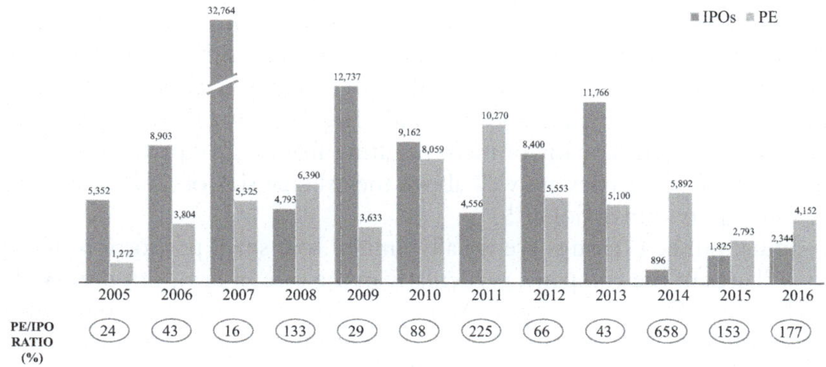

Fig. 1.3 IPOs vs. PE investments in Latin America ($MM)

region PE is far less developed than in advanced economies. Moreover, as the next section shows, PE is also a major source of external equity into firms in otherwise shallow capital markets.

1.2.1 PE Investment Volumes

Figure 1.3 compares annual private equity investments with capital raised through initial public offerings (IPOs) in Latin American stock markets.[18] IPOs are the process through which a private company goes public by selling its stock to the general public. Comparing private equity investments to the capital raised through initial listings seems natural: stock markets are the alternative to raising external equity financing.[19] It can be observed that, especially after a buoyant 2007 in Brazil,[20] public and private equity investments are of the same order of magnitude and roughly comparable. Beyond size, there are several reasons that arguably make private equity investments more consequential than IPOs.

[18] Bogotá, Buenos Aires, Lima, Mexico, Santiago, and São Paulo's stock exchanges.

[19] IPOs, as well as PE transactions, can be both "primary" and "secondary." Comparing private equity investments figures (a flow) with overall market capitalization or GDP (a stock) would not give an appropriate benchmark to grasp the relevance of this new asset class. "External" capital refers to investors from outside the firm, not necessarily foreign.

[20] Note that, for presentation purposes, the scale of the 2007 IPO bar is broken.

Private markets reach more companies. There are many more PE transactions than fundraising events in public markets. Stock markets often provide capital to much larger firms than the average company targeted by PE investors. IPO figures above include large banks, oil companies, and diversified holdings, many of them resulting from full or partial privatizations. These companies are well above the average size of Latin American private equity transactions.[21]

Initial public offerings are usually limited to a small proportion of the total shares of the company, particularly in the case of firms not previously backed by a financial investor. And these shares are usually bought by a large pool of passive investors, more detached from the governance of the firm. In contrast, PE investors often buy larger chunks of the total equity and in most cases have a more active role in leading the companies.

Importantly, IPOs are endogenous to previous private equity investments. As Chapter 3 shows, in Brazil, and to a lesser extent in Mexico, more than half of new listings are PE-backed companies that went public as part of the completion of their investment cycle (Minardi et al. 2013). The public market provides PE investors a feasible exit for their investments. Beyond blurring the comparison, this complementarity between private equity and stock markets has theoretical implications.

As the theory chapter discusses more thoroughly, at least in emerging markets, private equity functions less as a substitute and more as a complement to other forms of financing. PE is one of the main drivers of new stock market listings. PE investors also eventually need debt markets and banks to help finance their acquisitions. In this vein, I agree on the need to overcome the outdated dichotomy between bank and capital markets-based finance (Hardie et al. 2013). This dichotomy is a core assumption of classic comparative political economy (Zysman 1983) that hardly applies to present-day emerging economies: commercial banks do not provide equity capital to firms, and even in their loan business, they are mostly focused on consumer financing (Beck et al. 2012). While PE firms are certainly a financial player representative of liberal market economies centered on shareholder value, their illiquid concentrated holdings resemble the block-holders of coordinated systems.

[21] During the 2005–2016 period, the average private equity transaction was of around $30 million (with a large dispersion), compared to an average of $470 million raised in an initial public offering (Lavca, EMPEA, and Capital IQ).

From a political science perspective concerned with how power is projected from the private sector into the political sphere, private equity is particularly interesting because it usually entails changes in firm ownership and control. Most political science work on finance is focused on bank debt and capital markets (Stallings and Studart 2006). Debt does not directly change firm ownership. On the contrary, it mostly leverages the stake of incumbents. And the free-float[22] of Latin American listed companies is usually limited to a minority portion of their total shares (De La Cruz et al. 2019). Therefore, public equities transactions are usually less consequential in terms of control. Chile is a good example: public market capitalization figures are impressive and reach levels comparable to those of developed countries as the main business groups and several multinationals are listed in the domestic stock market. But the portion of total shares that are traded in the market is low.[23] Family-controlled groups often retain a majority and therefore have control over decision-making.

Overall, private equity seems to be a relevant asset class, both in value and in the number of companies invested. In a context of shallow public equity markets, private capital funds are a significant source of external equity into companies. And even if the magnitude of PE in Latin America is incipient compared to other regions, there are good methodological and substantive reasons that make it worthy of study.

1.3 Data and Research Methods

The prominence of business as a key economic and political actor in Latin America contrasts with its absence from the region's research agenda. This void exists not only in political science, but it is widespread to other disciplines. It is argued that this gap responds, at least in part, to methodological reasons. Outside of the US, the costs of acquiring systematic information on business are high (Schneider 2014). This is especially true for the type of investors we are focusing on: "private equity" encompasses a group of private asset classes defined in opposition to public securities. Public securities are traded in open and transparent markets where information is widely available; instead, private companies have

[22] Proportion of outstanding shares that are available to the public for trade.

[23] At the end of 2017, the average free float in Chile's listed companies is of only 16% of the total shares, see De La Cruz et al. (2019). Relatedly, its stock market turnover and liquidity ratios are also relatively low.

less demanding—if at all—disclosure requirements. If PE is in general an opaque asset class (Brown et al. 2015; Jeng and Lerner 2016), this is even more the case in low-institutionalized markets such as Latin America (Leeds 2015, 8).

The lack of information makes it particularly cumbersome when evaluating the financial performance of private investment funds.[24] The study of "abnormal returns" (i.e. the difference between the actual and the expected return of an asset) is the focus of empirical finance. The relative returns of PE investments are not the focus of this research, more interested in the question of its origins and development, although it is contextually relevant as it affects the sustainability of the business model. To build the country case studies that are the empirical backbone of the book, I triangulated several data sources.

I complemented a firm-level manually-collected dataset with reports and data compiled by the two regional private equity industry associations, EMPEA and LAVCA. Information from national private equity associations in each country is also leveraged throughout the book, even though comparisons are not always straightforward given the heterogeneity in regulations and the lack of standards and common definitions about what is considered private equity. Other providers of financial information such as Preqin and Capital IQ also helped identify private equity partnerships in the region and some of their portfolio companies. These sources helped measure the relative penetration of private equity in each country. I am not aware of other academic comparative analysis of the emergence and institutionalization of PE/VC across Latin America. Still, there are several industry reports, case studies, and multilateral's program evaluations (e.g. Rodríguez Guzmán et al. 2015), as well as some—mostly finance-oriented—academic literature that helped me build the case studies. Most of these sources are country specific. Brazil is the case that has more secondary sources available, given it is the country with the oldest and most institutionalized PE industry.

Most importantly, all these secondary sources of information were augmented with extensive primary fieldwork. I traveled to the business centers of the five countries that are the focus of the book: Bogotá (Colombia), Buenos Aires (Argentina), Mexico City (Mexico), Santiago (Chile), and São Paulo and Rio de Janeiro in Brazil. In each of these cities,

[24] See Harris et al. (2014); for this discussion applied to the Brazilian case, see Minardi et al. (2014).

I conducted semi-structured interviews with relevant actors involved in the sector in order to better understand the emergence of their private equity market. On the private sector side, I interviewed fund managers and other businesspeople, pension fund executives, entrepreneurs, and lawyers. I also engaged with the private equity business association of each country, as well as with the regional industry association. Regarding the public sector, I interviewed current and former officers of domestic and multilateral development financial institutions, securities, and pension regulators, among others.

The empirical leverage comes mostly from the detailed case studies that trace the development of domestic private capital markets between the early 2000s and 2017, approximately, in each of Latin America's largest countries: Argentina, Brazil. Chile, Colombia, and Mexico. These cases exhibit some common patterns that support the book's main arguments: the presence of government-related investors, the public sponsorship of business associations, and the "quiet politics" logic of the industry's regulation. The arguments are also backed by cross-national comparisons. Institutional variables cannot fully explain the variation observed across cases. Instead, where there was an earlier and more systematic support for the industry, private equity markets are also more developed—even considering the many flaws public investment programs have. Within case, cross-time comparisons also provide some extra leverage for parts of the overall argument.

This qualitative approach, in line with the comparative political economy tradition, is well suited to understand the role of actors, which is central to address the "origins" question. This approach can also lead to more concrete policy implications, as it is closer to the trade-offs faced by the different actors. Since private equity is still an incipient phenomenon in many emerging economies and data quality is challenging, it is harder to take a broader cross-national approach.

A micro-level approach is best suited to study the "consequences" and not the origins of private equity. In order to evaluate some of the implications of this corporate governance model, the otherwise qualitative approach is complemented with firm-level analyses. I collected raw data from each country's securities regulator and systematized it. The result is a novel dataset of the detailed ownership structure and family ties of all companies that listed in Latin American stock markets since the early 2000s until 2017. High-quality data from listed companies, together with individual-level biographical data, enabled the evaluation of the relationship between private equity and corporate governance at the micro-level. This analysis, displayed in Chapter 3, suggests that PE investors are indeed a driver of more modern corporate governance models: PE investors are behind a large proportion of new stock market listings and companies backed by PE investors appear to have a more dispersed shareholder structure and fewer kinship ties within their leadership positions.

Finally, I also gathered primary and secondary data on a variety of emerging and developed countries outside of Latin America, in order to contextualize the case studies and provide external validity to the book's arguments. In particular, I inventoried both present and historical government-related programs aimed toward the development of private equity markets in the US, Europe, and Asia, and also benchmarked the argument about the politics behind the emergence of private equity markets with cases outside the region. Chapter 6 presents these analyses.

1.4 Plan of the Book

In the last couple of decades, Latin American countries have liberalized both economically and politically, and passed reforms granting investor protections—conditions identified as key determinants for financial development. Still, their capital markets exhibit limited progress. To explain capital market development, this book proposes to focus directly on the role of institutional investors, rather than just focusing on institutional environments. To develop the argument, it narrows the object of study to the emergence of private equity markets. This first chapter introduced the PE investing model and discussed its relevance. Then, it presented the methodological approach centered on five case studies that cover Latin America's largest economies, and complemented by firm-level evidence.

Following this introduction, Chapter 2 presents the book's main theoretical contributions. It connects the question about the origins of private equity markets with the broader literatures on financial development and corporate governance reform. Institutional arguments focused on the long-term determinants of investor protections cannot fully account for the emergence of private capital markets. To complement this approach, the book emphasizes the role of different types of institutional investors—multilateral and domestic development banks, and pension funds—and discusses how they nurture capital markets. With respect to existing approaches to corporate governance reform, it discusses the literature's focus on macro-societal variables such as regime type or the strength of organized labor. Instead, it highlights the "quiet politics" role played by asset-specific industry associations. These business associations, which emerge with strong public support, then lobby to create a working regulatory framework. This policy-based argument also contributes to update arguments that associate state intervention in financial markets with bank-based financial systems, and introduces a novel model for financial productive—industrial—policymaking.

The theory section is followed by four empirical chapters. Chapter 3 provides firm-level evidence to support the argument that private equity investors are indeed drivers of more institutional—as an alternative to family-centered—corporate governance structures. PE-backed companies have more dispersed ownership structures and exhibit fewer kinship ties among its leadership. Moreover, this chapter ranks the penetration of private equity across Latin American countries by triangulating multiple data sources and shows it is not consistent with the main hypotheses from the literature. For example, Brazil, the most closed and interventionist country in the region, is the leader in the industry and overtakes other countries who outperform in most of the variables that the literature associates with the development of capital markets.

Chapters 4 and 5—the core empirical sections of the book—introduce and analyze the case studies. Chapter 4 shows how government-related financial institutions, domestic and multilateral, have attempted to promote the private capital industry by channeling capital into privately-managed equity funds. This is the case, for example, of BNDESPAR in Brazil, *Fondo de Fondos* in Mexico, and CORFO in Chile. The case studies also suggest that the entrance of pension funds into the market is an essential step for the nascent PE industry.

Chapter 5 explores the politics behind the key regulations that helped institutionalize the emerging private capital industry. It shows how domestic and multilateral agencies promoted fund managers' collective action and helped them establish asset-specific business associations. In turn, it describes how these industry associations lobbied to obtain some key regulations. In particular, they pushed for the creation of tax-incentivized investment vehicles and to access pension fund's resources. Notably, these business associations tried to keep their policy arena outside of the domain of Congress and large partisan politics. Suggestively, this "quiet politics" behavior is at odds with the mechanisms implicit in arguments that associate democratic politics with financial development and corporate governance reform.

Chapter 6 extends the scope of the arguments outside of Latin America and explores cases from other regions. Indeed, it finds evidence that governments also acted as early investors in the US, Europe, and Asia, playing an important role in the emergence of private equity markets in those regions. In most of the cases analyzed, government-related financial institutions together with pension funds are the largest investors in the asset class. This provides external validity to the findings from the Latin American cases and shows that more successful cases outside this region also exhibit a pervasive role of government-related financial institutions during early stages of market development. Beyond the state's role as an investor, outside of Latin America, public agencies also helped organize PE fund managers into asset-specific industry associations. In turn, these associations had an important role co-producing the industry's regulatory environment. And more generally, outside of Latin America, most of the reforms that help structure private capital markets also appear to follow a quiet politics logic.

To wrap up, the conclusion discusses the main contributions of the book, explores its implications, and acknowledges some of its limitations. Most importantly, it emphasizes the nodal role of institutional investors in shaping firm ownership and corporate governance practices and proposes a research agenda on the political economy of financial development and corporate governance reform based on the role of pension funds.

References

Abiad, Abdul, Enrica Detragiache, and Thierry Tressel. 2010. A New Database of Financial Reforms. *IMF Staff Papers* 57 (2): 281–302.

Acharya, Viral V., Oliver F. Gottschalg, Moritz Hahn, and Conor Kehoe. 2013. Corporate Governance and Value Creation: Evidence from Private Equity. *The Review of Financial Studies* 26 (2): 368–402.

Agrawal, Ashwini, and Prasanna Tambe. 2016. Private Equity and Workers' Career Paths: The Role of Technological Change. *Review of Financial Studies* 29 (9): 2455–2489.

Aguilera, Ruth V., and Rafel Crespi-Cladera. 2016. Global Corporate Governance: On the Relevance of Firms' Ownership Structure. *Journal of World Business* 51 (1): 50–57.

Alfaro, Laura. 2017. Gains from Foreign Direct Investment: Macro and Micro Approaches. *The World Bank Economic Review* 30: S2–15.

Aminadav, Gur, and Elias Papaioannou. 2020. Corporate Control around the World. *The Journal of Finance* 75 (3): 1191–1246.

Appelbaum, Eileen, and Rosemary Batt. 2014. *Private Equity at Work: When Wall Street Manages Main Street*. New York: Russell Sage Foundation.

Beck, Thorsten, Berrak Büyükkarabacak, Felix K. Rioja, and Neven T. Valev. 2012. Who Gets the Credit? And Does It Matter? Household vs. Firm Lending across Countries. *B.E. Journal of Macroeconomics* 12 (1): 1–46.

Berle, Adolf, and Gardiner Means. 1932. *The Modern Corporate and Private Property*.

Bernstein, Shai, and Albert Sheen. 2016. The Operational Consequences of Private Equity Buyouts: Evidence from the Restaurant Industry. *Review of Financial Studies* 29 (9): 2387–2418.

Bernstein, Shai, Josh Lerner, and Antoinette Schoar. 2013. The Investment Strategies of Sovereign Wealth Funds. *Journal of Economic Perspectives* 27 (2): 219–238.

Bernstein, Shai, Josh Lerner, and Filippo Mezzanotti. 2019. Private Equity and Financial Fragility During the Crisis. *The Review of Financial Studies* 32 (4): 1309–1373.

Bernstein, Shai, Josh Lerner, Morten Sorensen, and Per Strömberg. 2017. Private Equity and Industry Performance. *Management Science* 63 (4): 1198–1213.

Bertrand, Marianne, and Antoinette Schoar. 2006. The Role of Family in Family Firms. *Journal of Economic Perspectives* 20 (2): 73–96.

Bloom, Nicholas, et al. 2013. Does Management Matter? Evidence from India. *The Quarterly Journal of Economics* 128 (1): 1–51.

Bloom, Nicholas, and J. Van Reenen. 2007. Measuring and Explaining Management Practices Across Firms and Countries. *The Quarterly Journal of Economics* 122 (4): 1351–1408.

Bloom, Nicholas, Raffaella Sadun, and John Van Reenen. 2015. Do Private Equity Owned Firms Have Better Management Practices? *American Economic Review* 105 (5): 442–446.

Bloom, Nicholas, and John Van Reenen. 2010. Why Do Management Practices Differ across Firms and Countries? *Journal of Economic Perspectives* 24 (1): 203–224.

Boucly, Quentin, David Sraer, and David Thesmar. 2011. Growth LBOs. *Journal of Financial Economics* 102 (2): 432–453.

Brander, J.A., Q. Du, and T. Hellmann. 2015. The Effects of Government-Sponsored Venture Capital: International Evidence. *Review of Finance* 19 (2): 571–618.

Braunstein, Juergen. 2019. *Capital Choices. Sectoral Politics and the Variation of Sovereign Wealth Funds*. Ann Arbor, MI: University of Michigan Press.

Brown, Gregory W. et al. 2015. What Do Different Commercial Data Sets Tell Us About Private Equity Performance?. *SSRN Electronic Journal*.

Bruhn, Miriam, Dean Karlan, and Antoinette Schoar. 2010. What Capital Is Missing in Developing Countries? *American Economic Review* 100 (2): 629–633.

Campello, Daniela. 2015. *The Politics of Market Discipline in Latin America: Globalization and Democracy*. Cambridge: Cambridge University Press.

Caselli, Francesco. 2014. *The Latin American Efficiency Gap*.

Cendrowski, Harry., James P. Martin, Louis W. Petro, and Adam A. Wadecki. 2011. *Private Equity History, Governance, and Operations*. Wiley.

Chandler, Alfred Dupont. 1977. *The Visible Hand : The Managerial Revolution in American Business*. Cambridge: Belknap Press.

Chemmanur, Thomas J., Karthik Krishnan, and Debarshi K. Nandy. 2011. How Does Venture Capital Financing Improve Efficiency in Private Firms? A Look Beneath the Surface. *Review of Financial Studies* 24 (12): 4037–4090.

Cohn, Jonathan, and Erin Towery. 2013. *The Determinants and Consequences of Private Equity Buyouts of Private Firms: Evidence from U.S. Corporate Tax Returns*.

Cohn, Jonathan B., Nicole Nestoriak, and Malcolm Wardlaw. 2019. *Private Equity Buyouts and Workplace Safety*.

Cohen, Stephen D. 2007. *Multinational Corporations and Foreign Direct Investment : Avoiding Simplicity, Embracing Complexity*. Oxford: Oxford University Press.

Colpan, Asli M., and Takashi Hikino. 2018. *Business Groups in the West: Origins, Evolution, and Resilience Business Groups in the West: Origins, Evolution, and Resilience*. Oxford: Oxford University Press.

Davis, Gerald F. 2009. *Managed by the Markets: How Finance Re-Shaped America*. Oxford: Oxford University Press.

Davis, Gerald F., and Suntae Kim. 2015. Financialization of the Economy. *Annual Review of Sociology* 41 (1): 203–221.

Davis, Steven J., et al. 2014. Private Equity, Jobs, and Productivity. *The American Economic Review* 104: 3956–3990.

———. 2019. *The Economic Effects of Private Equity Buyouts*.

De La Cruz, A., A. Medina, and Y. Tang. 2019. *Owners of the World's Listed Companies*. OECD Capital Market Series, Paris.

Eaton, Charlie, Sabrina T. Howell, and Constantine Yannelis. 2019. When Investor Incentives and Consumer Interests Diverge: Private Equity in Higher Education. *The Review of Financial Studies* 33 (9): 4024–4060.

Fracassi, Cesare, Alessandro Previtero, and Albert Sheen. 2020. *Barbarians at the Store? Private Equity, Products, and Consumers*.

Fuller, Douglas B. 2016. *Paper Tigers, Hidden Dragons: Firms and the Political Economy of China's Technological Development*. New York: Oxford University Press.

Fukuyama, Francis. 2014. *Political Order and Political Decay*. ed. Straus and Giroux Farrar.

Girma, S., and A. Shortland. 2007. The Political Economy of Financial Development. *Oxford Economic Papers* 60 (4): 567–596.

Gompers, Paul A. 1994. The Rise and Fall of Venture Capital. *Business and Economic History* 23 (2): 1–24.

Guillén, Mauro F., and Laurence Capron. 2016. State Capacity, Minority Shareholder Protections, and Stock Market Development. *Administrative Science Quarterly* 61 (1): 125–160.

Haber, Stephen H., Douglass C. North, and Barry R. Weingast. 2008. *Political Institutions and Financial Development*. Stanford: Stanford University Press.

Haggard, Stephen, and Sylvia Maxfield. 1996. The Political Economy of Financial Internationalization in the Developing World. *International Organization* 50 (01): 35.

Haggard, Stephan, and Robert R. Kaufman. 2008. *Development, Democracy, and Welfare States : Latin America, East Asia, and Eastern Europe*. Princeton: Princeton University Press.

Haggard, Stephan, Andrew MacIntyre, and Lydia Tiede. 2008. The Rule of Law and Economic Development. *Annual Review of Political Science* 11 (1): 205–234.

Hardie, Iain, David Howarth, Sylvia Maxfield, and Amy Verdun. 2013. Banks and the False Dichotomy in the Comparative Political Economy of Finance. *World Politics* 65 (04): 691–728.

Harris, Robert S., Tim Jenkinson, and Steven N. Kaplan. 2014. Private Equity Performance: What Do We Know? *The Journal of Finance* 69 (5): 1851–1882.

Heng, Dyna et al. 2016. *Advancing Financial Development in Latin America and the Caribbean*.

Herrera, Ana Maria, and Eduardo Lora. 2005. Why So Small? Explaining the Size of Firms in Latin America. *The World Economy* 28 (7): 1005–1028.

Hirschman, Albert O. 1970. *Exit, Voice, and Loyalty : Responses to Decline in Firms, Organizations, and States*. Cambridge: Harvard University Press.

Hotchkiss, Edie, David C. Smith, and Per Strömberg. 2010. *Private Equity and the Resolution of Financial Distress*. National Bureau of Economic Research, Inc.

Huang, Yongfu. 2010. Political Institutions and Financial Development: An Empirical Study. *World Development* 38 (12): 1667–1677.

Inoue, Carlos F.K.V.., Sergio G. Lazzarini, and Aldo Musacchio. 2013. Leviathan as a Minority Shareholder: Firm-Level Implications of State Equity Purchases. *Academy of Management Journal* 56 (6): 1775–1801.

Ivashina, Victoria, and Anna Kovner. 2011. The Private Equity Advantage: Leveraged Buyout Firms and Relationship Banking. *The Review of Financial Studies* 24 (7): 2462–2498.

Jensen, Michael C., and William H. Meckling. 1976. Theory of the Firm: Managerial Behavior, Agency Costs and Ownership Structure. *Journal of Financial Economics* 3 (4): 305–360.

Jensen, Michael Cole. 1989. The Eclipse of the Public Corporation. *Harvard Business Review*, September.

Jeng, Leslie, and Josh Lerner. 2016. Making Private Data Accessible in an Opaque Industry: The Experience of the Private Capital Research Institute. *American Economic Review* 106 (5): 157–160.

Johnston-Ross, Emily, Song Ma, and Manju Puri. 2020. *Private Equity and Financial Stability: Evidence from Failed Bank Resolution in the Crisis.*

Kaplan, Steven N. 1989. The Effects of Management Buyouts on Operating Performance and Value. *Journal of Financial Economics* 24 (2): 217–254.

Kaplan, Steven N., and Per Strömberg. 2001. Venture Capitalists as Principals: Contracting, Screening, and Monitoring. *The American Economic Review* 91: 426–430.

Kaplan, Steven N., and Per Strömberg. 2009. Leveraged Buyouts and Private Equity. *Journal of Economic Perspectives* 23 (1): 121–146.

Kerner, Andrew. 2014. What We Talk About When We Talk About Foreign Direct Investment. *International Studies Quarterly* 58 (4): 804–815.

Khanna, Tarun, and Yishay Yafeh. 2007. Business Groups in Emerging Markets: Paragons or Parasites? *Journal of Economic Literature* 45 (2): 331–372.

Klonowski, Darek. 2013. Private Equity in Emerging Markets: The New Frontiers of International Finance. *Journal of Private Equity* 16 (2): 20–37.

Kochan, Thomas A. 2013. The American Jobs Crisis and Its Implication for the Future of Employment Policy: A Call for a New Jobs Compact. *ILR Review* 66 (2): 291–314.

KPMG-ABVCAP. 2016. Consolidação de Dados. Indústria de Private Equity e Venture Capital No Brasil—2016.

La., Porta, Florencio Lopez-de-Silanes. Rafael, Andrei Shleifer, and Robert W. Vishny. 1998. Law and Finance. *Journal of Political Economy* 106 (6): 1113–1155.

Lazonick, William, and Mary O'Sullivan. 2000. Maximizing Shareholder Value: A New Ideology for Corporate Governance. *Economy and Society* 29 (1): 13–35.

Leeds, Roger. 2015. *Private Equity Investing in Emerging Markets Private Equity Investing in Emerging Markets: Opportunities for Value Creation*. New York: Palgrave Macmillan US.

Lemos, Renata, and Daniela Scur. 2012. *Management Practices, Firm Ownership, and Productivity in Latin America.*

Lerner, Josh. 2009. *Boulevard of Broken Dreams: Why Public Efforts to Boost Entrepreneurship and Venture Capital Have Failed, and What to Do About It*. Princeton: Princeton University Press.

Lerner, Josh, Alex Hoye, and Gonzalo Pacanins. 1997. The Exxel Group.

Lerner, Josh, Morten Sorensen, and Per Strömberg. 2011. Private Equity and Long-Run Investment: The Case of Innovation. *The Journal of Finance* 66 (2): 445–477.

Leslie, Phillip, and Paul Oyer. 2008. Managerial Incentives and Strategic Change: Evidence from Private Equity. *National Bureau of Economic Research.*

Levine, Ross. 2005. Finance and Growth: Theory and Evidence. In *Handbook of Economic Growth*, ed. Philippe Aghion and Steven Durlauf, 865–934. Amsterdam: Elsevier.

Levine, Ross, Norman Loayza, and Thorsten Beck. 2000. Financial Intermediation and Growth: Causality and Causes. *Journal of Monetary Economics* 46 (1): 31–77.

Menaldo, Victor, and Daniel Yoo. 2015. Democracy, Elite Bias, and Financial Development in Latin America. *World Politics* 67 (04): 726–759.

Minardi, Andrea Maria, Guilherme Lopes Ferrari, and Pedro Carvalho Araújo-Tavares. 2013. Performances of Brazilian IPOs Backed by Private Equity. *Journal of Business Research* 66 (3): 448–455.

Minardi, Andrea Maria, Accioly Fonseca, Ricardo Vinicius Kanitz, and Rafael Honório Bassani. 2014. Private Equity and Venture Capital Industry Performance in Brazil: 1990–2013. *The Journal of Private Equity* 17: 48–58.

Mosley, Layna. 2003. *Global Capital and National Governments*. Cambridge: Cambridge University Press.

Musacchio, Aldo, and Sérgio. G. Lazzarini. 2014. *Reinventing State Capitalism: Leviathan in Business*. Brazil and Beyond: Harvard University Press.

Musacchio, Aldo, Sérgio. G. Lazzarini, and Ruth V. Aguilera. 2015. New Varieties of State Capitalism: Strategic and Governance Implications. *Academy of Management Perspectives* 29 (1): 115–131.

OECD. 2008. *OECD Benchmark Definition of Foreign Direct Investment —4th Edition.*

Pagés, Carmen. 2010. Big Questions about Small Firms. In *The Age of Productivity*, ed. Carmen Pagés, 207–222. New York: Palgrave Macmillan US.

Phalippou, Ludovic. 2020. *An Inconvenient Fact: Private Equity Returns & The Billionaire Factory.*

Philippon, Thomas. 2015. Has the US Finance Industry Become Less Efficient? On the Theory and Measurement of Financial Intermediation. *American Economic Review* 105 (4): 1408–1438.

Phalippou, Ludovic, Christian Rauch, and Marc Umber. 2018. Private Equity Portfolio Company Fees. *Journal of Financial Economics* 129 (3): 559–585.

Polanyi, Karl. 1944. *The Great Transformation: The Political and Economic Origins of Our Time*. Boston, MA: Beacon Press.

Puri, Manju, and Rebecca Zarutskie. 2012. On the Life Cycle Dynamics of Venture-Capital- and Non-Venture-Capital-Financed Firms. *The Journal of Finance* 67 (6): 2247–2293.

Rajan, Raghuram G., and Luigi Zingales. 1998. Financial Dependence and Growth. *The American Economic Review* 88: 559–586.

Rajan, Raghuram G., and Luigi Zingales. 2003. The Great Reversals: The Politics of Financial Development in the Twentieth Century. *Journal of Financial Economics* 69 (1): 5–50.

Remes, Jaana et al. 2019. *Latin America's Missing Middle.*

Rin, Marco da, Thomas Hellmann, and Manju Puri. 2013. A Survey of Venture Capital Research. In *Handbook of the Economics of Finance*, 573–648. Amsterdam: Elsevier B.V.

Rodríguez Guzmán, Guillermo, Juan Carlos Elorza, and Diana Mejia. 2015. *Private Equity y Venture Capital En America Latina.*

Samila, Sampsa, and Olav Sorenson. 2011. Venture Capital, Entrepreneurship, and Economic Growth. *Review of Economics and Statistics* 93 (1): 338–349.

Schmukler, Sergio L., Juan Carlos Gozzi, and Augusto De la Torre. 2007. Capital Market Development: Whither Latin America ?

Schneider, Ben Ross. 2008. Economic Liberalization and Corporate Governance: The Resilience of Business Groups in Latin America. *Comparative Politics* 40: 379–97.

Schneider, Ben Ross. 2009. A Comparative Political Economy of Diversified Business Groups, or How States Organize Big Business. *Review of International Political Economy* 16: 178–201.

Schneider, Ben Ross. 2013. *Hierarchical Capitalism in Latin America: Business, Labor, and the Challenges of Equitable Development.* Cambridge: Cambridge University Press.

Schneider, Ben Ross. 2014. Studying Political Economy in Latin America: Gaps and Methods. *Latin American Politics and Society* 56: 20–23.

Schrank, Andrew. 2007. Asian Industrialization in Latin American Perspective: The Limits to Institutional Analysis. *Latin American Politics and Society* 49 (2): 183–200.

Stallings, Barbara. 2006. *and Rogelio Studart. Finance for Development: Latin America in Comparative Perspective*. Washington, DC: Brookings Institutions Press.

Storm, Servaas. 2018. Financialization and Economic Development: A Debate on the Social Efficiency of Modern Finance. *Development and Change* 49 (2): 302–329.

Stulz, René M., and Rohan Williamson. 2003. Culture, Openness, and Finance. *Journal of Financial Economics* 70 (3): 313–349.

Taylor, March Zachary. 2016. *The Politics of Innovation. Why Some Countries Are Better than Others in Science & Technology*. New York: Oxford University Press.

Wellhausen, Rachel L. 2014. *The Shield of Nationality*. New York: Cambridge University Press.

Yang, Benhua. 2011. Does Democracy Foster Financial Development? An Empirical Analysis. *Economics Letters* 112 (3): 262–265.

Zysman, John. 1983. *Governments, Markets and Growth: Financial Systems and the Politics of Industrial Change*. Ithaca: Cornell University Press.

CHAPTER 2

Private Equity, Financial Development, and Corporate Governance Reform

Even after democratization and widespread liberalization, Latin American capital markets are underdeveloped, and other than through privatizations, corporate governance models remained mostly unchanged (Aguilera et al. 2012; Schneider 2008). Stock markets are shallow, and the ownership of the region's largest firms is concentrated among business groups, multinational companies, and the state (De La Cruz et al. 2019). The prevalence of firms organized around families has proved enduring, and kinship ties remain widespread in the corporate world. Lack of external finance[1] and traditional corporate governance models are arguably related to the region's low levels of investment, scant firm creation, weak competition, poor management practices (Lemos and Scur 2012), firms small size (Beck et al. 2008; Pagés 2010), low levels of innovation (Remes et al. 2019; Schneider 2013), and high levels of labor informality (Bruhn and Love 2014; Catão et al. 2009)—all factors that affect the region's long-run economic growth, disparity in income distribution, and incidence of poverty.

While most of the literature focuses on explaining the continuity of this low-level equilibrium (e.g. Schneider 2013), this book studies the sources

[1] For "external finance," I refer to funds obtained outside—external—to the firm (e.g. bank loan, equity investor), not necessarily from external—foreign—countries.

I. Puente, *Private Equity and Financial Development in Latin America*, Latin American Political Economy,
https://doi.org/10.1007/978-3-030-88983-8_2

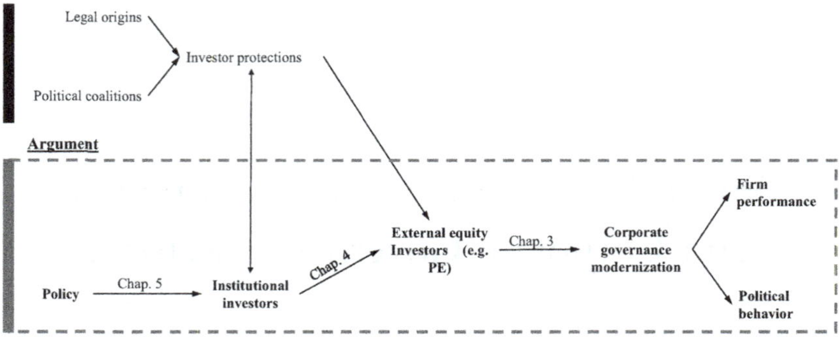

Fig. 2.1 Argument diagram

of corporate governance change. In order to do so, it focuses on Latin America's emerging private equity markets. As a key source of arms-length equity into companies, private equity investors are one of the few drivers of institutional equity investments and more professional management.

In line with a recent wave of research that argues for paying more attention to business and the private sector as an explanatory variable when thinking about development,[2] this research highlights the importance of bringing back finance into the productive development debate. More specifically, it helps introduce a new type of investor, asset managers focused on private equities, into the development debate (Fuller 2016). The main goal of the chapter is to frame the book's contributions into the broader literatures about financial development and corporate governance reform. To do this, first it discusses how a focus on private equity in emerging economies is relevant to these broader topics. Then, it engages with these two literatures and lays out the main contributions of this research. The main argument is sketched in Fig. 2.1.

As portrayed at the top of Fig. 2.1, most of the existing work on financial development focuses on the long-term more structural determinants of investor protections. As discussed below, arguments can be broadly grouped in two types: the legal origins (La Porta et al. 1998) and the political institutions views (Haber et al. 2008; Rajan and Zingales 2003). With adequate investor protections, financial markets will develop and

[2] See, for example, Fuller (2016), Jones Luong and Weinthal (2010), Post (2014), Taylor (2016), Wang (2015), and Yadav and Mukherjee (2016).

capital will flow into firms and drive more modern models of corporate governance.

But there is more to equity market development than institutional environments. To complement this approach, this book's argument shown in the bottom of the diagram has a shorter timeframe and focus on one narrower asset class: private equity. To justify this focus, Chapter 3 shows private equity investors are among the few drivers of institutional ownership in companies and ultimately of more "modern" corporate governance models. Chapter 4 focuses on the role of institutional investors who nurture private capital markets. As noted by the vertical arrow, investor protections—and the institutional environment more generally—certainly affect institutional investors, as, for example, they are recurrent targets of government expropriation. But as Chapter 4 shows, many of the early investors in the asset class are not just markets players. This is the case of multilateral and domestic development banks, as well as pension funds. And while analyzing the politics behind the emergence of this industry, the findings depart from existing hypotheses about corporate governance reform. Instead of focusing on macro-societal variables such as regime type or the strength of organized labor, my case studies highlight micro-level dynamics. In particular, Chapter 5 shows that in addition to the role as investors, public and multilateral agencies also foster private sector collective action and help organize the incipient industry. In turn, these industry-specific business associations, established as instances of private–public collaboration, help "co-create" the regulatory framework that institutionalizes the asset class.

This chapter engages with two intimately-related bodies of scholarship: on the one side the political economy literature on financial development; on the other, the literature on corporate governance reform. These literatures can be viewed as two sides of the same coin, at least in the developing world. External finance into companies, in particular in the form of equity, is the object of financial development. And changes in the types of ownership and control of firms driven by these external investments are a core corporate governance question.

These two bodies of literature come from somewhat different traditions. Financial development is associated with new economic institutionalism. Its main argument is aligned with an institutional approach to development centered on the importance of the rule of law, property rights, and contract enforcement. With a thin theory of change and functionalist mechanisms, the implications of institutional arguments are also more detached from active policymaking. While the book does not challenge the overall importance of property rights for development, it argues they are insufficient as an explanation/institution, at least for the case of equity markets (Guillén and Capron 2016). To explain the emergence of domestic private equity markets, it presents an actor-based argument that emphasizes the role of government-related institutional investors, in particular development banks and pension funds. These institutional investors, it is important to highlight, are not just intermediaries in a longer causal chain that goes from investor property rights protections to firm-level outcomes. Their origin is hardly market based, even if once in operation, they follow a more or less "commercial" approach to investing (and are, of course, recurrent targets of state expropriation). Development banks are, by definition, policy driven. And as for pension funds, they emerge as a by-product of the social security system. They raise funds from mandatory—forced—savings and their operations are heavily regulated. Different to institutional-based arguments, usually related to minority shareholder rights, this study focuses directly on the role of a specific type of investor and shows how, by organizing, they also help drive regulatory reform.

Arguments focused on corporate governance reform, on the other hand, come from a comparative political economy tradition that is more actor-based, usually having a macro-coalitional focus around the balance between labor and capital (Gourevitch and Shinn 2005; Roe 2003). In contrast, the book takes a micro-level approach that highlights the "quiet politics" (Culpepper 2010) role played by government-related domestic and multilateral financial institutions that help organize the emergent industry participants, who, in turn, lobby to access pension funds resources and to establish the legal and fiscal basis of the industry.

The argument is better portrayed as the emergence of a new industry rather than as a reform. Private equity in Latin America plays a different role than in more advanced economies. In the US as well as in other advanced economies, private equity grows as a reaction to managerial extensive autonomy. It concentrates ownership in order to reduce agency costs and better align the incentives of managers and shareholders (Michael Cole Jensen 1989; Kaplan and Strömberg 2009). But as Chapter 3 shows, in Latin America, private equity drives relatively more dispersed shareholding structures. With only a few widely-held (i.e. with a dispersed shareholder base) companies to begin with, without a relevant role for autonomous management, in Latin America, private equity is an alternative to the prevalence of family firms and arguably empowers more professional management. Private equity investors are related to arms-length, as opposed to kin-based, relationships across firm's leadership and owners, and generate more institutional and dispersed ownership structures.

Corporate governance has varying meanings across audiences, fields, and regions. In the US, where institutional capital is widespread and large companies usually have dispersed ownership structures, corporate governance research usually focuses on the micro-level behaviors and regulations underlying the relationship between shareholders and managers (e.g. poison pills, staggered boards, executive compensation, etc.), a topic mostly approached by corporate lawyers and financial economists (Bebchuk and Weisbach 2010). From a political economy perspective interested in comparative development, I do not conceptualize corporate governance just as the mechanisms to solve the agency problems that arise from the separation between ownership and control. Instead, I take a broader approach that compares corporate governance models prevalent outside the US and that deals with more fundamental questions related to the type of firm ownership and control, ultimately centered around who holds decision-making power across corporations: families, professional managers, banks, or bureaucrats (Morck 2005).

The rest of this chapter, first, justifies the focus on private equity financing and explain how it is related to financial development and corporate governance reform; second, discusses the literature's focus on investor protections; third, contrasts different—macro-societal—hypotheses regarding the sources of corporate governance reform; and fourth, engages with the literature about the role of the state in financial markets. Each of these sections also review the implications of the different hypotheses of the literature when applied to Latin America.

2.1 Financial Development and Private Equity

The connection between finance, economic growth, and overall development is well established. Historical arguments around the relationship between capital accumulation and development (e.g. Gerschenkron 1962; Goldsmith 1969) were augmented in the recent decades by a large empirical literature in economics. Addressing issues of causal identification through innovative research designs and rigorous econometrics, a series of studies presented conclusive evidence to support the claim that the availability of capital is an important causal antecedent of economic performance, and not just its consequence (Rajan and Zingales 1998; Samila and Sorenson 2011).[3] Finance fosters new investments, firm entry, and competition and through that, determines economies' long-run growth. While this literature mostly agrees there is a causal relationship between finance, growth, and economic development, the discussion about the political economy drivers of financial development is less settled. This book proposes to complement rule-based arguments built around investor protection with an actor-based argument centered on institutional investors.

My working definition of financial development is one focused on the availability of external capital for firms and entrepreneurs (Rajan and Zingales 2003), rather than on individual's access to financial services—for example, on access to banking or the digitalization of payment methods.[4] Within firms and entrepreneurs' access to arms-length external financing, I focus on the availability of external sources of equity financing. More specifically, the book focuses on a particular type of equity financing: one that is provided privately, as an alternative to just considering "public" stock markets. The rest of this section, first, explains the focus on equity investors rather than on external capital more broadly. And second, it discusses the relevance of private investors as opposed to more standard investors focused on public equities.

Equity holders are owners. And business owners are key political economy actors. This is the ultimate reason to focus on equity financing. As owners, equity-holders often have political rights (i.e. voting rights on issues such as board of director membership, the establishment of corporate objectives and policy, etc.) that grant them influence over a firm's decision-making (Aguilera and Crespi-Cladera 2016). As opposed to equity, debt or bank loans do not affect firms' ownership structure directly. And their holders do not get political rights besides some more broadly-defined covenants and therefore have only an indirect influence

[3] See King and Levine (1993), Levine et al. (2000), Beck et al. (2008), and Ayyagari et al. (2021). For a summary, see Levine (2005) and for a more recent evaluation of capital markets growth Laeven (2014).

[4] For a comprehensive discussion of the multiple dimensions of financial development, see World's Bank Global Financial Development framework (Cihak et al. 2012). Latin America has reasonable levels of access to financial services, at least given its level of development. But its financial markets, in particular the region's equity markets, are significantly underdeveloped, see Heng et al. (2016).

on decision-making. Equity holders are the ones who have a central role in the governance of the firm and determine the firm's management. In particular, external equity investors, those unrelated to the firm's founder, drive arms-length management and control of firms, help modernize corporate governance, and crowd-out kinship ties.

Importantly, this type of ownership and management—institutional as opposed to family-based—has been convincingly related to firm's productivity and performance (Bloom and Van Reenen 2007, 2010; Bloom et al. 2015; S. J. Davis et al. 2019; Parise et al. 2018). And beyond management practices and productivity, different ownership types affect firm's political behavior. For example, family businesspeople are often more connected politically than professional managers (Balan et al. 2021; Morck and Yeung 2004; Post 2014; Schneider 2013).

Related to the distinction between debt and equity, the literature on comparative capitalisms presents a sharp dichotomy between bank-based and capital market-based financial systems (Bril-Mascarenhas 2016; Hall and Soskice 2001; Zysman 1983). This dichotomy seems outdated, and banks can hardly function as a reliable source of patient capital any longer. As argued by Hardie et al. (2013), banks themselves are now much more market based and are less able to mitigate the impact of financial market pressures on their long-term client relationships, which was the key defining characteristic of banks as patient capital providers in coordinated market economies. Banks are increasingly focused on household lending (e.g. consumer credit and mortgages) rather than on long-term corporate loans (Beck et al. 2012). Relatedly, it is very hard for commercial banks to invest directly into the equity portion of businesses. The Basel Framework has homogenized banking regulation and limits the ability of banks to hold in their balance sheets long-term loans as well as stock of non-financial firms, given the enhanced risk and illiquidity, even from listed companies (Center for Global Development 2019). At least in Latin America, banks rarely hold any third-party stocks in their balance sheets and their loan business is mostly consumer-oriented. Moreover, the sharp increase in the participation of foreign banks in Latin America (Moguillansky et al. 2004) not always favored firm's access to credit.[5] So no matter the role banks played in postwar coordinated market

[5] Instead, there is some evidence that foreign bank entry limited firm and household access to finance. For example, Beck and Martinez Peria (2008) associate the increase of foreign banks participation in Mexico with a decline in bank's outreach. Beck et al.

economies or in East Asian developmental states—arguably providing long-term loans and holding equity stakes in non-financial firms with which they had established relationships—this can hardly be their role in contemporary Latin America. In terms of patient capital, it is clear that there is no bank-based substitute for an active equity market.

Indeed, private equity is usually associated with the heavy use of debt financing. In order to optimize a firm's capital structure, part of the private equity playbook includes leveraging portfolio companies with abundant debt (Kaplan and Strömberg 2009). This helps concentrate ownership and discipline management, and can magnify investor returns at the expense of increasing companies' risk profiles. In emerging economies such as those in Latin America, where corporate debt markets are not as developed and macroeconomic conditions more volatile, highly-leveraged private equity buyouts are rarer (Leeds 2015). Therefore, the association between private equity and debt is less straightforward. In fact, debt is less associated with private equity than with family ownership. As Chapter 3 shows using a cross-section of firms that listed in Latin American stock markets since the 2000s, and in line with empirical work in finance in Brazil and Chile, high leverage levels are correlated not with private equity but, if any, with family control.[6]

External equity into companies may come either through private or public equity markets. As showed in the first chapter, private capital markets are in terms of volume, at least, as relevant as public markets. Moreover, private equity investors are a significant driver of firms listing in the stock market. Therefore, PE could be thought of as an important antecedent condition for the growth of public equity markets: PE-backed companies appear to be more prone to listing in the public market, and when they do, they are more likely to have a more dispersed shareholder base and a larger free-float (i.e. proportion of the outstanding

(2018) show that foreign bank loans in Bolivia have shorter maturity than domestic bank loans (to the same group of firms) while relying more on collateral. Also see Mian (2006) and Gormley (2010). For a review of the literature on foreign banks, see Claessens and Van Horen (2014).

[6] See, for example, for the Chilean case, Larrain and Urzúa (2016) and Donelli et al. (2013), who show that ownership structure for business groups in Chile, most of them family controlled, did not change while the economy liberalized extensively. In terms of capital structure, if any, these groups seem to have concentrated their ownership structure and increased leverage. In Brazil, Kayo et al. (2018) show that family-owned firms tend to be more leveraged than non-family firms.

shares of a company owned by the investor public). Given their larger—and more illiquid—stakes, private equity investors are more involved in decision-making at the firm level, in contrast to portfolio investors in listed equities, who usually take a more passive approach to governance. And related to this activism and the illiquidity of their stakes, they are also usually more patient investors, holding their stakes for several years.

In more developed capital markets, the growth of private equity appears to be related to the decline in the number of listed companies (Doidge et al. 2017; Ewens and Farre-Mensa 2019; Mauboussin and Callahan 2020; McKinsey & Company 2019). Take-private buyouts delist companies from stock markets, and increasingly larger private fundraising rounds delay—or avoid altogether—IPOs. This trend also influences emerging economies. The "end-state" firm model is not necessarily the Berle-Means type of corporation, with atomized shareholdings and an absolute separation between ownership and management; instead, it most likely involves the coexistence of several large, institutional, block-holders.[7]

Without vigorous public markets to substitute, in an emerging context the main distinction in terms of corporate governance is less about public vs. private equities and more about the extent to which institutional investors replace traditional corporate governance models organized around individuals and family ownership, either through public or private equity stakes. Ownership and control type—institutional vs. individual/family—is therefore arguably a more fundamental variable than, for example, ownership concentration. The presence of institutional shareholders seems to be a more basic distinction than how dispersed these shareholders are, even if institutional investors raise their own agency issues (Bebchuk et al. 2017; Çelik and Isaksson 2013). While the Berle and Means model of atomized ownership structures empowers autonomous management, institutional ownership, even when concentrated, also creates room for professional management unrelated to the ultimate owners and crowds out kinship within the firm, modernizing corporate governance (Aggarwal et al. 2011; Hellmann and Puri 2002).

[7] The lack of atomized shareholders shifts corporate governance problem from a principal-agent to a principal-principal one. The key relationship is no longer the relationship between professional managers and dispersed shareholders but rather between controlling shareholders and minority shareholders (see, for example, Young et al. 2008).

Overall, studying private equity capital markets, broadly defined as to include all segments of this market (e.g. venture capital, growth equity, and buyouts), allows me to engage the broader literatures on financial development and on corporate governance reform. Moreover, certain attributes—adjectives—of alternative sources of capital are often highlighted: institutional origin, riskiness, and patience. As illustrated in Fig. 2.2, private equity arguably displays these attributes.

Raising capital from institutional sources such as pension funds and managed by professional investors, private equity funds are a distinctive source of ***institutional capital***, as an alternative to family and individual-related capital, otherwise prevalent in the developing world. Investing in the more risky tranches of a firm's capital structure, and different than providing loans against some collateral, PE also provides firms with ***risk capital***. Moreover, given the illiquidity of their holdings and the more active approach to management, private equity investors usually have relatively long holding periods, arguably warranting being classified as a source of ***patient capital***, at least among the class of financial investors, compared, for example, with portfolio investors (Ivashina and Lerner 2019). The sources of patient capital are a core political economy question that is widely discussed in comparative political literature (Deeg

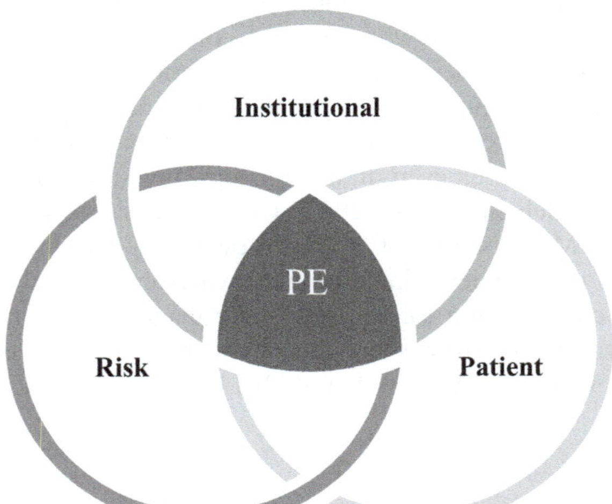

Fig. 2.2 Capital with adjectives

and Hardie 2016). Patient capital is associated with the VOC literature with bank-based finance in coordinated market economies. Highlighting the centrality of large pools of institutional capital, this book contributes to update this discussion and make it extensive to emerging contexts. Also, it elucidates the role of different actors in the investment chain, who are sometimes confused (e.g. portraying pension funds and private equity funds as alternative models, when pension funds are usually the largest source of capital then deployed by private equity firms). In sum, when considering the intersection between the three sets that contain alternative forms of financing that share some key characteristics—institutional, risk, and patient—in Fig. 2.2, there are hardly any substitutes for—broadly defined—private equity.

Across Latin America, the absence of external capital into firms, in particular in the form of equity, is notorious. The region's stock market is shallower than what it would be expected given the region's middle-income development levels, as shown in Fig. 2.3 that plots country-level data on stock market capitalization and liquidity as a proportion of GDP (Latin American countries are highlighted in orange). And private equity is only timidly emerging. The interventionist ISI period generated concentrated shareholdings and scant external capital; capital markets were re-launched only after the liberalization that started in the late

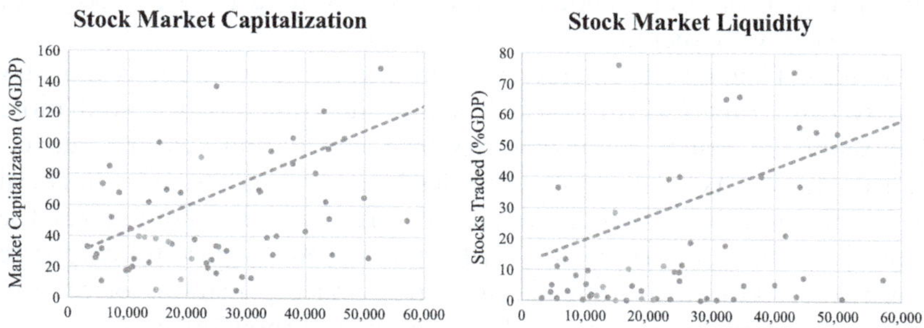

Fig. 2.3 Stock market development—cross-national comparison (*Note* Latin American countries are highlighted in orange. Data is from World Bank's Development Indicators)

eighties. But more than twenty years after extensive macro- and micro-level reforms, the Latin American financial systems remain underdeveloped and, if any, primarily bank based (Beck 2016; Heng et al. 2016; Stallings and Studart 2006).

The initial enthusiasm that followed successful programs of macroeconomic stabilization and extensive financial liberalization during the nineties soon gave room to disappointment. Despite intense micro-level reform efforts across the region (Abiad et al. 2010), that included changes in corporate law, privatizations, and pension system reforms, high expectations were not met and equity markets remain underdeveloped (Heng et al. 2016; Schmukler et al. 2007). Relatedly, after close to three decades of extensive liberalization, we do not observe major changes in corporate governance models other than those resulting from privatization programs (e.g. Aldunate et al. 2020).

The under-development of Latin American financial markets, particularly when it comes to its capital markets, does not make the topic less relevant, but arguably more pressing. Their continued shallowness despite the consolidation of democracy and extensive efforts of liberalization and reforms is in itself theoretically puzzling and calls for explanations alternative to those that focus exclusively on institutional environments. More substantively, scant levels of external capital into firms are arguably one of the key bottlenecks to the region's private sector development, affecting firm productivity and competitiveness, and the long-term prospects for economic development.

While explaining the emergence of an incipient private equity industry across Latin America, my research shines light on broader—and more important—questions about financial development and corporate governance reforms. As an alternative to rules-based arguments about financial development based on investor protections, this book emphasizes the more proximate role of institutional investors. And regarding corporate governance reform, it argues against structural explanations of reform. Instead, it zooms into micro-level regulations and shows extensive public-private collaboration behind the creation of the new industry.

2.2 Beyond Investor Protections

As part of the consensus around the long-term causes of development that focus on the importance of the rule of law, contract enforcement, and the overall protection of property rights (Shirley 2005), the research agenda on financial development appears to have settled around the centrality of investor protections. Together with macroeconomic stability, most explanations agree that well-established property rights, in particular the protection of minority shareholder rights, are the key mechanism behind the growth of financial markets (Haber et al. 2008).[8] While there are competing hypothesis around the origins of investor protections, there is not much discussion of whether or not this is the key causal mechanism driving financial development.

The logic underlying the investor protections argument is straightforward (e.g. La Porta et al. 2002). Investors will only allocate their capital into a company (in the case of equity investments with no guarantee of fixed return, just the claim to residual cash flows after every other claimant such as workers, government, suppliers, and debt holders has been paid) if they are confident they will not be expropriated by managers, majority shareholders, or the state. Specific pieces of legislation that protect shareholder rights and improve information transparency are enacted to lower monitoring costs, and penalize and discourage the expropriation of outsider investors. Countries who have stronger investor protections in place and enforce them more effectively would experience more external capital flowing into its companies. Otherwise, firms will receive less "outside" investment and will therefore have more concentrated ownership structures.

It would be foolish to try to refute the overall soundness of this argument. As the Argentinean case illustrates bluntly, chronic experiences of expropriation and a weak judiciary, paired with macroeconomic and political instability, are for sure not conducive toward financial development (Roe and Siegel 2011). A strong corporate governance framework, transparent accounting rules, and diligent bankruptcy courts are most certainly important elements for the development of more complete capital markets. Still, they seem not to be enough. As shown in the introduction, legal rules by themselves have limited explanatory capacity (Guillén and Capron 2016), at least during the last couple of decades. This book proposes to shift the analytical focus from the institutional settings to the more proximate actors that can drive external equity investments into companies: institutional investors. In particular, it focuses

[8] For private equity, see how property rights affect the type of instrument used to make investments (Lerner and Schoar 2005), in Latin America, see Chong and Lopez-de-Silanes (2007) and Khoury et al. (2015).

on a group of development financial institutions which, together with pension funds, can help the emerging private capital industry and anchor other domestic and international investors. While institutions cannot be ignored, much can be gained by occasionally pushing them into the analytical background in order to develop a more business-centered understanding of market development (Puente and Schneider 2020).

The institutionalist literature barely discusses the mechanisms that connect rules with firm-level outcomes. Explanations are mostly functionalist; their underlying logic implicitly assumes that if rules are in place, actors will then follow. But the origins and investment logic behind many of the most important institutional investors who are the cornerstone players of modern capital markets, such as pension funds, do not necessarily follow the mechanisms that underlie institutional arguments. As mentioned, some of the actors identified as key drivers of equity markets—domestic and multilateral development financial institutions together with pension funds—are hardly pure market players. The origin of these actors is not market-based and does not follow the enactment of investor protection rules. And their operating logics, while in some cases is certainly market-driven (and often subject to state expropriation), it is also heavily regulated.

Moreover, a specific focus on private equity makes minority shareholders rights arguably less relevant (Pandya and Leblang 2017). Given their concentrated equity stakes, even without having full control, private equity investors have the incentives and the capacity to monitor management and other shareholders, making weak minority protections and pervasive contract incompleteness somewhat less problematic. This does not deny the importance, from the investor's perspective, of governments ensuring the rule of law and securing the enforcement of contracts; rule of law affects all types of investors. PE investors would also favor the strengthening of minority shareholders' protections. They often take minority stakes (in particular in VC and growth equity type of investments), and private and public markets complement each other.

But legal shareholder rights have limited explanatory capacity. We need therefore to think about alternative—complementary—hypotheses beyond standard institutional explanations keeping in mind that by holding concentrated stakes private equity may have the capacity to penetrate more disorganized political economies and adapt to different institutional environments. Again, given its characteristics, private equity seems to be less demanding in terms of the enforcement of "within the firm" property rights, in particular those concerning minority shareholder protections. This makes it a form of external capital well suited to operate in less strongly institutionalized environments as well as investing in smaller and less formalized firms (N. Berger and F. Udell 1998).

While minority shareholder rights may not be the key mechanisms driving the emergence of private equity, it is still worth to engage with more general arguments about the political economy determinants of investor protections. Here too, there is also a parallelism with the arguments made in the literature on the political origins of inclusive, as opposed to extractive, economic institutions. Within this literature, there are two families of explanations for how financial systems develop over time and across countries: we can distinguish between historically-minded "deep institutional" arguments focused on countries' legal origins and shorter-term "political economy" explanations based on political institutions.

In line with the colonial origins argument (Acemoglu et al. 2001; Dell 2010), a prominent literature on financial development highlights the origins of each country's legal system as the key long-term determinant of the depth of its capital market (Aminadav and Papaioannou 2020; La Porta et al. 1998). Other things equal, common law countries, which have a legal tradition more protective of investors, would have stronger financial systems compared to civil law countries which are less protective of external investors. Countries which transplanted their legal framework from the French civil law family exhibit less protective shareholder and creditor rights, and therefore have less external investment and more concentrated ownership structures. In line with the long-term focus of legal origin arguments, other research has focused on how country's religious origins (Stulz and Williamson 2003), and more broadly, on cultural factors associated with social capital (Guiso et al. 2004) and family values (Bertrand and Schoar 2006) affect financial development.

It may well be the case that the historical analysis of legal and cultural traditions in Latin America indeed illuminates some long-term trend that jeopardized development (Mahoney 2010). Latin American countries' common Iberian—Spanish and Portuguese—colonization experiences inaugurated a legal tradition based on French civil law that arguably offered weaker investor protections, therefore possibly undermining the region's overall development of its financial markets. Similarly, its Christian legacy may have also affected creditors' protections negatively (Stulz and Williamson 2003). And Latin America's culture of strong family values may shape the organization of business away from external investors (Bertrand and Schoar 2006). The case selection of this book focused on a region that broadly shares all these structural factors, and its time frame, comparing the paths of Latin America's five largest economies after their liberalization, does not allow for a thorough assessment of these arguments. Still, these cases exhibit variation in the development of private equity markets, unexplained by these longer-term causes. And Chapter 6 explores cases outside Latin America, providing external validity to the book's main arguments.

Even though path dependence in the development of financial markets could exist, critics of investor protections as an exogenous variable note that countries experienced extensive legal reforms over time, and lawmakers many times purposely borrowed institutions from other legal traditions, such as the American securities law (Coffee 1999). To explain within-country variations in both legal rules and outcomes, it requires to go beyond a quasi-constant such as legal family. Treating investor protections as an endogenous policy choice, scholars then focused on the type of political institutions that drives investor protections and hence, financial development (Haber et al. 2008; Menaldo and Yoo 2015; Musacchio 2009; Rajan and Zingales 2003; Roe and Siegel 2009). And again, in line with broader institutional arguments about development (Acemoglu et al. 2005), this literature usually associates inclusive political institutions—basically democracy—with property rights and therefore with financial development. Development is thought as a dispute between entrenched insiders and outsiders. Outsiders favor the broader availability of arms-length capital, while insiders block the development of capital markets in order to maintain their privileges (Li and Resnick 2003; Menaldo and Yoo 2015). Empowering outsiders and restraining insiders, democracy is argued to be associated with financial development (Girma and Shortland 2007).

More specifically, there are two types of arguments about democracy—and political institutions more generally—and financial development: one centered on constraints on the executive and the other one on the expansion of "vertical" electoral accountability (Cox and Weingast 2018; Simison 2019). Regarding the first one, Haber et al. (2008) explain that "unless there are self-enforcing political institutions that limit the government's authority and discretion, it will have strong incentives to govern the financial system as to facilitate its own political survival, at the expense of the development of the securities markets and banking system that can finance the private economy" (p. 2). As for the political institutions necessary to constrain public officials' expropriatory temptations that inhibit the development of markets, they list "federalism, separation of powers, electoral suffrage and party competition" (p. 5).

The second argument highlights democracies' enhanced responsiveness to broader publics. The median voter is assumed to be an asset holder—actual or potential—who would induce policymaker's push for the expansion of capital markets, break the elite's privileged access to capital, induce competition, and foster economic growth. "As shareholdings by the median voters increase, for instance because of the economic success of the middle class or the emergence of capitalized pension systems, political support should move towards favoring equity markets with riskier corporate strategies" (Perotti and von Thadden 2006, 147).

Beyond sharing a common colonial origin, from a political institutions perspective, all Latin American countries during the time period covered are considered to be full electoral democracies. While they exhibit some differences in their electoral institutions, party systems, and Constitutions, institutions that can bias democracies toward elites preferences and therefore undermine financial development (Menaldo and Yoo 2015; Pagano and Volpin 2005), all of them were ruled by democratically-elected governments during the time period under analysis. Therefore, the cross-section of cases does not allow to directly evaluate a regime-type hypothesis. Still, Chapter 3 shows that, at least within Latin America, overall differences on executive constraints can hardly explain variation across cases. And Chapters 5 and 6 provide evidence from both Latin America and Europe that indicate relevant regulations are—purposefully—enacted far from congress and the electoral debate.[9] Overall, these chapters' findings tend to rebut the mechanisms behind the hypotheses that highlight democracy as a leading force toward the development of financial markets.

[9] Using individual-level survey data, Kerner (2018) shows that the expansion of the population who owns corporate securities through pension reforms did not increase support for pro-market reforms in Latin America and "neoliberalism," against one of the possible mechanisms that could connect democracy and financial reforms.

Compared with theories about financial development over long periods, this book takes a shorter-term approach.[10] It advances an intermediate range argument that spans over around two decades in Latin America's largest countries. And instead of focusing on cross-national regressions on a variety of broad indicators (e.g. market capitalization and bank assets as a proportion of GDP), it focuses on a narrow—and opaque—asset class through detailed case studies. This approach allows to go beyond institutional environments and to forefront actors.

2.3 Corporate Governance Reform

In contrast to the literature on financial development, scholarly work on corporate governance reform is indeed more actor-based. As part of the comparative analysis of advanced capitalisms, this literature is also framed in a relatively shorter time period than century-long legal origins' hypothesis. Arguments are more mindful of alternative models of organizing financial markets and firm governance. They are mostly focused on, first, explaining the divergence between corporate governance models in liberal and coordinated market economies, and then, on how each model reacted to financial globalization and the extent to which each country trended toward more active markets for corporate control with a larger role for financial investors external to firms. Still, this literature is rarely focused on development. And while the goal of this book is less about explaining conflict and reform and more about the emergence of an asset class and the creation of new markets, discussing the role of each of the main actors in these theories will help frame my argument within the broader literature and introduce alternative hypotheses.

[10] Given the shorter time span of the book's analysis, it could be argued some of the reforms still have to mature in order to observe changes in firm-level ownership structures and governance models: with time, ownership structures would gradually become more dispersed and institutional. But this is not in line with the evidence. While business groups in Latin America indeed appear to have professionalized their management, their ownership structure has remained mostly unchanged, even when the institutional conditions for change appear to be fulfilled. When looking at large "incumbent" companies in Chile during the last thirty years, Larrain and Urzúa (2016) find that rather than dispersing, owners—typically families—have concentrated their ownership stakes through debt financing. More "open" models of governance appear to come through new companies that have grown with PE financing rather than through the gradual reform of incumbent firms.

Arguments regarding corporate governance reform highlight how different configurations of social actors affect corporate governance outcomes within market-based democracies. In particular, they discuss the role of labor, managers, as well as in some cases, institutional investors.[11]

2.3.1 Labor

Most political economy arguments on corporate governance reform set apart a protagonic role for labor. Still, the impact of labor's strength is somewhat undetermined. While most of this literature argues about the relationship between strong labor and the persistence of concentrated firm ownership structures, others emphasize the role of labor pushing for the extension of financial markets.

Aiming to explain the political origins of the divergence between American widely-held firms and the European block-holding model, Roe (2003) argues that in a social-democracy the cost for owners of granting managers autonomy is higher, outweighing the value they obtain by diffusing their ownership stakes. Social-democracy raises the pressures on managers to abandon the shareholder's side and couple with employees to do what managers want to do all along: expand and avoid risk and rapid change at the expense of owners. Moreover, social-democracy hinders the mechanisms that could be used by shareholders to control managers such as take-overs and manager's incentive compensation. Considering a strong organized labor as the key pre-requisite for social-democracy, strong labor blocks the path to firms with dispersed shareholders and managerial autonomy. This would be one of the drivers of the postwar difference between the continental and the US corporate governance model, where, in the latter, weak labor loosens the agency problem between owners and managers and therefore makes possible the separation between ownership and control. This argument is validated empirically, for example, by the correlation found between labor strength and ownership concentration (Aminadav and Papaioannou 2020; van Essen et al. 2013). In a more limited comparison, but showing directionally similar results, Goyer (2011) uses the strength of labor inside firms to explain the different—lower—penetration of financial investors—contingent capital—in Germany than in France.

[11] For reviews of this literature, see Aguilera and Jackson (2010) and Roe and Vatiero (2015).

In Roe's class-based model of corporate governance, capital and labor cannot be part of the same coalition. Gourevitch and Shinn (2005), instead, propose a cross-class argument. They agree labor strength may have blocked shareholder dispersion in the postwar era, but propose an alternative three-actor coalitional explanation of this outcome in which labor allied with management in a corporatist agreement, and owners accommodated by maintaining concentrated block-holdings. In line with VOC's argument about electoral systems, this corporatist compromise is facilitated by proportional electoral systems that incentivize coalitions between different parties and actors.[12]

But Gourevitch and Shinn's three-actor framework has substantial consequences when thinking about reform, since it also conceive a cross-class alliance between labor and owners. This coalition will push for reforms that extend the role of financial markets, facilitate the monitoring of management, and allow firms to open their capital structure and disperse their ownership. In this line, other scholarly works argue labor-based parties, in particular when workers have their pensions invested in the financial market, can lead a "transparency coalition" that, together with investors, intends to curb managerial opportunism and push for increased investor rights against corporate insiders. For example, Cioffi and Höpner (2006) provide evidence that center-left political parties have pushed for pro-shareholder corporate governance reform in the 1990s and 2000s. Against the conventional wisdom, they show that the pro-business right has generally resisted reform to protect established forms of organized capitalism and concentrated corporate stock ownership, as their interests are mostly aligned with managers. Moreover, Pinto et al. (2010) find evidence that left-leaning governments are more likely to be associated with higher stock market capitalizations. And Barker and Rueda (2007) show that the weakening of "insider" labor, and strengthening of "outside" labor, undermines the corporatist coalition and pushes for reforms in the financial markets as a way to favor new entrants and make markets more competitive.

At least in Latin America, we do not observe more open corporate governance models in those countries where organized labor is relatively weaker, for example in Colombia and Mexico. And labor-based

[12] Pagano and Volpin (2005) also propose a model—and provide evidence—about the relationship between proportional electoral systems, weaker investor protections, and more concentrated shareholdings.

parties, even those more oriented to outsider labor, do not appear to push for "neoliberal" reforms that would extend the scope of financial markets either. Instead, the left is in general skeptical of the expansion of finance. I do not find micro-level evidence about the relevance of labor either facilitating more open and institutionalized forms of ownership in Latin America directly, at least through the creation of more active private equity markets. Organized labor indeed participated in designing a pension system during market reforms. For example, as Etchemendy (2011) argues, labor, when strong, usually pressed to obtain compensations that strengthened their organization. Beyond these reforms, in some cases, unions have a role in the management of pension systems, particularly in the case of defined benefit plans. The management of individual capitalization plans is usually less related to organized labor.

That organized labor has not directly pushed or hampered the micro-level reforms that promoted more dynamic capital markets does not counter arguments about the valence between labor relations and corporate governance models. Family firms may be better able to cope with conflictive labor and therefore relatively more prevalent in countries with hostile labor relations (Mueller and Philippon 2011), even if they do not actively promote labor conflict. Business across the board does not favor extending labor regulations. But PE's restructuring role may be more easily conducted in contexts with more flexible labor protections. Most interestingly, several interviewees pointed out private equity investors avoid getting involved in sectors with high levels of labor—and tax—informality. Given their more stringent compliance standards related to the institutional origin of their capital, PE investors are arguably more sensible to labor liabilities. And competition from informal firms prevents them to overcome atomization and foster the consolidation of a sector, a usual investment strategy.[13]

2.3.2 Managers

Other than labor, political economy models of corporate governance also grant managers a pivotal role. In order to protect their positions, and

[13] Beyond just refraining from high-informality industries, a former executive from one of the largest PE funds in Brazil described me how they researched in detail which sectors/industries government was tightening the enforcement of taxation and regulations to then deploy a "buy-and-build" investment strategy.

preserve their autonomy, managers can side with either owners or labor. While the relevance of managers may be valid in a context where management already exists as an actor, as it is the case in both coordinated and liberal market economies, this literature is not as useful in a developing context. Given the prevalence of concentrated ownership and hierarchical governance models (Schneider 2013), there is no management as an autonomous group to begin with. Autonomous managers are precisely one of the key outcomes of financial development, therefore hardly its cause. Without external investors that inject professionalism into firms, management typically remains closely subordinated to the firms' ultimate owners. As Chapter 5 shows, public agencies had to aid fund managers' collective action and sponsor their business association, arguably helping them "become an actor" that could then push for reform. Once again, my argument is less about reform and insiders vs. outsiders than about the creation of a new industry through private-public collaboration.

2.3.3 *Institutional Investors*

Finally, representing "outsider capital" (Barker and Rueda 2007), institutional investors such as pension funds are portrayed by the literature to be unequivocally called to limit the influence of corporate insiders and block-holders. But after more than 20 years from pension system reform, in Latin America, pension funds have yet to play that role. With portfolios fully loaded with public debt and/or increasingly attracted by diversified global investment strategies free of "headline-risk," their engagement with more activist forms of domestic investing, such as private/public equity, is far from automatic. Getting access to pension fund resources is one of the key outcomes and a core goal for both policy interventions and private capital industry associations.

While there is some recent political science work on institutional investors in the region (Bril-Mascarenhas 2016; Bril-Mascarenhas and Maillet 2019), I am not aware of any systematic comparative research on the political economy of pension fund investment strategies, and this topic has yet to permeate into the more mainstream literature on financial development (Scharfstein 2018). Engaging with pension funds as corporate governance actors in an emerging context is one of the contributions of this research.

Pension fund's mandate is to generate financial returns to face pensioners' retirements. Developmental "market-making" role is in most cases not within pension fund's stated goals. PE's role is to enhance traditional stock and bonds portfolios by generating excess returns (i.e. alpha). Long-term private equity commitments match well the distinctively long-term liabilities held by pension funds and would enable them to obtain a liquidity premium. While there is a debate on the extent of the "alpha" generated by the PE asset class during the recent stock market super-cycle (e.g. Bain & Company 2020) and on the conflict of interest between pension fund and PE managers (Phalippou 2020), generating financial returns and beating the market are pension funds' main goal when investing in the asset class.[14]

Pension systems are structured in different ways. Broadly, two models can be distinguished. On the one side, publicly-managed systems, that can be pay-as-you-go or partially funded schemes. Their public sector status creates a tension between maximizing financial returns, the need to attract top financial talent to do so, and pressure from politicians to invest in projects that may not maximize financial returns, but benefit them, electoral or privately. Still, public pension funds are among the most active private equity investors. The most successful of them have resolved this tension granting their managers a substantial degree of autonomy from politicians and bureaucracies, best exemplified by Canadian pension funds (Little 2008; World Bank 2017). As Chapter 4 discusses, this tension is also clearly exemplified by the more politicized Brazilian pension funds.

On the other hand, fully-funded individual capitalization pension systems accumulate the largest pools of capital and are managed by private administrators. By design, they intend to insulate pensioner's savings from political pressure and prevent becoming government's captive investors. Still, portfolio allocation quotas—as well as many other parameters—are heavily regulated. Managers' incentives to take risk, compete and differentiate from each other, and prioritize longer-term investments over short-term securities are not easily generated (e.g. as discussed for the

[14] As mentioned, the number of listed companies in Latin American stock markets is quite small. Firms typically have a controlling shareholder, dual shares, and pyramidal structures. These features generate a gap between political and cash flow rights that incentivize controllers to expropriate minority shareholders (Dyck and Zingales 2004; Nenova 2003). From this perspective, and notwithstanding the agency problem between PE fund managers and institutional investors, private equity may have an advantage over domestic public equities.

Chilean case by Opazo et al. [2014]). And pensioners' discretion to re-allocate their individual savings can also bias portfolios toward liquid securities (Da et al. 2018).

Different systems raise distinct governance issues, but the overall challenge is similar: to create the channels that connect large pools of capital into long-term projects while generating risk-adjusted market returns, i.e. without expropriating pensioners. Far from automatic, these channels are the result of extensive public-private collaboration.

2.4 Quiet Politics

As an alternative to macro-societal theories of corporate governance reform, Culpepper (2010) makes a "quiet politics" argument centered on the preferences of managers rather than on the relative power of social actors. Culpepper points out that it would be a mistake "treating corporate control like any other high-profile battle in democracies, where public opinion and legislative votes are the most valuable currencies" (p. 3). In low saliency and technically opaque policy areas, in particular when execution and implementation are more relevant than legal reform, as it would be the case for corporate governance, Culpepper argues that managerial organizations have an advantage. Given their superior knowledge and technical lobbying capacity, outcomes would tend to follow manager's input.

However, Culpepper's outcomes are still based on societal considerations, since in his argument, managerial preferences are ultimately a function of the strength of within-firms labor organization. So, notwithstanding the level on which each of these arguments identifies the corporate governance policy arena—quiet or open—all of the arguments presented are mostly societal, with the role of labor being at the core of most models. They rarely acknowledge any role for public policy besides implementing the winning coalition's preferred position in a rather automatic way. It is not clear from reading this literature what are the mechanisms through which societal actors operate and how, or which, policies are implemented. The different arguments are not explicit on the specific policies driving change and if any, are mostly centered on legal reforms. For example, are the policies implemented by alternative socio-economic coalitions change to corporate law, specific pieces of administrative-level regulations, or the increased enforcement of existing rules? Or, rather, they push for alternative pension fund regulations, privatizations, or a new direction in the strategy of development banks? Diving into detailed case studies allows to weigh these alternative "mechanisms" to then connect them back to the broader hypotheses in the literature.

My argument is indeed located in the "quiet politics" arena, as an alternative to macro-coalitional theories. While my detailed focus does not allow for the large-n type of evaluation to make a full quantitative assessment, I do not observe the connection between the macro-coalitional politics discussed by the literature and the micro-level issues that are more relevant in the case studies. First, as mentioned, labor has not played a direct role pushing for financial market reform in Latin America. And second, explanations focused on the role of managers seem less relevant for an argument about the development of a new market. Without an autonomous management group to start with, the emergence of a private capital market is less about conflict and reform, and more about the creation of a new industry. Therefore, a macro-societal approach does not appear to be as helpful as in other contexts.

Given the smaller scale of the object of study—private equity in a region where it is yet emerging—and the micro-level and highly technical regulations that affect it, a quiet politics approach seems trivially true. But as Chapter 5 discusses in detail, even for a low-salience topic, the "quiet politics" bureaucratic arena is not always the natural setting for this type of issues. Actors in the PE industry purposefully chose to keep their policy working space outside Congress and party politics, even if that means paying a cost in the—second-best—outcomes they may obtain. Moreover, Chapter 6 shows the logic behind PE regulation in more developed markets also follows a similar logic.

Beyond societal arguments on reform, my explanation focuses on the role of government-related players for the emergence of a new industry. First, development financial institutions act as investors in this emerging asset class and try to attract other institutional investors, such as pension funds, into the new industry (Chapter 4). Second, some of these public agencies also foster the industry's collective action by sponsoring business associations that represent fund managers, who, in turn, then lobby for a workable regulatory environment (Chapter 5). The policymaking roles played by domestic and multilateral development financial institutions, substantially more active than the one granted by institutionalist arguments, are central to explain the emergence and institutionalization of private capital markets.

2.5 Update: State and Finance

Beyond a set of market-conforming policies, mainstream institutionalism considers the state not as an enabler but mostly as a barrier to development. This tradition grants business a more functionalist role: firms will germinate to take advantage of market opportunities if the state's expropriation impulses are checked by an institutional framework that protects property rights and allows market competition. Similarly, in the financial sector, capital market development would follow from the rules that protect investors and constrain executive power. If the correct institutional environment is in place, investors and intermediaries will emerge in a decentralized way to invest into firms, and owners will open their firm's capital structure to external investors in order to reduce the cost of capital and to diversify their wealth. The role of the state is limited to the—at all trivial—tasks of enforcing the law and guaranteeing a sound regulatory framework. Beyond that, government's role in markets crowds out private investment.

Oddly, the countries that exhibited the highest growth in capital markets in the last couple of decades exhibit a rather statist political economy, comparatively less constrained executives and prominent government-related investors (OECD 2018). Such is the case in China but also in Singapore, Korea, and Malaysia (Gomez et al. 2018; Klingler-Vidra 2018; Yong 2012). State-related actors such as sovereign wealth funds, development banks, and publicly-managed pension funds function as cornerstone investors in many of these markets. As Chapter 6 documents, state-related sources of capital funding private equity investments are ubiquitous not just in emerging markets but also in the developed world.

Latin America is a non-obvious choice to advance an argument with state and policy at its core. Not only have Latin America states been historically weaker than their Asian counterparts (Fukuyama 2014; Stephan Haggard and Kaufman 2008; Schrank 2007), but also, after extensive liberalization in the 1990s, Latin American political economies are thought as less statist than they were in the past. If anything, state presence in the financial sector is mostly restricted to commercial banking (Etchemendy and Puente 2017; Yeyati et al. 2007). Of course, Brazil is an exception with its well-known development bank, BNDES, one of the largest of its kind in the developing world (Hochstetler and Montero 2013; Lazzarini et al. 2015; A. Leslie 2017; Torres and Zeidan 2016).

Even though Latin America may be an unexpected region to focus on, it exhibits interesting variation across countries and time that can provide empirical leverage to support my argument. As in other cases in both the developed and developing world, if we analyze the investors behind some of the pioneer private equity funds, even in Latin America, we notice the presence of government-related financial institutions, both multilateral and domestic.

As an investor, the state can participate in private equity markets in two main ways: directly and indirectly. First, occasionally, government-related financial institutions can function themselves as private equity investors and participate directly as shareholders. This model is thoroughly described in Musacchio and Lazzarini's (2014) "Leviathan as a minority shareholder" model that uses the Brazilian case as an example. In contrast to more traditional state-owned enterprises, in these cases the state usually holds minority, though concentrated, equity stakes in firms, co-investing alongside a variety of business partners. While state investments generally have an explicit policy purpose, and there might be some guidance and monitoring through participation in the board of directors, companies are mostly managed by the state's business partners (Musacchio et al. 2015).

Second, government-related financial institutions often function as investors—as limited partners (LPs)—in privately-managed private equity funds. These funds pool capital from multiple sources and in turn participate as shareholders—majority or minority—in multiple portfolio companies. This extra layer of intermediation that outsources ultimate capital allocation decision-making to a third-party fund manager provides a more detached model of intervention. It allows the limited partners to reach smaller, but larger number of firms, in an arms-length way. Acting as an anchor investor and aiming to crowd-in other domestic and international investors, through PE investments government-related financial institutions also often aim to achieve narrower, sector-specific policy goals, while imposing themselves some level of market discipline. Chapter 4 discusses different private equity government-sponsored initiatives throughout Latin America.

Policymakers promoting private equity have intertwined goals. More generally, they aim to develop more complete capital markets and improve firms' access to finance, in particular in the form of equity capital, otherwise notably absent from the financing menu. As just mentioned, access to finance in some cases is combined with sectoral goals; equity funds serve as targeted policy instruments to promote innovation, transition to green technologies, among others (Mazzucato and Penna 2016). Development financial institutions in general do not invest alone, but their goal is to anchor resources from other institutional investors. Most importantly, in most cases, they intend to leverage pension funds' vast pools of capital.

Beyond these programmatic goals, and regarding individual-level motivations, senior public officials at both development banks and regulators most likely consider their career paths that often combine public service with private sector positions. The fund management industry, and the professional services surrounding it, is a common path for senior technocrats to go into business. So gaining expertise and embedding themselves in the industry networks can help them advance in their careers. This seems to be the case across Latin America and probably elsewhere.

Beyond the focus on capital markets, there is, of course, a large literature that addresses the role of the state owning corporate assets, focused on the discussion around state-owned enterprises (SOEs). There are compelling arguments both in favor and against market interventions.[15] SOEs indeed appear to face multiple governance issues, as raised by an agency perspective usually skeptical of governments' developmental efforts. Efficiency and profitability are often in tension with the social objectives that motivated state intervention in the first place, and SOEs thus have multiple and potentially contradictory goals. Their managers typically lack high-powered incentives that would align their goals with societal goals. The ultimate principals, politicians, are tempted to use their authority over SOEs for their personal gain and to benefit their cronies. Lack of proper monitoring, either from an independent board of directors or from the market, further complicates these agency problems. SOEs can also distort competition and crowd-out other private sector participants. And poorly managed SOE can lead to chronic increases in the fiscal burden. In contrast to a more cautious approach to state intervention, the defenders of an industrial policy view conceive state investment as a way to promote development beyond what is possible under the free market. Governments can help firms develop new capabilities by reducing capital constraints, subsidizing part of the research and development expenses and solving coordination and rent appropriation

[15] For a more complete assessment of this debate, see Musacchio and Lazzarini's (2014) Chapter 3. Also see Mazzucato and Penna (2016), Musacchio et al. (2015) and Yeyati et al. (2007).

problems, and encouraging firms to pursue new projects with potentially high spillovers.

The relative merits of each of these arguments, and ultimately the quality of interventions, are likely a function of the capacity and autonomy of the bureaucratic organizations that implement them (Fukuyama 2013). And while co-investing with private sector players and the intermediation of professional managers may ease some concerns, the policy programs considered in Chapters 4 and 5 certainly suffer from the agency challenges and trade-offs discussed by the literature. But beyond these concerns, the case studies suggest that government policymaking has a significant role to play in the emergence of private equity markets. Without a more active role than the one implied by the institutionalist literature, private capital markets can hardly take off. This is not the same as arguing that state intervention is always positive or exempt of rent-seeking, nor minimizing the capabilities required to run a successful program in this realm. The empirical chapters go into the agency challenges of programs specifically aimed at equity markets and discuss how different organizational designs try to resolve them.

Interestingly, most of the private equity policy programs established throughout Latin America were built by each country's long-standing development financial institutions. This is the case of the largest of these programs, such as BNDESPAR, part of BNDES in Brazil, *Fondo de Fondos*, affiliated to Nafinsa in Mexico, and Corfo's risk capital program in Chile, that exemplify one of the more novel roles development financial institutions have (Griffith-Jones and Ocampo 2018; Lazzarini et al. 2015). The importance of these legacy institutions signals the organizational costs of starting these programs and therefore, their path-dependent nature. These financial institutions grant government-sponsored investment programs some autonomy from politics and standard bureaucracy, the relationships with the private sector, and may employ the type of officials—with experience in finance that spans the private and public sector—that lead these initiatives.

More generally, by focusing on equity investment rather than on bank loans, the book also contributes to update the literature on the state's role in finance.[16] As mentioned, the literature on comparative capitalisms presented a dichotomy between bank-based and capital

[16] For a theoretical discussion on the state's role in finance, also see Mazzucato and Penna (2016).

market-based financial systems. This literature also associates state intervention with a bank-based system argument (e.g. industrialization in France and Germany (Gerschenkron's 1962), postwar industrial policy (Zysman 1983), and East Asian development (Woo-Cumings 1991)). Capital markets are portrayed as the reign of more liberal political economies (Storm 2018). Characteristically short-sighted, they would be unable to overcome the multiple market failures that plague development. As explained above, this bank vs. capital market dichotomy is at best outdated. The association between banks and state interventions also seems old-fashioned. While development banks continue to be major lenders, many of them are also active players in capital markets. The sharp dichotomy between bank-based and capital market-based financial system does not seem to hold, nor does the exclusive affinity between banks and government intervention.

Mainstream institutionalism is also skeptical of close business-government relationships, as opportunities for entrenchment, capture, and rent-seeking would outweigh any potential gains from closer coordination. The main role for the state is to serve an arms-length regulator. This includes strengthening regulators' capacity, improving transparency and information flows, and reducing overall transaction costs. Beyond these, close relationships between bureaucrats and their private sector counterparts are treated with suspicion, many times certainly with good reasons to do so.

But as the case of private equity industry associations illustrates, the role played by domestic and multilateral public agencies in the organizational dimension, again, contrasts with this hands-off approach. In tandem with its role as an investor, and beyond state's role as a regulator, in most countries there is an active participation of a variety of public agencies that, together with multilateral financial institutions, promote the emerging private capital industry's collective action. They help create asset-specific business associations which will then lobby for regulatory reforms.

This is in line with arguments about the importance of private-public collaboration for effective productive policymaking. Together with the crucial issue of public sector capabilities, the aspects that determine the success or failure of public-private cooperation appear to be less structural and more practical issues around the collaboration between the private sector and public agencies (Fernández-Arias et al. 2016). And as Fernández-Arias et al. (2016) emphasize, private sector organizations are often a pre-requisite for successful policymaking, since industry associations are key to foster cooperation among firms and to allow more stable and legitimate interactions with the government (Schneider 2015). The private capital industry is a clear example where public agencies play a more political role facilitating collective action in order to have an organized business counterpart that can aid policy design and implementation (Schneider 2004). Chapter 5 analyzes the origins of each country's business associations and their role behind some key regulatory issues.

Beyond its contribution to the academic literature on financial development and corporate governance reform, by emphasizing the role of institutional investors, this work can also provide relevant—though still high-level—inputs for policymaking. Mainstream arguments about financial development are more detached from policy. They prescribe, if anything, strengthening regulatory agencies and legal reform. While developing strong and competent regulatory agencies is crucial, this book focuses on the role of the state not just as a regulator but as an investor through public and semi-public institutions (e.g. sovereign wealth funds, domestic and multilateral development banks, and pension funds), helping create an institutional framework for capital accumulation and the channels that connect large capital pools with firms. It also discusses a more "political" role for public agencies: that of fostering collective action through industry associations to establish a more fluid public–private working relationship. These business associations, in turn, advocate for the creation of specific corporate vehicles, push for favorable taxation, and lobby for accessing pension fund resources. Discussing these different roles can contribute to more practical questions around the capabilities required and trade-offs faced when trying to foster private equity, and capital markets more generally.

2.6 Conclusion and Roadmap

This chapter connected the book's focus on the development of private equity markets in Latin America to broader questions about financial development and corporate governance reform in an "emerging" context. Other than private equity—that can certainly accommodate various models—there is no clear alternative form of financing that combines three important characteristics: institutional origin, riskiness, and patience. In contrast to its role in more developed capital markets, where private equity concentrates ownership as a way to check managers' autonomy, in emerging economies it is an alternative to governance models organized around families and individuals.

In order to explain the emergence of this new market, the book emphasizes the role of institutional investors as an alternative to just focusing on institutional environments. Property rights and investor protections are most definitely important for development, but they are not enough, at least for the case of equity markets. As the empirical chapters make clear, an exclusive focus on institutions "as rules" cannot fully explain the emergence of private equity markets in Latin America. Instead, in all cases analyzed, we observe a more active role of policymakers than the ones portrayed by mainstream arguments about financial development. In particular, I distinguish government's role as an investor (Chapter 4), from policymaker's role helping the emerging industry organize into asset-specific business associations (Chapter 5).

Next, Chapter 3 introduces firm-level evidence to support the arguments on the role of private equity made throughout this chapter. PE investors are behind a majority of stock market listings, crowd-out kinship ties within firms, and induce more dispersed ownership structures. It also presents data on the relative penetration of private capital investors in each country and score cases on a set of alternative hypothesis (e.g. investor protections, trade protections, regime type, and labor strength), laying out the stylized facts of the country case studies developed in Chapters 4 and 5.

References

Abiad, Abdul, Enrica Detragiache, and Thierry Tressel. 2010. A New Database of Financial Reforms. *IMF Staff Papers* 57 (2): 281–302.

Acemoglu, Daron, Simon Johnson, and James A. Robinson. 2001. The Colonial Origins of Comparative Development: An Empirical Investigation. *American Economic Review* 91 (5): 1369–1401.

———. 2005. Institutions as a Fundamental Cause of Long-Run Growth. In *Handbook of Economic Growth*, ed. Philippe Aghion and Steven Durlauf, 385–472. Amsterdam: North-Holland.

Aggarwal, Reena, Isil Erel, Miguel Ferreira, and Pedro Matos. 2011. Does Governance Travel around the World? Evidence from Institutional Investors. *Journal of Financial Economics* 100 (1): 154–181.

Aguilera, Ruth V., and Rafel Crespi-Cladera. 2016. Global Corporate Governance: On the Relevance of Firms' Ownership Structure. *Journal of World Business* 51 (1): 50–57.

Aguilera, Ruth V., and Gregory Jackson. 2010. Comparative and International Corporate Governance. *Academy of Management Annals* 4 (1): 485–556.

Aguilera, Ruth V., Ricardo L. Kabbach De Castro, Jun Ho Lee, and Jihae You. 2012. Corporate Governance in Emerging Markets. In *Capitalisms and Capitalism in the Twenty-First Century*, ed. Glenn Morgan and Richard Whitley. Oxford: Oxford University Press.

Aldunate, Felipe, Felipe Gonzaalez, Mounu Prem, and Francisco Urzua. 2020. *Privatization and Business Groups: Evidence from the Chicago Boys in Chile.*

Aminadav, Gur, and Elias Papaioannou. 2020. Corporate Control around the World. *The Journal of Finance* 75 (3): 1191–1246.

Ayyagari, Meghana, Pedro Juarros, Maria Soledad Martinez Peria, and Sandeep Singh. 2021. Access to Finance and Job Growth: Firm-Level Evidence Across Developing Countries. *Review of Finance* 25 (5): 1473–1496.

Bain & Company. 2020. *Global Private Equity Report 2020.*

Balan, Pablo, Juan Dodyk, and Ignacio Puente. 2021. *The Political Behavior of Family Firms: Evidence From Brazil.*

Barker, Roger, and David Rueda. 2007. SSRN Electronic Journal *The Labor Market Determinants of Corporate Governance Reform.* Elsevier BV.

Bebchuk, Lucian A., Alma Cohen, and Scott Hirst. 2017. The Agency Problems of Institutional Investors. *Journal of Economic Perspectives* 31 (3): 89–112.

Bebchuk, Lucian A., and Michael S. Weisbach. 2010. The State of Corporate Governance Research. *Review of Financial Studies* 23 (3): 939–961.

Beck, Thorsten. 2016. *Long-Term Finance in Latin America.*

Beck, Thorsten, Berrak Büyükkarabacak, Felix K. Rioja, and Neven T. Valev. 2012. Who Gets the Credit? And Does It Matter? Household vs. Firm Lending across Countries. *B.E. Journal of Macroeconomics* 12 (1): 1–46.

Beck, Thorsten, Asli Demirguc-Kunt, Luc Laeven, and Ross Levine. 2008. Finance, Firm Size, and Growth. *Journal of Money, Credit and Banking* 40 (7): 1379–1405.

Beck, Thorsten, Vasso Ioannidou, and Larissa Schäfer. 2018. Foreigners vs. Natives: Bank Lending Technologies and Loan Pricing. *Management Science* 64 (8): 3792–3820.

Beck, Thorsten, and Maria Soledad Martinez Peria. 2008. *Foreign Bank Acquisitions and Outreach: Evidence from Mexico.*

Berger, Allen N., and Gregory F. Udell. 1998. The Economics of Small Business Finance: The Roles of Private Equity and Debt Markets in the Financial Growth Cycle. *Journal of Banking & Finance* 22(6–8): 613–673.

Bertrand, Marianne, and Antoinette Schoar. 2006. The Role of Family in Family Firms. *Journal of Economic Perspectives* 20 (2): 73–96.

Bloom, Nicholas, and J. Van Reenen. 2007. Measuring and Explaining Management Practices Across Firms and Countries. *The Quarterly Journal of Economics* 122 (4): 1351–1408.

———. 2010. Why Do Management Practices Differ Across Firms and Countries? *Journal of Economic Perspectives* 24 (1): 203–224.

Bloom, Nicholas, Raffaella Sadun, and John Van Reenen. 2015. Do Private Equity Owned Firms Have Better Management Practices? *American Economic Review* 105 (5): 442–446.

Bril-Mascarenhas, Tomás. 2016. *How States Shape Markets in Latin America*. PhD Dissertation. University of California, Berkeley.

Bril-Mascarenhas, Tomás, and Antoine Maillet. 2019. How to Build and Wield Business Power: The Political Economy of Pension Regulation in Chile, 1990–2018. *Latin American Politics and Society* 61 (1): 101–125.

Bruhn, Miriam, and Inessa Love. 2014. The Real Impact of Improved Access to Finance: Evidence from Mexico. *Journal of Finance* 69 (3): 1347–1376.

Catão, Luis A.V., Carmen Pagés, and María Fernanda Rosales. 2009. *Financial Dependence, Formal Credit and Informal Jobs: New Evidence from Brazilian Household Data*.

Çelik, Serdar, and Mats Isaksson. 2013. *Institutional Investors as Owners: Who Are They and What Do They Do?*

Center for Global Development. 2019. *Making Basel III Work for Emerging Markets and Developing Economies*.

Chong, Alberto, and Florencio Lopez-de-Silanes. 2007. *Investor Protection and Corporate Governance: Firm-Level Evidence across Latin America*. Stanford: Inter-American Development Bank/Stanford University Press.

Cihak, Martin, Asli Demirguc-Kunt, Erik Feyen, and Ross Levine. 2012. Benchmarking Financial Systems around the World, 1–58.

Cioffi, John W., and Martin Höpner. 2006. The Political Paradox of Finance Capitalism: Interests, Preferences, and Center-Left Party Politics in Corporate Governance Reform. *Politics & Society* 34 (4): 463–502.

Claessens, Stijn, and Neeltje Van Horen. 2014. Foreign Banks: Trends and Impact. *Journal of Money, Credit and Banking* 46 (s1): 295–326.

Coffee, John C. 1999. The Future as History: The Prospects for Global Convergence in Corporate Governance and Its Implications. *Northwestern University Law Review* 93 (3): 641–707.

Cox, Gary W., and Barry R. Weingast. 2018. Executive Constraint, Political Stability, and Economic Growth. *Comparative Political Studies* 51 (3): 279–303.

Culpepper, Pepper D. 2010. *Quiet Politics and Business Power: Corporate Control in Europe and Japan*. Cambridge: Cambridge University Press.

Da, Zhi, Borja Larrain, Clemens Sialm, and José Tessada. 2018. Destabilizing Financial Advice: Evidence from Pension Fund Reallocations. *The Review of Financial Studies* 31 (10): 3720–3755.

Davis, Steven J. et al. 2019. *The Economic Effects of Private Equity Buyouts*.

De La Cruz, A., A. Medina, and Y. Tang. 2019. *Owners of the World's Listed Companies*. OECD Capital Market Series, Paris.

Deeg, Richard, and Iain Hardie. 2016. What Is Patient Capital and Who Supplies It? *Socio-Economic Review* 14 (4): 627–645.

Dell, Melissa. 2010. The Persistent Effects of Peru's Mining Mita. *Econometrica* 78 (6): 1863–1903.

Doidge, Craig, G. Andrew Karolyi, and René M. Stulz. 2017. The U.S. Listing Gap. *Journal of Financial Economics* 123 (3): 464–487.

Donelli, Marcelo, Borja Larrain, and I. Francisco Urzúa. 2013. Ownership Dynamics with Large Shareholders: An Empirical Analysis. *Journal of Financial and Quantitative Analysis* 48 (2): 579–609.

Dyck, Alexander, and Luigi Zingales. 2004. Private Benefits of Control: An International Comparison. *The Journal of Finance* 59 (2): 537–600.

Etchemendy, Sebastián. 2011. *Models of Economic Liberalization: Business, Workers, and Compensation in Latin America, Spain, and Portugal*. Cambridge: Cambridge University Press.

Etchemendy, Sebastián, and Ignacio Puente. 2017. Power and Crisis: Explaining Varieties of Commercial Banking Systems in Argentina, Brazil and Mexico. *Journal of Politics in Latin America* 9 (1): 331.

Ewens, Michael, and Joan Farre-Mensa. 2019. *The Deregulation of the Private Equity Markets and the Decline in IPOs By*.

Fernández-Arias, Eduardo, Charles F. Sabel, Ernesto Stein, and Alberto Trejos. 2016. *Two to Tango: Public-Private Collaboration for Productive Development Policies*. Washington, DC: Inter-American Development Bank.

Fukuyama, Francis. 2013. What Is Governance? *Governance* 26 (3): 347–368.

———. 2014 *Political Order and Political Decay*. New York: Straus and Giroux Farrar.

Fuller, Douglas B. 2016. *Paper Tigers, Hidden Dragons: Firms and the Political Economy of China's Technological Development*. New York: Oxford University Press.

Gerschenkron, Alexander. 1962. *Economic Backwardness in Historical Perspective: A Book of Essays*. Cambridge: Harvard University Press.

Girma, S., and A. Shortland. 2007. The Political Economy of Financial Development. *Oxford Economic Papers* 60 (4): 567–596.

Goldsmith, Raymond. 1969. *Financial Structure and Development*. New Haven: Yale University Press.

Gomez, Edmund Terence, et al. 2018. *Minister of Finance Incorporated: Ownership and Control in Corporate Malaysia*. Singapore: Palgrave Macmillan.

Gormley, Todd A. 2010. The Impact of Foreign Bank Entry in Emerging Markets: Evidence from India. *Journal of Financial Intermediation* 19 (1): 26–51.

Gourevitch, Peter, and James Shinn. 2005. *Political Power and Corporate Control: The New Global Politics of Corporate Governance*. Princeton: Princeton University Press.

Goyer, Michel. 2011. *Contingent Capital Short-Term Investors and the Evolution of Corporate Governance in France and Germany*. Oxford: Oxford University Press.

Griffith-Jones, Stephany, and José Antonio Ocampo, eds. 2018. 1 *The Future of National Development Banks*. Oxford: Oxford University Press.

Guillén, Mauro F., and Laurence Capron. 2016. State Capacity, Minority Shareholder Protections, and Stock Market Development. *Administrative Science Quarterly* 61 (1): 125–160.

Guiso, Luigi, Paola Sapienza, and Luigi Zingales. 2004. The Role of Social Capital in Financial Development. *American Economic Review* 94 (3): 526–556.

Haber, Stephen H., Douglass C. North, and Barry R. Weingast. 2008. *Political Institutions and Financial Development*. Stanford: Stanford University Press.

Haggard, Stephan, and Robert R. Kaufman. 2008. *Development, Democracy, and Welfare States: Latin America, East Asia, and Eastern Europe*. Princeton: Princeton University Press.

Hall, Peter A., and David W. Soskice. 2001. *Varieties of Capitalism: The Institutional Foundations of Comparative Advantage*. Oxford: Oxford University Press.

Hardie, Iain, David Howarth, Sylvia Maxfield, and Amy Verdun. 2013. Banks and the False Dichotomy in the Comparative Political Economy of Finance. *World Politics* 65 (04): 691–728.

Hellmann, Thomas, and Manju Puri. 2002. Venture Capital and the Professionalization of Start-Up Firms: Empirical Evidence. *The Journal of Finance* 57 (1): 169–197.

Heng, Dyna, et al. 2016. *Advancing Financial Development in Latin America and the Caribbean*.

Hochstetler, Kathryn, and Alfred P. Montero. 2013. The Renewed Developmental State: The National Development Bank and the Brazil Model. *Journal of Development Studies* 49 (11): 1484–1499.

Ivashina, Victoria, and Joshua Lerner. 2019. *Patient Capital: The Challenges and Promises of Long-Term Investing*. Princeton: Princeton University Press.

Jensen, Michael Cole. 1989. The Eclipse of the Public Corporation. *Harvard Business Review*, September.

Jones Luong, Pauline, and Erika Weinthal. 2010. *Oil Is Not a Curse: Ownership Structure and Institutions in Soviet Successor States*. Cambridge: Cambridge University Press.

Kaplan, Steven N., and Per Strömberg. 2009. Leveraged Buyouts and Private Equity. *Journal of Economic Perspectives* 23 (1): 121–146.

Kayo, Eduardo K., et al. 2018. Capital Structure Adjustment in Brazilian Family Firms. *Revista de Administração Contemporânea* 22 (1): 92–114.

Kerner, Andrew. 2018. Pension Returns and Popular Support for Neoliberalism in Post-Pension Reform Latin America. *British Journal of Political Science* 50 (2): 1–36.

Khoury, Theodore A., Marc Junkunc, and Santiago Mingo. 2015. Navigating Political Hazard Risks and Legal System Quality. *Journal of Management* 41 (3): 808–840.

King, R.G., and R. Levine. 1993. Finance and Growth: Schumpeter Might Be Right. *The Quarterly Journal of Economics* 108 (3): 717–737.

Klingler-Vidra, Robyn. 2018. *The Venture Capital State: The Silicon Valley Model in East Asia*. Ithaca: Cornell University Press.

Laeven, Luc. 2014. *The Development of Local Capital Markets: Rationale and Challenges*.

La Porta, Rafael, Florencio Lopez-de-Silanes, Andrei Shleifer, and Robert W. Vishny. 1998. Law and Finance. *Journal of Political Economy* 106 (6): 1113–1155.

La Porta, Rafael, et al. 2002. Investor Protection and Corporate Governance: Origins, Consequences, Reform. *Journal of Financial Economics* 58(1–2): 3–27.

Larrain, Borja, and I. Francisco Urzúa. 2016. Do Business Groups Change with Market Development? *Journal of Economics & Management Strategy* 25 (3): 750–784.

Lazzarini, Sérgio. G., Aldo Musacchio, Rodrigo Bandeira-de-Mello, and Rosilene Marcon. 2015. What Do State-Owned Development Banks Do? Evidence from BNDES, 2002–09. *World Development* 66: 237–253.

Leeds, Roger. 2015. *Private Equity Investing in Emerging Markets: Opportunities for Value Creation*. New York: Palgrave Macmillan US.

Lemos, Renata, and Daniela Scur. 2012. *Management Practices, Firm Ownership, and Productivity in Latin America*.

Lerner, Josh, and Antoinette Schoar. 2005. Does Legal Enforcement Affect Financial Transactions? The Contractual Channel in Private Equity. *The Quarterly Journal of Economics* 120 (1): 223–246.

Leslie, Armijo. 2017. The Public Bank Trilemma: Brazil's New Developmentalism and the BNDES. In *Democratic Brazil Divided*, ed. Peter R. Kingstone and Thimoty J. Power. Pittsburgh: University of Pittsburgh Press.

Levine, Ross. 2005. Finance and Growth: Theory and Evidence. In *Handbook of Economic Growth*, ed. Philippe Aghion and Steven Durlauf, 865–934. Amsterdam: Elsevier.

Levine, Ross, Norman Loayza, and Thorsten Beck. 2000. Financial Intermediation and Growth: Causality and Causes. *Journal of Monetary Economics* 46 (1): 31–77.

Li, Quan, and Adam Resnick. 2003. Reversal of Fortunes: Democratic Institutions and Foreign Direct Investment Inflows to Developing Countries. *International Organization* 57 (1): 175–211.

Little, Bruce. 2008. *Fixing the Future: How Canada's Usually Fractious Governments Worked Together to Rescue the Canada Pension Plan*. Toronto: University of Toronto Press.

Mahoney, James. 2010. *Colonialism and Postcolonial Development: Spanish America in Comparative Perspective*. Cambridge: Cambridge University Press.

Mauboussin, Michael J., and Dan Callahan. 2020. *Public to Private Equity in the United States: A Long-Term Look.*

Mazzucato, Mariana, and Caetano C.R. Penna. 2016. Beyond Market Failures: The Market Creating and Shaping Roles of State Investment Banks. *Journal of Economic Policy Reform* 19 (4): 305–326.

McKinsey & Company 2019. *Private Markets Come of Age: McKinsey Global Private Markets Review 2019.*

Menaldo, Victor, and Daniel Yoo. 2015. Democracy, Elite Bias, and Financial Development in Latin America. *World Politics* 67 (04): 726–759.

Mian, Atif. 2006. Distance Constraints: The Limits of Foreign Lending in Poor Economies. *The Journal of Finance* 61 (3): 1465–1505.

Moguillansky, Graciela, Rogerio Studart, and Sebastián Vergara. 2004. Foreign Banks in Latin America: A Paradoxical Result. *Cepal Review* 82: 19–35.

Morck, Randall. 2005. *A History of Corporate Governance around the World: Family Business Groups to Professional Managers*, ed. Morck Randall. Chicago: University of Chicago Press.

Morck, Randall, and Bernard Yeung. 2004. Family Control and the Rent-Seeking Society. *Entrepreneurship Theory and Practice* 28 (4): 391–409.

Mueller, Holger M., and Thomas Philippon. 2011. Family Firms and Labor Relations. *American Economic Journal: Macroeconomics* 3 (2): 218–245.

Musacchio, Aldo. 2009. *Experiments in Financial Democracy*. Cambridge: Cambridge University Press.

Musacchio, Aldo, and Sérgio G. Lazzarini. 2014. *Reinventing State Capitalism: Leviathan in Business, Brazil and Beyond*. Cambridge: Harvard University Press.

Musacchio, Aldo, Sérgio. G. Lazzarini, and Ruth V. Aguilera. 2015. New Varieties of State Capitalism: Strategic and Governance Implications. *Academy of Management Perspectives* 29 (1): 115–131.

Nenova, Tatiana. 2003. The Value of Corporate Voting Rights and Control: A Cross-Country Analysis. *Journal of Financial Economics* 68 (3): 325–351.

OECD. 2018. *OECD Equity Market Review of Asia 2018.*

Opazo, Luis, Claudio Raddatz, and Sergio L. Schmukler. 2014. *Institutional Investors and Long-Term Investment: Evidence from Chile*. The World Bank.

Pagano, Marco, and Paolo F. Volpin. 2005. The Political Economy of Corporate Governance. *The American Economic Review* 95: 1005–1030.

Pagés, Carmen. 2010. Big Questions About Small Firms. In *The Age of Productivity*, ed. Carmen Pagés, 207–222. New York: Palgrave Macmillan US.

Pandya, Sonal, and David Leblang. 2017. Risky Business: Institutions vs. Social Networks in FDI. *Economics & Politics* 29 (2): 91–117.

Parise, Gianpaolo, Fabrizio Leone, and Carlo Sommavilla. 2018. *Family First? Nepotism and Corporate Investment*.

Perotti, Enrico C., and Ernst-Ludwig von Thadden. 2006. The Political Economy of Corporate Control and Labor Rents. *Journal of Political Economy* 114 (1): 145–175.

Phalippou, Ludovic. 2020. *An Inconvenient Fact: Private Equity Returns & The Billionaire Factory*.

Pinto, Pablo M., Stephen Weymouth, and Peter Gourevitch. 2010. The Politics of Stock Market Development. *Review of International Political Economy* 17 (2): 378–409.

Post, Alison E. 2014. *Foreign and Domestic Investment in Argentina: The Politics of Privatized Infrastructure*. Cambridge University Press.

Puente, Ignacio, and Ben Ross Schneider. 2020. Business and Development: How Organization, Ownership and Networks Matter. *Review of International Political Economy*: 1–25.

Rajan, Raghuram G., and Luigi Zingales. 1998. Financial Dependence and Growth. *The American Economic Review* 88: 559–586.

———. 2003. The Great Reversals: The Politics of Financial Development in the Twentieth Century. *Journal of Financial Economics* 69 (1): 5–50.

Remes, Jaana, et al. 2019. *Latin America's Missing Middle*.

Roe, Mark J. 2003. *Political Determinants of Corporate Governance: Political Context, Corporate Impact*. Oxford: Oxford University Press.

Roe, Mark J., and Jordan I. Siegel. 2009. Finance and Politics: A Review Essay. *Journal of Economic Literature* 47 (3): 781–800.

———. 2011. Political Instability: Effects on Financial Development, Roots in the Severity of Economic Inequality. *Journal of Comparative Economics* 39 (3): 279–309.

Roe, Mark J., and Massimiliano Vatiero. 2015. Corporate Governance and Its Political Economy. In *Oxford Handbook of Corporate Governance*, ed. Jeffrey N. Gordon and Wolf-Georg Ringe. New York: Oxford University Press.

Samila, Sampsa, and Olav Sorenson. 2011. Venture Capital, Entrepreneurship, and Economic Growth. *Review of Economics and Statistics* 93 (1): 338–349.

Scharfstein, David. 2018. Presidential Address: Pension Policy and the Financial System. *The Journal of Finance* 73 (4): 1463–1512.

Schmukler, Sergio L., Juan Carlos Gozzi, and Augusto De la Torre. 2007. Capital Market Development: Whither Latin America ?

Schneider, Ben Ross. 2004. *Business Politics and the State in Twentieth-Century Latin America*. Cambridge University Press.

———. 2008. Economic Liberalization and Corporate Governance: The Resilience of Business Groups in Latin America. *Comparative Politics* 40: 379–397.

———. 2013. *Hierarchical Capitalism in Latin America: Business, Labor, and the Challenges of Equitable Development*. Cambridge: Cambridge University Press.

———. 2015. *Designing Industrial Policy in Latin America: Business-State Relations and the New Developmentalism*. New York: Palgrave Macmillan US.

Schrank, Andrew. 2007. Asian Industrialization in Latin American Perspective: The Limits to Institutional Analysis. *Latin American Politics and Society* 49 (2): 183–200.

Shirley, Mary M. 2005. Institutions and Development. In *Handbook of New Economic Institutionalism*, ed. Mary M. Shirley and Claude Menard. Boston: Springer.

Simison, Emilia. 2019. *Democracies, Dictatorships, and Policy Change*.

Stallings, Barbara, and Rogelio Studart. 2006. *Finance for Development: Latin America in Comparative Perspective*. Washington, DC: Brookings Institutions Press.

Storm, Servaas. 2018. Financialization and Economic Development: A Debate on the Social Efficiency of Modern Finance. *Development and Change* 49 (2): 302–329.

Stulz, René M., and Rohan Williamson. 2003. Culture, Openness, and Finance. *Journal of Financial Economics* 70 (3): 313–349.

Taylor, March Zachary. 2016. *The Politics of Innovation: Why Some Countries Are Better than Others in Science & Technology*. New York: Oxford University Press.

Torres, Ernani, and Rodrigo Zeidan. 2016. The Life-Cycle of National Development Banks: The Experience of Brazil's BNDES. *The Quarterly Review of Economics and Finance* 62: 97–104.

van Essen, Marc, J. (Hans) van Oosterhout, and Pursey P.M.A.R. Heugens. 2013. Competition and Cooperation in Corporate Governance: The Effects of Labor Institutions on Blockholder Effectiveness in 23 European Countries. *Organization Science* 24 (2): 530–551.

Wang, Yuhua. 2015. *Tying the Autocrat's Hands: The Rise of the Rule of Law in China*. New York: Cambridge University Press.

Woo-Cumings, Meredith. 1991. *Race to the Swift: State and Finance in Korean Industrialization*. New York: Columbia University Press.

World Bank. 2017. *The Evolution of the Canadian Pension Model: Practical Lessons for Building World-Class Pension Organizations*.

Yadav, Vineeta, and Bumba Mukherjee. 2016. *The Politics of Corruption in Dictatorships*. Cambridge: Cambridge University Press.

Yeyati, Eduardo Levy, Alejandro Micco, and Ugo Panizza. 2007. A Reappraisal of State-Owned Banks. *Economía* 7: 209–259.

Yong, Kwek Ping. 2012. *Private Equity in China: Challenges and Opportunities*. Wiley.

Young, Michael N., et al. 2008. Corporate Governance in Emerging Economies: A Review of the Principal-Principal Perspective. *Journal of Management Studies* 45 (1): 196–220.

Zysman, John. 1983. *Governments*. Markets and Growth: Financial Systems and the Politics of Industrial Change. Cornell University Press.

CHAPTER 3

Private Equity and Latin America

This chapter presents data about private equity in Latin America to support both the theoretical arguments from the previous chapter and the case studies developed in Chapters 4 and 5. It makes three main points.

First, it presents firm-level evidence to support the relationship between private equity, financial development, and corporate governance reform. In particular, it provides evidence that indicates that: (1) PE is an important driver of stock market listings; (2) PE-backed companies exhibit a more dispersed—and more institutional—ownership structure; (3) PE investors crowds-out family members from corporate leadership positions; (4) family ownership, and not private equity, is associated with more leveraged capital structures (i.e. with more intense use of debt financing); and, (5) the mere passage of time, measured as firm's age, does not necessarily drive companies to become more institutionalized. This exercise provides an empirical validation to the arguments about private equity made in Chapter 2.

Second, it shows Brazil is, by far, the largest private equity market in the region. This second section displays fundraising and investment figures gathered by industry associations, and other metrics related to the relative penetration of the asset class by country. Brazil dominates the regional private equity industry, even after normalizing by the size of its economy. Chile, that otherwise has the most developed financial markets

I. Puente, *Private Equity and Financial Development in Latin America*, Latin American Political Economy,
https://doi.org/10.1007/978-3-030-88983-8_3

in the region, exhibits a relatively lower penetration of PE investors. These figures confirm evidence gathered from the IPOs and are also consistent with data on the penetration of PE into business elites, as well as with the material gathered through interviews with market participants and other secondary sources.

And third, it shows alternative hypotheses do not reconcile easily with the ordering of the cases regarding the penetration of PE investors. Latin American countries are benchmarked on a set of indicators that illustrate alternative hypothesis from the literature: investor protections, financial and trade openness, regime type, and labor strength. Even within a small sample we could expect the development of private equity markets—as a key component of a more developed financial system—to be more closely related with stronger investor protections, more deregulated financial systems, trade openness, democracy, and relatively weaker labor organizations. But Latin American country's relative ordering in these dimensions do not match well the development of each country's PE markets. For example, while Brazil is the largest country in the region, its scores low on investor protections, it is quite protectionist and has strong organized labor, at least relatively to its Latin American peers. Moreover, it discusses the role of country's size and scale as another possible explanation for the relative penetration of PE in Latin America.

Private equity is, by definition, an opaque industry. Given the private nature of its investments, data is mostly proprietary and not easily available (L. Jeng and Lerner 2016). Moreover, there are significant measurement challenges that make data from different sources hardly comparable (G. W. Brown et al. 2015). For example, it is not always clear what type of investors are considered part of the asset class (e.g. government-related funds are rarely included), which sectors are covered (e.g. infrastructure or real estate), and how investment figures are calculated (e.g. with or without leverage). Beyond definitional congruence, the information collected by industry associations can also be biased since it is mostly used for promotional purposes. In order to overcome these limitations, and being mindful of the advantages and limitations of different data sources, I triangulate multiple sources of information: firm-level data from stock market listings, aggregate data from regional industry associations, and individual-level data from businesspeople. Moreover, the main findings are corroborated with interviews and secondary sources.

Overall, the goal of the chapter is both to present evidence that validates some of the arguments made in the theory chapter and to introduce the stylized facts of the country case studies that will be developed in subsequent chapters. The first section displays the empirical exercise using firm-level data from all companies that listed in Latin American stock markets in the 2002–2106 period. Private equity investors, indeed, appear to help modernize corporate governance at the firm level. Second, it presents different data sources to determine the relative penetration of PE at the country level. Third, it compares these countries on a series of indicators that illustrate alternative hypothesis. Finally, it concludes and introduces the case studies developed in Chapters 4 and 5.

3.1 PE and Stock Markets: Evidence from IPOs in Latin America

To assess the penetration of private equity across countries, and compare PE-backed[1] with non-PE-backed firms, I gathered the prospectus of all companies that listed their shares in Latin American stock markets in the last fifteen years. The sample comprises around 250 companies in six countries—Argentina, Brazil, Chile, Colombia, Mexico, and Peru—spanning from 2002 to 2017.[2] A prospectus is a document that companies are required to file in each country securities regulator before their initial public offering. These documents contain detailed information on the firm's ownership structure and board of directors, providing a snapshot of the company before going public, while still privately-held.

It would be extremely hard to obtain equivalent information on a larger sample of private companies. From the prospectus I can identify who are each firm's pre-IPO owners and gather a battery of firm-level covariates. I classify ownership type into five categories: family/individuals, multinationals, government, private equity, and shares owned by public investors; and compute this variable before and after the listing. This is not data that is readily available in off-the-shelf sources, but

[1] A PE-backed IPO is the initial selling to the public of shares in a company that has been previously funded by private equity investors. See, for example, Wilhelmus and Lee (2019) that also compare PE-backed from non-PE-backed companies.

[2] Given the relatively shallow capital markets in the region, the number of companies is not large. To identify the companies that listed in Latin American stock markets, many of them later de-listed, I triangulated data from Capital IQ with the information of each country's security regulators. Then, I downloaded the prospectus for each company from either the regulator's portal or the company's investor relations site, and hand-coded the different variables.

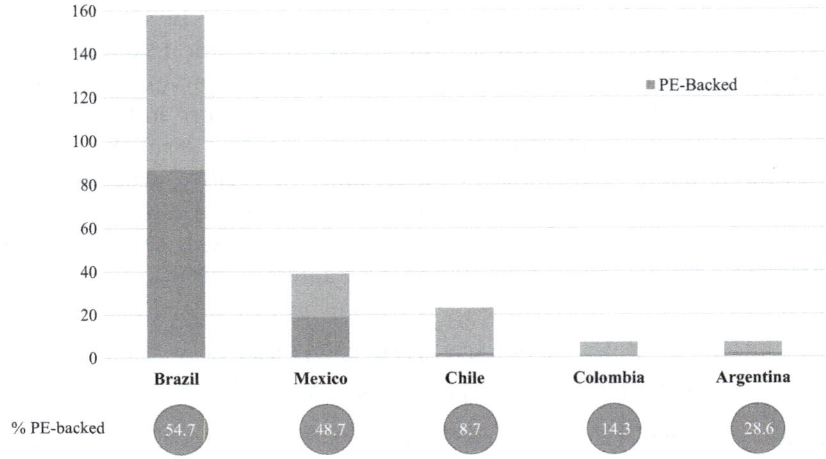

Fig. 3.1 #IPOs per country (2002–2017) (*Source* Capital IQ, securities regulators)

has to be collected manually. Prospectus contain richer and more accurate information than standard sources of firm-level data such as Bureau van Dijk and Capital IQ, but in a raw format.

Figure 3.1 shows the number of listings by country and distinguishes between companies that had PE backing before the IPO from those that did not. Private equity is an important investor in companies that list in public markets. Pooling across all countries and years, 47% of all the companies that listed had a—broadly defined—private equity investor among its pre-IPO shareholders. This figure is somewhat lower than comparable figures outside the region,[3] but still substantial. Cross-country differences are noteworthy. Brazil concentrates around two-thirds of the total listings (67%) but more than three-quarters (78%) of all the PE-backed IPOs in the region; more than half (54.7%) of the companies that listed in Brazil throughout the period had PE backing. On the other hand, only two of the 23 companies that listed in Chile (8.7%) had a private equity shareholder when they went public. The country-level average is of 31%. The two countries that concentrate most of the

[3] Relatedly, see Kaplan and Lerner (2010) that find that around 60% of IPOs in the US between 1999 and 2009 were venture-backed.

listings, Brazil and Mexico, are also where the proportion of PE-backed companies is higher. These findings are consistent with the complementarity between private and public markets.[4] Private equity investors "feed" stock markets of companies, and stock markets provide PE investors a feasible exit option for their investments.

The evidence in Fig. 3.1 is also in line with arguments gathered during fieldwork. An executive from the Brazil's stock exchange highlighted the importance of private equity investors as a driver of listings:

> Around 60% of IPOs in the last decade have been PE-backed, and in the last couple of years this figure has been larger, over 70%. PE is the key factor for new listings! This is our working hypothesis.

Similarly, in Mexico, a former official from the banking and securities regulator explained, when discussing the—scant—development of the local stock market:

> I am not sure how we can accelerate the process, but there is one thing that is very clear: every IPO from the last couple of years was backed by a PE fund. So we don't have to re-invent the wheel, but to promote private capital. We need to feed the stock market of companies. [...]They [grupos] don't need to raise money. You need a private equity fund that changes the culture of the company, and then sponsors the IPO. If a company reaches the stock market, it will likely be because it is backed by a PE fund. Achieving a listing without them is unusual.

Beyond cross-national differences, this dataset is also useful to compare firm-level characteristics of private equity backed companies at the time of the IPO. In particular, I focus on evaluating ownership concentration, the presence of kinship ties and leverage.[5]

First, regression analysis indicates that private equity backed companies tend to have more dispersed shareholding structures, one of the metrics usually associated with financial development (e.g., in La Porta et al. 1998), before listing. The likelihood of having a controlling shareholder (an investor who by itself controls more than 50% of the voting rights) is

[4] See, for example, Jeng and Wells (2000) that show IPOs (and not overall market capitalization) are crucial determinants of VC/PE finance.

[5] For an analysis of firm and country-level corporate governance features and valuation, see Chong and Lopez-de-Silanes (2007).

Table 3.1 Private equity and majority control

	Majority pre-IPO	*Majority post-IPO*
PE (dummy)	−0.225***	−0.148***
PE (%)	−0.004***	−0.003***

01 "***" 0.05 "**" 0.1 "*"

Note Majority is defined as one shareholder having more than 50% of voting rights and not by its economic rights. Regression models include country fixed effects and controls by year, assets (ln), sector (infrastructure and financial), and firm's age. Post-IPO regressions in the second column also control by the stake of the largest shareholder before the IPO

significantly lower for PE-backed companies. Using a binary measure for PE, results in Table 3.1 show PE-backed companies have a 22.5% lower probability of having majoritarian control before they do the IPO (0.6 of the standard deviation). IPOs, of course, modify firms' ownership structure. Following the IPO, PE-backed companies are also less likely (14.8 percentage points) to have a controlling shareholder, even after controlling by the pre-IPO concentration level.[6] Relatedly, PE-backed companies are associated with larger free floats and more dispersed ownership, as shown in Table 3.4 in the Appendix of this chapter. These are relevant results: the empirical literature on finance and development coincides that what is relevant for economic growth, capital accumulation, and productivity is market liquidity—related to larger free floats and more dispersed ownership structures—and not market size/overall market capitalization (Beck and Levine 2004; Levine and Zervos 1998).

Indeed, it appears PE can introduce some dispersion in otherwise highly concentrated ownership structures. Still, it is clear that in Latin America, the end line in terms of ownership concentration is not the Berle and Means model of atomized shareholders. Most companies in Latin America have a controlling shareholder (see data in De La Cruz et al. 2019), with a few exceptions in Brazil, in most cases of companies that had at some point government-related investors among its main shareholders (e.g. Embraer, BRF). Following the IPO, the largest shareholder owns, on average, 56% of the company. There is some variation across

[6] All these regression outcomes are from models that include country fixed effects and controls by year and firm's age, industry, and size. For the post-IPO models in the second column, they also control for the largest shareholder prior to the IPO.

countries: companies that listed in Brazil and Mexico are somewhat more dispersed compared to the ones that listed in Chile and Colombia. Still, firms throughout the region exhibit concentrated ownership structure relative to international standards.

I also find evidence suggesting that a higher proportion of—more institutional—private equity investors before the IPO also drives a more "modern" corporate governance, measured by the number of kinship ties in the board.[7] PE-backed companies tend to have fewer family ties among the board of directors. The presence of institutionalized investors is inversely related with the presence of family ties within a firm's board and management. Equity holdings usually grant political rights and give shareholders a say on the appointment of board members and top management. Thus, shareholders can encourage the replacement of family members in leadership positions with professionals. Figure 3.2 displays the negative relationship between the percentage of private equity ownership prior to the firm's initial public offering (IPO) and the—residualized—number of family members in the company's board across Latin America. Companies controlled by private equity investors rarely exhibit any family ties within their leadership, in line with the argument that private equity is a driver of firm professionalization.

To corroborate this relationship, I regress both binary and continuous measures of family ties within a firms' board on a—binary and continuous—measures of PE ownership. Table 3.2 shows the results from the four resulting models. All models include country fixed effects (that are not significant under most specifications suggesting this correlation is not country-specific), as well as controls for year, and firm's industry, age, and size (measured by both assets and revenues). The presence of family-related individuals within a firm's board is negatively—and highly significantly—correlated with the percentage of shares owned by PE investors. The same results hold true when using a binary indicator of private equity and of family ties. At the time of listings, companies that have a PE investor have 24 percentage points lower probability of exhibiting kinship ties within their board (around half a standard deviation of the binary metric of kinship ties). Thus, this data supports the

[7] For an evaluation of the effectiveness of PE/VC funds promoting best practices in corporate governance in SMEs in Brazil, see Latini et al. (2014).

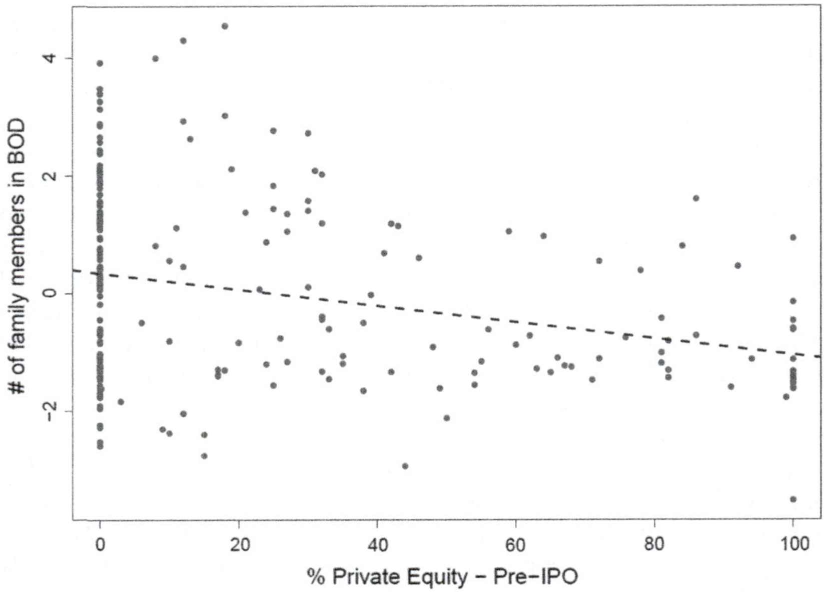

Fig. 3.2 Private Equity and family ties (*Note* Each dot the graph represents a firm. Y-axis exhibit the residuals obtained after regressing the number of members with family ties on each company's board of directors on country fixed effects, controls for year, assets [ln], sector [infrastructure and finance], and age [years since its foundation])

Table 3.2 Private equity and family ties

	Family ties (#)	*Family ties (binary)*
PE (dummy)	−0.653***	−0.242***
PE (%)	−0.014***	−0.004***

01 "***" 0.05 "**" 0.1 "*"

Note Regression models include country fixed effects and controls by year, firm's age, assets (ln), and sector (infrastructure and financial)

Table 3.3 Ownership type and leverage

	Leverage (%)	*Leverage (%)*
PE (%)	−0.00072	
	(0.0005)	
Family (%)		0.00073*
		(0.004)

01 "***" 0.05 "**" 0.1 "*"

Note Regression models include country fixed effects and controls by year, firm's age, assets (ln), and sector (infrastructure and financia)

claim that institutional forms of ownership and investment such as private equity have the potential to break the kin-based control of firms.[8]

This dataset also supports the argument made in Chapter 2 regarding capital structures. I regress a measure of firm leverage[9]—or indebtedness—at the time of the IPO on both the percentage of the company owned by private equity investors, and by families or individuals, together with a battery of controls. Results in Table 3.3 do not show statistically significant evidence of a relationship between private equity ownership and leverage, at least at the moment of listing (see left column). Instead, I do observe a positive relationship between family/individual ownership and leverage, even when including in the regression country fixed effects, and firm age, asset size, and industry controls (see right column). One possible explanation is that family members value retaining control over their firm more than other type of owners. Thus, they try to avoid diluting their control by selling an equity stake to external investors. Debt can help retain control. This correlation is in line with the findings of some applied finance work on Latin America that I discussed in Chapter 2 (Kayo et al.

[8] With cross-sectional data alone it is not possible to know if the negative relationship between PE investors and kinship ties comes from the "within firm" effects of PE investors institutionalizing family firms, or just from the composition effect (i.e., PE investing in and helping mount non-family firms). In order to strengthen the plausibility of a causal connection between ownership structure and kinship ties, a separate co-authored paper using across-time data from Brazilian listed companies finds evidence of the former. Exploiting variation in firm ownership over time, the paper tracks the evolution of kinship ties across time (at both the board and top executive levels). Including firm fixed-effects, coefficients are negative and significant at the 5% level. These results give more credence to the argument that as a firm's ownership becomes more institutional through PE investments, it displays fewer family ties. See Puente et al. (2021).

[9] Leverage is measured as the ratio between total liabilities and total assets (book value).

2018; Larrain and Urzúa I. 2016). Overall, leverage seems to be more associated with family ownership than with private equity.

Finally, I analyze how firms' age impact corporate governance. If change at the firm level is slow and reforms take time to mature, it could be expected existing firms will gradually drift to a more dispersed shareholding base and slowly professionalize their corporate leadership. But this does not seem to be the case. A firm's age (measured as the number of years since foundation) is not related to ownership dispersion, nor to the professionalization of its leadership. Instead, age is correlated positively both with the size of the stake of the largest shareholder and with the probability of having kinship ties in the board, even if not consistently statistically significant at conventional levels (again, controlling by a battery of firm-level covariates and country fixed effects). Table 3.5 in the Appendix to this chapter shows the results of models using age and age (ln). These results are in line with evidence about the stickiness in the ownership structure of business groups (Larrain and Urzúa, I. 2016) that show a remarkable stability in ownership structures, even after going public.

I use this dataset for two different purposes: (1) to evaluate the relative penetration of PE in each market/country and (2) to assess the impact of this type of investor on the firms' ownership structure, governance, and leverage. As explained above, this empirical exercise was based on data extracted from IPO prospectus. The richness of this information is, of course, at the expense of only including in the sample companies about to be listed, that "selected" into the capital markets. For the cross-country comparisons (e.g. which country has more PE?) the sampling of this dataset would be problematic if private equity investors in one country are more or less likely to exit their investments through the public markets. I did not find indications to believe so and next section validates this dataset's findings using several other sources.

For the firm-level assessments (e.g. how are PE-backed companies "different"?), this dataset misses the comparison between PE-backed and non-PE-backed companies that remain private. But, if one considers that non-PE-backed companies that list in the stock market are more institutionalized than the ones that do not, then, by focusing the comparison only on companies that go public, we are creating a more stringent test for PE-backed companies. If this is the case, then this sample would underestimate the already noteworthy relationship between private equity investors and corporate governance modernization shown in this section.

3.2 PE Investment by Country

Figure 3.1 presented data about the relative penetration of private equity across multiple Latin American countries. Brazil appears to be, by far, the largest market. As (Leeds 2015) asserts, "even accounting for the country's dominant size (…) its share of total Latin American private equity has long dwarfed the rest of the Southern Hemisphere" (p. 195).

This assessment is consistent with the information gathered from interviews across the region. When asked to rank Latin American countries in terms of the development of their private equity markets, interviewees unanimously indicated Brazil as the leader in the region (even though interviews occurred during a time when Brazil was going through a severe political and economic crisis); Mexico usually followed.

For example, a corporate lawyer working throughout the region, and actively involved in the PE/VC business associations, answered "Brazil, then Mexico—we'll see what happens with AMLO—then Colombia, finally Argentina. And then Chile, well, they play in a different league." Similarly, a Colombian partner of a fund with operations across the region agreed on Brazil's dominance: *"Brazil is the most developed and institutionalized market in the region, by far!"*

While data from public listings could introduce some biases, the general ordering of cases is also corroborated by data gathered by the two regional industry associations: EMPEA, that brings together fund managers from across all emerging markets, and LAVCA, that focuses on Latin America. Since transaction-level data was not available, I use the aggregates they make public. I do not show time trends by country, but average them out. When relevant, the case studies in Chapter 4 leverage the within-country temporal dimension. For example, the timing of the Mexican case illustrates my main argument about the development of private capital markets: the market only emerges after local pension funds are allowed to invest in private capital funds in 2009.

Figure 3.3 presents fundraising values. It aggregates all the capital committed to funds dedicated to each country. Although capital commitments come from both local and international investors, this metric is arguably a good proxy for the development of a domestic private capital industry as it only takes into account funds raised with a mandate to invest in one particular country. It does not include regional or global fund managers conducting one-off transactions. Both in terms of total volume and when scaled by GDP, Brazil is the largest market, followed by Mexico

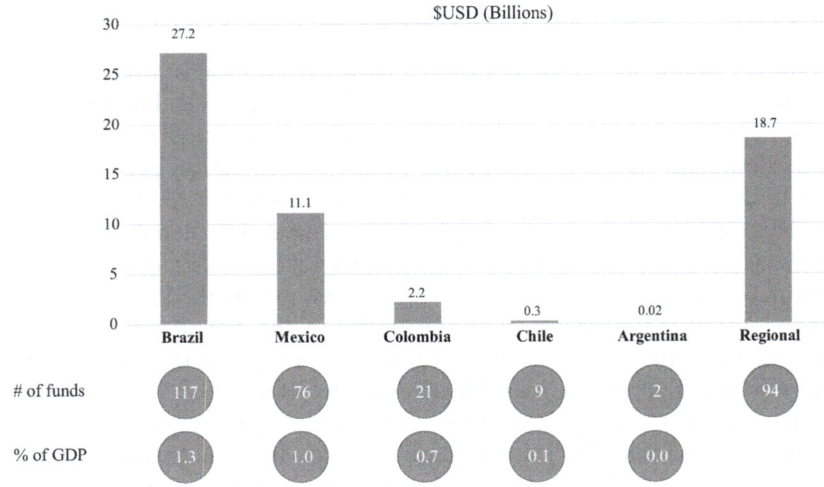

Fig. 3.3 Private equity fundraising by country (2008–2016) (*Source* EMPEA)

and then Colombia. Of course, this metric may be biased against smaller countries such as Chile, as its smaller scale makes it less attractive for dedicated funds. Indeed, Chile shows low "dedicated" fundraising volumes, only surpassing Argentina's null fundraising activity.

In terms of private equity investment volumes, the data exhibited in Fig. 3.4 corroborates Brazil's lead, followed by Mexico, then Colombia, Argentina, and finally Chile. Chile, in turn, appears to receive substantial private capital for infrastructure investments. To facilitate comparability figures are scaled by the size of the economy (GDP), as well as by the gross capital formation levels in each country. I present figures compiled by LAVCA,[10] the Latin American association that encompasses the whole period of my case studies (2002–2018), a longer period of time that figures computed by EMPEA (2008–2016). While at first sight scaling by GDP seems reasonable, this approach could be questionable at the early stages of development of the industry (particularly without correcting by other factors (such as GDP per capita) that can also affect the industry

[10] From LAVCA Scorecards. Data on PE/VC stocks in 2006 was "distributed" evenly across the 6 previous years.

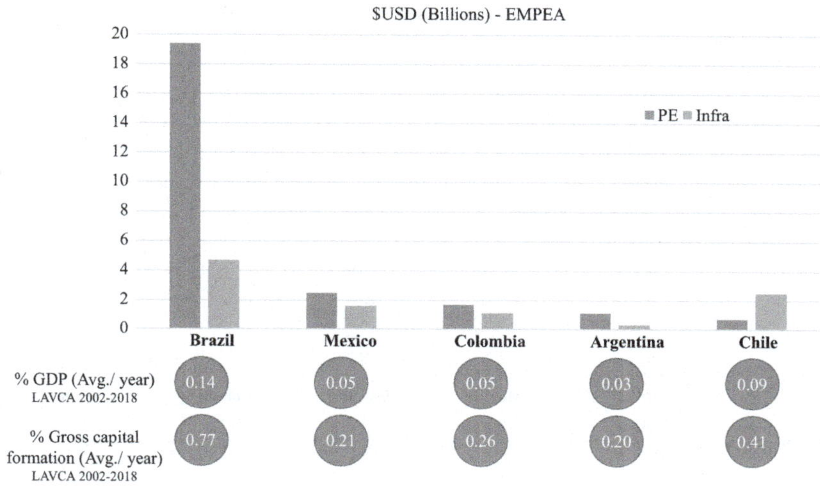

Fig. 3.4 Private equity investments by country (2008–2016) (*Source* EMPEA, LAVCA)

from the demand side). Adjusting by gross capital formation levels amplifies Brazil's lead.[11] Chile, the smallest economy, ranks second, arguably driven, at least in part, by a handful of large infrastructure investments made by foreign fund managers. Colombia and Mexico follow, and Argentina is—consistently—last.[12] As explained by LAVCA's director, responsible for collecting these numbers:

> Chile is not the largest market, but is able to attract a couple of hundred million dollars a year just because it has many natural resources. Once in a while, a foreign fund manager invests $500M in a solar plant or in some other renewable energy. Given the size of the economy, that inflates their investment over GDP ratio.

[11] It is important to note these figures do not include BNDESPAR's (BNDES private equity arm) quite sizable direct private equity investments.

[12] On normalizing by GDP, it is remarkable China, where PE has undoubtedly boomed well beyond Latin America levels (Fuller 2016; Leeds 2015; Yong 2012), would show similar (in some years lower) by GDP metrics than Brazil/Chile.

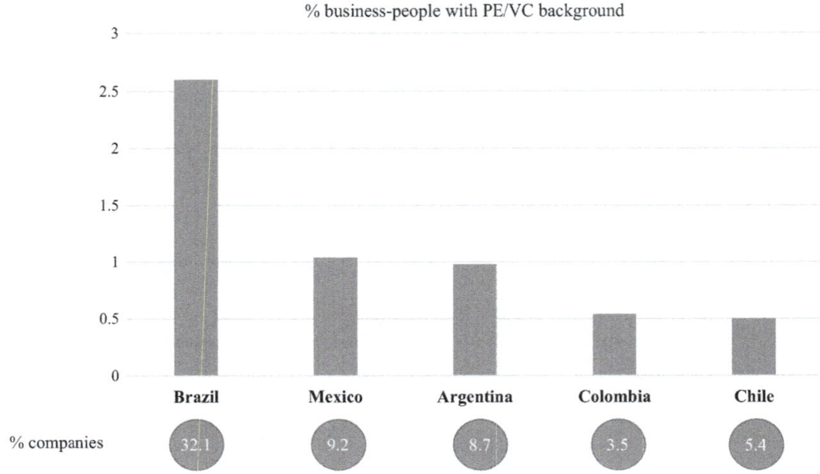

Fig. 3.5 Penetration of PE/VC in business communities (*Source* Capital IQ)

3.2.1 Evidence from Business Elites

In order to provide further evidence on the relative ordering of cases, I analyze the penetration of private equity professionals in each business community. To do so, I collect the bios of top business executives and board members from all Latin American companies under the supervision of securities regulators (i.e. those that issue stock and/or debt in public markets) in 2017, available through Capital IQ. The dataset comprises the bios of 8,020 unique individuals from 946 firms. Arguably, this extensive list is representative of most top businesspeople in each country, with some bias driven by the different levels of capital market development across the region. I then count how many unique individuals have experience working in the private equity industry and normalize this number by the total amount of individuals from each country included in the dataset.[13] The prevalence of businesspeople with a background in private equity can serve as another proxy for the relative penetration of private capital in each country. The pattern is consistent with the figures presented above. Figure 3.5 shows that Brazil is, by far, the country where

[13] I use a simple text function over the bios of each businessperson, where I search for the words "private equity" and/or "venture capital."

the private equity model is most extended among the business community, with a frequency 2.5 times higher than in Mexico and Argentina,[14] and more than five times than Colombia and Chile.[15] Not surprisingly, the same exercise as above but aggregating the data at the company level find the same pattern. These figures are displayed at the bottom of Fig. 3.5.

3.3 Alternative Explanations

The following section presents country-level data on a set of variables that illustrate alternative hypothesis: countries' institutional environments, their trade openness, regime type, and the strength of their labor organizations. This data allows to evaluate some of the arguments introduced in Chapter 2, when discussed the literature on financial development and corporate governance reform. It also provides context for the case studies. It is important to highlight that the empirical leverage that supports my findings does not come mostly from this cross-sectional analysis, but from the detailed case studies that, through time, exhibit similar patterns throughout the region. This exercise illustrates the ordering of cases in some key dimensions. It does not attempt to substitute more thorough empirical tests and does not refute the overall importance of some of these dimensions for the healthy development of financial markets. Still, it shows that the relative penetration of private equity in Latin America is not in line, and sometime even at odds, with what would be expected according to these hypotheses. Brazil, the Latin American country where private equity is most extended, is also consistently among the lowest-ranked in terms of its institutional environment, the least liberalized in terms of trade and capital flows, and where labor is also more strongly organized.

The analysis begins with a cross-national evaluation of each country's institutional environment. Institutional-based rankings are in line with

[14] Argentina's relatively high ranking is likely a legacy of its pioneering industry during the 90s, when the PE model was booming.

[15] Also, a comparative analysis of each country's corporate networks using board interlocks shows private equity professionals among the top connectors in Brazil (also, see Lazzarini 2010). This contrasts with Chile's interlock network. While Chile's network shows an extremely cohesive business community, the businesspeople that connected were mostly executives from family-owned business groups.

country's trade and financial openness. It then turns to political variables, and score the cases on regime type and evaluate the strength of organized labor in each country. Finally, I discuss the role of size and demand-side factors.

Figure 3.6 scores each of the countries in three metrics: World Bank's overall "ease of doing business" score, Fraser's Institute index on economic freedom/rule of law, and World Bank's score on minority shareholder rights and investor protections—more focused on financial markets. A similar pattern is observed across these three metrics where Chile, together with Mexico and Colombia, scores higher than Brazil and Argentina. Beyond the Argentinean case, whose weak investor protections, chronic episodes of expropriations and chaotic macro-economy frustrated all forms of investment into the country, by themselves, hypotheses only based on property rights and overall investor protections cannot explain the relative ordering of cases in PE dimensions.

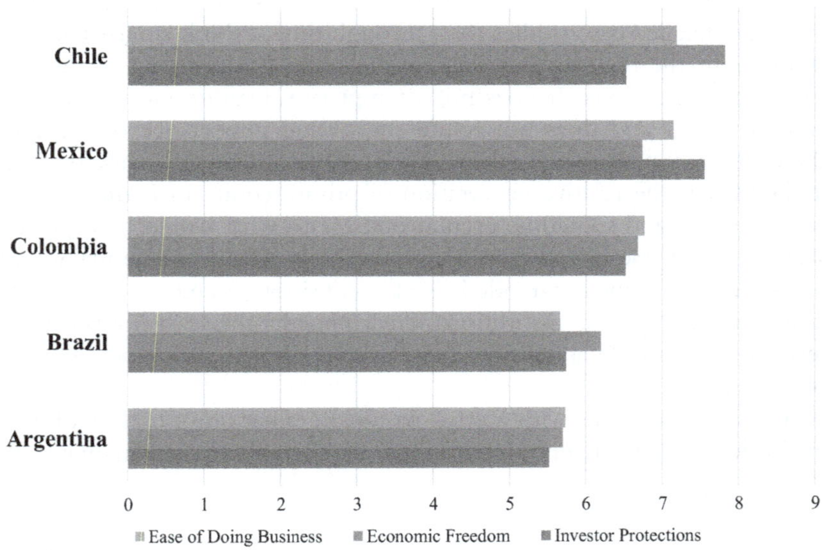

Fig. 3.6 Institutional environments (*Note* Investor Protections [2006–2017], Ease of Doing Business Score [2010–2017], and Economic Freedom Index [2002–2017]. *Source* Ease of Doing Business [World Bank]; Fraser Institute)

Rajan and Zingales's (2003) seminal paper focuses on cross-border capital and trade flows as key elements that drive the extension of arms-length financing (i.e. financial development). The rationale behind these hypotheses is that liberalization intensifies competition and weaken the incumbents' opposition to capital market development. Data from IMFs financial reform index (Abiad et al. 2010) ranks Mexico, together with Chile and Argentina high, and Brazil low (in addition to showing significant liberalization and "convergence" during the 1980s/1990s). Data on trade liberalization, as a proxy for the intensity of cross-border competition, is also not consistent with the ordering of my cases. Brazil appears to be the most protectionist country in the region and the one that has liberalized the least. Mexico and Chile are more open, as measured by total trade—imports and exports—as a proportion of GDP (and score higher in the financial liberalization index), as shown in Fig. 3.7.

As discussed in the theory chapter, political economy arguments about financial development connect inclusive political institutions—democracy—with growth in capital markets. After Fox's 2000 election in Mexico, the five Latin American countries analyzed are classified as democracies, at least when considering binary classifications (Cheibub et al. 2010). Throughout this period all countries are also

Fig. 3.7 Trade openness (2002–2017) (*Source* World Bank Development Indicators)

above the 0.5 cut-off in the—continuous—polyarchy indicator from V-DEM (Coppedge et al. 2019). In this classification, Chile together with Argentina and Brazil rank above Mexico and Colombia. Polity IV indicator, more associated with horizontal constraints, grants Chile full scores, followed by Argentina, Brazil, Mexico, and Colombia. And if focused just on constraints on the executives rather than on broader dimensions of democracy, again, for most of this period Chile appears to have a slight advantage over its Latin American peers. So overall, and at least by itself, a regime-type hypothesis does not fit well the outcomes. Chapter 5 further engages in the discussion on democracy and its mechanisms.

Beyond regime type, as argued in the theory chapter, Brazil (together with Argentina) seems to have the most powerful labor organizations in the region. This is illustrated by ILOs data that measures the coverage of collective bargain agreements as well as union membership, shown in Fig. 3.8. Argentina and Brazil appear to have the most conflictive labor relations, as suggested by the higher average number of stoppages per year. Chile ranks as the intermediate case, and in Colombia and Mexico, organized labor appears to be weak. Strong—and conflictive—labor organizations can be somehow related to Argentina's capital market

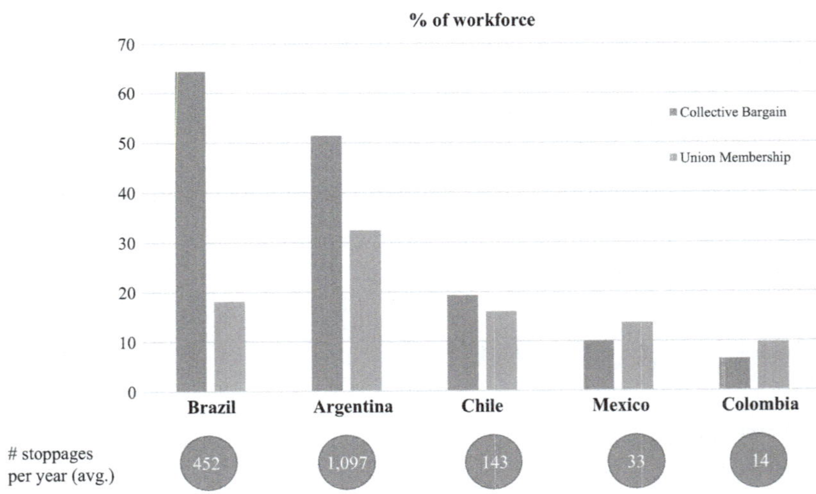

Fig. 3.8 Labor strength (*Source* ILO)

underdevelopment, but does not seem to have prevented the consolidation of a PE market in Brazil. And as for the rest of the cases, the strength of organized labor does not seem to be the most relevant factor to explain their relative underdevelopment.

Even though most of the metrics presented are somehow normalized, size seems as a plausible explanation for relatively more developed equity markets in Brazil, the region's largest economy. Data about the penetration of PE using IPOs is normalized by the total number of companies listed, PE/VC businesspeople data is scaled by the total number of business executives, and fundraising and investment figures are divided by GDP and gross capital formation. Still, there could be some scale effects that could favor the development of capital markets in larger countries (e.g. Panizza and Borensztein, Eduardo Eichengreen 2006). But, as argued below, this can hardly explain all the variation observed across Latin America.

First, it is worth highlighting some counter-examples. There are numerous countries with dynamic capital markets that are not large. For example, Singapore, Malaysia, and Israel are relatively small in terms of population and GDP but have sizable equity markets. Chapter 6 expands my arguments on cases outside of Latin America and shows evidence that suggests they hold beyond this region.[16]

Even if PE/VC financing is particularly well-suited for small—growing—companies, at least relative to public equity markets, one could argue that smaller countries lack a pool of companies large enough to become attractive to external investors. But this does not seem to explain the Chilean case. Notably, even the total number of listed companies in Chile is quite large (and therefore their total stock market capitalization high), especially when normalized by the size of the economy or population.

A related mechanism through which an economy's size could condition the development of the private equity market would be through its visibility to international investors. Small, peripheral markets could arguably be outside of the radar of large international investors, who are important players for the development of PE markets. Again, this does not seem to be Chile's case. For example, the difference between fundraising

[16] The World Bank identifies a minimum GDP of \$20B for an economy to be able to develop a viable stock market (Demekas and Nerlich 2020), a threshold that is way below the size of the five cases analyzed in the book.

and investment levels shows that Chile indeed appears to have attracted international attention.[17] Local institutional investors are the ones notably absent from domestic private capital markets, and these are arguably less influenced by scale/information effects. Overall, even though a sizable internal market may help drive demand for private capital, there is much more than size to the development of capital markets, as the case studies will show.

There are definitely other "demand side" factors that affect the development of the private equity industry. Generally, growth and income levels of the economy are viewed as proxies for the "demand" of capital. During the commodity boom, all of these economies grew, followed by a deceleration, more pronounced in the case of Brazil and Argentina (crisis can actually create opportunities for PE investors, who have a competitive advantage in situations of corporate distress and restructuring).[18] Moreover, Chile's higher GDP per capita levels should skew demand-side explanations in its favor. There are other "demand side" factors that could possibly impact the development of the industry, many of them policy-related (e.g. privatizations, public support for R&D). While these are certainly plausible, they are mostly outside the scope of the book. And at best, can complement arguments based on the role of institutional investors.

3.4 Conclusion

This chapter's findings support some key arguments about the role of private equity advanced in the theory chapter. First, it provides firm-level evidence that suggests that PE investors are indeed drivers of more modern corporate governance models. PE appears to feed the stock market with new listings. Moreover, among companies that list in the stock market, those backed by PE investors appear to have a more dispersed shareholder base and fewer kinship ties within their leadership.

[17] Beyond PE/VC financing Chile is, by order of magnitude, the country that has received during the last two decades more FDI—as a proportion of GDP—in the region. See World Bank Development Indicators (BX.KLT.DINV.WD.GD.ZS).

[18] Colombia together with Chile have been the fastest growing economies of this group of countries, averaging between 2002 and 2017 4.1% and 3.9% annual GDP growth rates. This was followed by Argentina (3.0%, biased upwards by the base year) and then Brazil (2.5%) and Mexico (2.2%). See World Bank Development Indicators (NY.GDP.MKTP.KD.ZG).

Second, the chapter presented multiple data points about the PE markets in Latin America, triangulating between alternative data sources. In terms of penetration, Brazil is the most consolidated market. Mexico and then Colombia appear to follow. Chile receives some sizable international investments, mostly in infrastructure; otherwise, it appears to lag behind. Argentina, where the PE model was early adopted during the 1990s, exhibited limited activity after the 2000s. This ordering of cases is not aligned with what would be expected based on the main hypotheses from the literatures on financial development and corporate reform.

Next, Chapter 4 focuses on the more direct role of government-related financial institutions, who promote PE funds by investing in them and encouraging pension funds to follow their lead. And beyond its role as an investor, Chapter 5 shows how public agencies helped the incipient private capital industry organize into asset-specific business associations who then lobbied for regulatory—institutional—change.

Appendix

See Tables 3.4 and 3.5.

Table 3.4 PE and ownership concentration

	PE Ownership pre-IPO (%)	PE Ownership pre-IPO (binary)
Free float (%)	0.126***	4.025***
	(0.024)	(1.773)
Largest shareholder post IPO (%)	−0.333***	−21.891***
	(0.039)	(2.820)

0.01 "***" 0.05 "**" 0.1 "*"

Note Regression models include country fixed effects and controls by year, firm's age, assets (ln), and sector (infrastructure and financial)

Table 3.5 Firms age, ownership dispersion, and professionalization

	Largest shareholder (%)	*Family ties (binary)*
Age	0.047	0.002
	(0.056)	(0.001)
Age (ln)	2.703	0.107**
	(1.852)	(0.002)

0.01"***" 0.05 "**" 0.1 "*"

Note Regression models include country fixed effects and controls by year, firm's assets (ln) and sector (infrastructure and financial)

References

Abiad, Abdul, Enrica Detragiache, and Thierry Tressel. 2010. A New Database of Financial Reforms. *IMF Staff Papers* 57 (2): 281–302.

Balan, Pablo, Juan Dodyk, and Ignacio Puente. 2021. *The Political Behavior of Family Firms: Evidence From Brazil.*

Beck, Thorsten, and Ross Levine. 2004. Stock Markets, Banks, and Growth: Panel Evidence. *Journal of Banking and Finance* 28 (3): 423–442.

Brown, Gregory W., et al. 2015. What Do Different Commercial Data Sets Tell Us About Private Equity Performance? *SSRN Electronic Journal.*

Cheibub, José Antonio, Jennifer Gandhi, and James Raymond Vreeland. 2010. Democracy and Dictatorship Revisited. *Public Choice* 143 (1): 67–101.

Chong, Alberto, and Florencio Lopez-de-Silanes. 2007. *Investor Protection and Corporate Governance: Firm-Level Evidence across Latin America.* Stanford: Inter-American Development Bank/Stanford University Press.

Coppedge, Michael, et al. 2019. V-Dem [Country-Year/Country-Date] Dataset V9. *Varieties of Democracy (V-Dem).*

De La Cruz, A., A. Medina, and Y. Tang. 2019. *Owners of the World's Listed Companies.* OECD Capital Market Series, Paris.

Demekas, Dimitri, and Anica Nerlich. 2020. *Creating Domestic Capital Markets in Developing Countries: Perspectives from Market Participants.*

Fuller, Douglas B. 2016. *Paper Tigers, Hidden Dragons: Firms and the Political Economy of China's Technological Development.* New York: Oxford University Press.

Jeng, Leslie, and Josh Lerner. 2016. Making Private Data Accessible in an Opaque Industry: The Experience of the Private Capital Research Institute. *American Economic Review* 106 (5): 157–160.

Jeng, Leslie A., and Philippe C. Wells. 2000. The Determinants of Venture Capital Funding: Evidence across Countries. *Journal of Corporate Finance* 6 (3): 241–289.

Kaplan, Steven N., and Josh Lerner. 2010. It Ain't Broke: The Past, Present, and Future of Venture Capital. *Journal of Applied Corporate Finance* 22 (2): 36–47.

Kayo, Eduardo K., et al. 2018. Capital Structure Adjustment in Brazilian Family Firms. *Revista De Administração Contemporânea* 22 (1): 92–114.

La Porta, Rafael, Florencio Lopez-de-Silanes, Andrei Shleifer, and Robert W. Vishny. 1998. Law and Finance. *Journal of Political Economy* 106 (6): 1113–1155.

Larrain, Borja, and Urzúa I. Francisco. 2016. Do Business Groups Change with Market Development? *Journal of Economics & Management Strategy* 25 (3): 750–784.

Latini, Estevão Teixeira, Joaquim Rubens Fontes-Filho, and Eric L. Chambers. 2014. Private Equity and Corporate Governance: Managing Brazilian SMEs. *Corporate Governance* 14 (2): 220–237.

Lazzarini, Sérgio G. 2010. *Capitalismo de Laços*. Elsevier.

Leeds, Roger. 2015. *Private Equity Investing in Emerging Markets: Opportunities for Value Creation*. New York: Palgrave Macmillan US.

Levine, Ross, and Sara Zervos. 1998. Stock Markets, Banks, and Economic Growth. *American Economic Review* 88 (3): 537–558.

Panizza, Ugo, and Barry Borensztein, Eduardo Eichengreen. 2006. *Debt Instruments and Policies in the New Millennium: New Markets and New Opportunities*.

Rajan, Raghuram G., and Luigi Zingales. 2003. The Great Reversals: The Politics of Financial Development in the Twentieth Century. *Journal of Financial Economics* 69 (1): 5–50.

Wilhelmus, Jakob, and Willian Lee. 2019. *Private Equity IPOs. Generating Faster Job Growth and More Investment*.

Yong, Kwek Ping. 2012. *Private Equity in China: Challenges and Opportunities*. Wiley.

CHAPTER 4

Institutions: Rules and Investors

The main goal of this chapter is to provide evidence about the role of institutional investors nurturing the incipient private capital industry in Latin America. Going through each of the cases, it shows that government-related investors,[1] and not just international and private players, appear to catalyze the sector's growth. Among institutional investors, it highlights the initial role played by domestic and multilateral development banks, followed by pension funds.

The chapter provides support to the second argument from the introduction and shows that the role of institutional investors is an important factor to explain the emergence of PE. These PE investors, in turn, are arguably one of the few drivers of corporate governance reform in the region, as showed in the previous chapter. Mainstream explanations based on rules and environments do not grant much attention to the mechanisms behind their main causal hypothesis that connects legal rules to financial and corporate governance outcomes, and overlook the origin and role played by financial intermediaries.

It is important to note that this actor-based argument does not contradict some of the lessons from the institutionalist literature, nor suggest

[1] Institutional investors refer to organizations that invest on behalf of its usually large member's base. This chapter focuses primarily on pension funds, as well as on government-owned investment funds.

I. Puente, *Private Equity and Financial Development in Latin America*, Latin American Political Economy,
https://doi.org/10.1007/978-3-030-88983-8_4

all state interventions in this area are conducive to more vibrant equity markets. Needless to say, recurrent state expropriation indeed inhibits financial development; it is enough to look at the Argentinean chronic history of sovereign defaults, the recent nationalization of pension system and to the negligible size of its financial system (Datz 2012). A government aligned with promoting private initiative and developing capital markets indeed appears to be a necessary condition for the development of the industry. Some degree of macroeconomic stability seems to be a pre-requisite for developing a domestic financial sector, particularly one based on securities denominated in local currency. Fiscally responsible administrations that do not overload local asset manager's portfolios with government bonds (Menaldo 2016) allow them to invest in longer-term riskier private sector securities and a reasonably good working corporate governance framework that protects investors external to the firm seem to be a pre-requisite for attracting them. But these conditions are not enough to generate a more active equity-based risk capital market. These markets also appear to be incubated by more active public policies.

This chapter is focused on the supply-side of private capital and explores the role in each case of both multilateral and domestic financial institutions. It introduces the main investors in PE funds in each country and highlights the role of the institutional investors that promote the emergence of new funds. Among them, development financial institutions play an "incubating" role during the early stages of the PE industry, followed by pension funds. While this chapter is centered on capital providers, the next one dives into the politics of regulatory change that helped institutionalize the industry, where notably many of the same players that provide capital also had a protagonic role.

It is also important to re-emphasize that the development of the industry is not just a function of the supply of capital and its regulatory framework, and, among others, that there are important demand-side aspects that also drive the overall development of the industry. While certainly important, many potential demand-side factors go beyond the scope of my research, focused on the financial supply side. Still, the selected cases can roughly "control" for some of these factors. As mentioned, these are all countries in the same continent, with comparable macro-trajectories, sizable economies at broadly similar stages of development, and exposed to the same shocks and trends in the international political economy. Moreover, the private capital industry is throughout the region at its early stages of development, before the point where we could expect the overall size of the economy can function as a limiting factor.

The analysis spans all the segments of the private capital industry, including venture capital, private equity, and infrastructure-related funds. Aside of their peculiarities—some of them definitely relevant but outside the more general focus of my research—they all fit a broad definition of PE: they are financial investors who have a medium to long-term time horizon and an active role in strategic management. They generally use the same investment vehicles from a legal and tax perspective. Regarding their fundraising sources, they all strive to attract institutional capital. They are often represented in the same business associations, which tend to represent all segments of the private capital industry. Moreover, the governance model they promote is broadly the same, with a protagonic role for external financial investors and professional managers. And notably, the emergence of each of the different segments of the private capital market also follows broadly similar dynamics.

The development of private capital markets in Latin American countries displays similar trajectories, though their timing and intensity grant some empirical leverage from where to make inference. The first "modern" PE funds first appeared in the region during the nineties in Argentina and Brazil, largely related to international flows of capital that followed these countries liberalizations. In many cases they participated in the privatizations of former state-owned enterprises and started engaging local financial institutions. Even if at that time there were some attempts by domestic actors to engage with PE, most of the analysis is centered on the phase starting in the early 2000s, where PE firms' local footprint was more pronounced.

As an executive with vast experience in the market acknowledged, the main investors that backed a typical first-time fund were "*always multilateral development banks, the government and maybe some family money and fund-of-funds.*" Schematically, there are two key steps in the emergence and institutionalization of a local market for private equity. In the first one, development financial institutions (DFIs), domestic and multilateral, play an incubating role. The next step is the participation of local pension funds.

The chapter first analyzes multilateral development financial institutions, in particular the role of both the World Bank and Inter-American Development Bank's private sector arms, together with some international—mostly European—DFIs. Then, it introduces the main

Table 4.1 Main government-related institutional investors

	Development financial institutions	*Pension funds*
Brazil	Bndespar, Finep	Previ, Funcef, Petros, etc.
Mexico	Fondo de Fondos, Fonadin	Afores
Chile	CORFO	AFPs
Colombia	Bancoldex, FDN	AFPs
Argentina	Fondce	AFJPs (nationalized), FGS-ANSES
Multilateral DFIs	IFC, IDB, CAF	

government-related financial institutions in each country that have private equity programs, describe their main initiatives, compare them, and discuss their governance challenges. In the Brazilian case, it inquires on the role of its better-known development bank, BNDES, as well as of Finep, a federal agency devoted to the promotion of science and technology. Then, it explores the fund of funds model of Fondo de Fondos (FdF), closely related to Mexican development banks. In Chile, CORFO, its long-lasting development agency has been promoting the local venture capital industry since the late 1990s. In Colombia, this role was played in a more limited way by Bancoldex, a second-floor (i.e. that operates through commercial financial intermediaries) policy bank, together with its newly launched infrastructure-oriented development bank, FDN. And finally, Argentina's more recent Fondce is unlikely to substitute for the lack of any active—state or private—domestic institutional investors.

Table 4.1 provides an overview of the main institutional investors in the region addressed throughout the rest of the chapter.

Development financial institutions (DFIs) can have direct and indirect PE investment strategies. Direct strategies refer to those cases in which they participate directly as shareholders of otherwise privately-managed firms, and are not intermediated by a third-party fund manager. This is the state-as-a-minority-shareholder model as introduced by Musacchio and Lazzarini (2014). As shown below, Brazil's development bank together with some multilateral institutions, are the only cases in the region in which development financial institutions functioned as direct private equity providers, at least at a meaningful scale. DFIs can also have indirect strategies, where they invest through third-party fund managers that pool capital from different sources and then acquire equity stakes in companies. This "state as a limited partner" model can be thought as a particular—and outsourced—case of the state-as a minority-investor.[2]

Regarding the question around the goals of these policy interventions, conceptually, two main objectives can be distinguished. First, state-related financial institutions can invest in private equity funds as a way to promote the development of local capital markets. They aim to facilitate firms' access to risk—equity—capital outside public markets. Doing so, they also intend to nurture the otherwise anemic public equity markets with new companies, beyond what can be achieved through regulatory reform. With more of a "horizontal" goal these programs tend to invest in generalist PE funds with broad mandates, instead of promoting industry-specific funds or investing directly into companies. Second, policymakers can have sector-specific goals and use capital investments as a tool to pursue them. These "vertical" policy goals are varied and range from pushing for new "green" energy sources to tech-related digital ventures, including more classic industrial policy areas. Even if the differences are not always as clear in practice, different program designs found throughout the cases can be classified as more closely aligned to one of these two models.

In addition to the promotional role of government-related investors, the case studies explore the engagement of pension funds as a key next step for the institutionalization of private equity markets. Pension funds are usually the cornerstone actors in their local capital markets. This is even more the case for private capital markets, where the presence of retail investors is limited. Instead, public and private defined-benefit pension funds, who give little investment decision-making to pensioners—and not defined-contribution plans (e.g. 401(k))—are by far the most important investors (Cornelius 2011, 160). In Latin America, pension funds involvement with the asset class is still incipient, in an ongoing process of institutionalization and one of the big challenges the industry faces. Still, their involvement with private equity does not seem to be only a function of how they are structured. For example, distinct types of pension funds, such as the ones in Brazil and Mexico, have channeled more resources

[2] As a reminder, limited partners (LPs) are those investors in the fund that as opposed to the general partners (GPs), do not usually take an active role in its management.

to managers investing domestically than those in Chile, otherwise more similar in structure to the Mexican ones.

Going back to the literature discussion, it is important to note that pension funds are not pure market players, even in those cases where they are indeed privately managed. Their origin and up to certain extent also their operating logic are not market-based. Regarding their origin, the source of their resources is mandatory savings. Individuals are compelled to contribute as per government rules; they cannot opt-out from the pension system. And pension funds investment decisions are not completely market-based either, but are usually regulated through detailed guidelines that, for example, specify allocation quotas to each asset class in their portfolios. While each case study describes the involvement of the pension funds, Chapter 5 explores more closely their regulation.

Other than as pensioners, the retail investor capacity to participate in this asset class is limited. Given its illiquidity and riskiness, private equity does not have a good fit with retail investors. This is by no means just a Latin American phenomenon. The investor base of large international private equity is for the most part institutional, composed mainly of pension funds, endowments, sovereign wealth funds, and insurance companies. Outside institutional investors only high-wealth individuals and family offices access the asset class directly. Even in the most developed financial markets, attempts to commercialize private capital funds to the retail public have not worked and most regulators restrict PE firm's ability to fundraise outside accredited investors.

Instead of retail investors, wealthy individuals and families are core actors in the Latin American business scene. Investing through their family offices, they help mount most PE firms. The policy initiatives described below also aim to channel private non-institutional money into private equity/venture capital. But in general, family offices conduct investments by themselves and do not delegate to professional managers who pool money from multiple sources, including institutional money, in particular for private equity investments.[3] Instead, even if they hire their own team of professional managers, they prefer to act on their own. And if they invest into the more institutionalized private equity asset class,

[3] For an assessment of the—rather limited—role of family offices in Mexican private capital market, see Márquez and Sandoval-Arzaga (2017).

family offices tend to invest outside their local country in order to diversify their geographic exposure. Still, as mentioned in the Introduction, as part of the consolidation and diffusion of the private equity model, some of these family offices, particularly if they have already exited their core business, are becoming increasingly institutionalized and professionalized, and behave as long-term PE firms.

4.1 Multilateral DFIs

Multilateral development financial institutions (MDFIs) are public institutions, funded and owned by multiple member countries that provide financing to encourage economic development. Most of them are structured as development banks[4] and concentrate their activities in lending and policy advising. While governments are their main clients (and sponsors), development banks also support the private sector directly. In order to do so they have created separate organizations that offer investment, advisory, and asset-management services. Notably, these multilateral investment corporations have pushed for the introduction of new organizational forms in emerging economies, pioneering the private equity and venture capital model into new markets (Settel et al. 2009). As explained below, they did this by investing in PE funds as limited partners, as well as by providing equity finance directly to companies. Beyond providing capital, they promoted industry best practices and functioned as a vector for the diffusion of these more novel forms of financial policymaking.

As part of their broader menu of financial products, MDFIs often have both direct and indirect equity participations. In all cases, their involvement intends to catalyze further private investments. They aim to function as anchor investors that grant a seal of approval to help mobilize additional capital. When they hold an equity stake in a company directly, it is always in a non-controlling minority position. And when they invest indirectly through third-party managed PE funds, their participation is also limited, in general subscribing no more than 20% of fund's committed capital.[5]

[4] Even if none of them are banks in the sense of being deposit-taking institution.

[5] They only exceed this limit in the case of funds that invest in countries with embryonic capital markets, or when these funds have a specialized mandate that includes underserved segments, such as early-stage VC or some specific priority sector, and therefore, mobilizing a substantial portion of private capital is not possible.

Even if most of these multilateral institutions have existed for a longer time, they started to engage with private equity in the late 1980s and beginning of the 1990s (Ibanez 1989), and they functioned as vectors for the diffusion of this new model. As part of the global liberalization trend, MDFIs helped create several private equity funds as a way to support the privatization of state-owned enterprises and the expansion of capital markets to emerging economies, trying to fill a chronic gap in equity financing. Many of these efforts were focused in post-communist Eastern Europe, where the IFC, together with the European Bank for Reconstruction and Development (EBRD), had—and still have—an active role funding the transition from planned to market-oriented economies. Latin America was no exception in this global trend. And in this region too, multilateral investors backed private equity initiatives early-on, during the nineties. And still today, we can find this class of investors supporting many PE funds in the region. Among them, World Bank's IFC, the Inter-American Development Bank's IIC, and a group of European development institutions are the most prominent.[6]

The World Bank's private sector arm, the International Financial Corporation (IFC), offers private firms a full menu of financial products ranging from more detached trade finance instruments, to core equity products. Within their equity holdings, most of them are private rather than public equities, being the former more closely aligned with their market-failure-solving mission. The IFC was the pioneer supporter of private equity initiatives across the emerging world and served as anchor investor for several of the first PE funds that appeared in the region during the nineties (Lavelle 1999; World Bank 1996). It still invests in many regional funds and directly into companies and also functions as an asset-manager for third-party investors.[7] It also vividly promotes the asset

[6] For an overview of the equity investment strategies of different DFIs, see Michelitsch et al. (2017).

[7] First, the IFC is organized by industry verticals and as part of their menu of products, they may participate directly in firms within each sector through equity products. For example, through their Oil, Gas & Mining unit the IFC is a minority shareholder in several companies in that sector. Second, the financial services vertical also promotes PE firms, as an alternative type of financial intermediary. Third, through their asset-management unit—IFC's Asset Management Company—they leverage the IFC's industry knowledge and relationships and act as a private equity firm themselves, managing third-party resources. As of 2020, they managed 12 funds and fund-of-funds with activity all over the emerging world through which they invest directly into companies and participate

class among policymakers and the general public, for example, through research as well as sponsoring specialized publication, events and the emerging market's industry association (EMPEA).

The IFCs recruitment profile is the most similar to investment firms and is able to attract top talent. Employees exhibit a higher turnover with the private sector than what is the standard for government-related organizations in the developing world. Yet, the IFC exhibits a more patient behavior than private investors, may accept lower returns, and in each of its transactions aims to provide "additionalities" to its financing. When investing directly into companies, their average holding period is longer than the standard 5/7 years cycle of PE investments. They restrict their participation to minority stakes and have a relatively more passive role. Rather than going into the operational details of the companies they invest in, they push for a more general ESG agenda. For example, in terms of governance practices, they push for more open and transparent models, and when able, support the nomination of independent directors, usually outside experts not related neither to the company nor to the IFC.

The Inter-American Development Bank (IDB), dedicated to the Latin America and the Caribbean region, also played an active role in the emergence of an incipient PE industry and continues to do so. Structured similarly to the World Bank, but smaller in size and regionally focused, it has two main channels through which it promotes the private capital model. IDB's Multilateral Investment Fund (MIF) promoted as an "innovation laboratory" in finance makes some investments in early-stage VC funds. Beyond financing, they also provide grants to support institutional-building activities. As described in the next chapter, the MIF played a key ecosystem building role. It promoted the organization of associations

as quota-holders in other investment funds. Besides managing the IFC's own resources, each of these funds also fundraises capital from outside investors. Among several global, regional, and industry-specific funds, they also manage one country-specific fund. The $1.2 billion China-Mexico Fund, whose capital comes from sovereign sources of these two countries: one billion came from China Investment Corporation and China Development Bank, the rest from the Mexican state-owned financial institutions (Nafinsa and Fonadin-Banobras). Instead of channeling these resources directly into companies, governments outsource management/decision making to the IFC. It is mandated to make equity and quasi-equity investments in privately held Mexican companies. For the moment activity has been limited. The fund has investments in the energy and telecom industries, following these sector's recent reforms.

that group the private capital industry at the regional and country-level, serving as a vector for the diffusion of a set of policies and regulations that promote this novel form of financing and managing firms. And the Inter-American Investment Corporation (IIC), that in 2016 was rebranded as IDB Invest and consolidated all IDB's private sector operations, also invests through funds and more recently has also began doing some direct equity and mezzanine investments, as part of its broader product offering. Given its smaller size, it usually makes earlier-stage investments and has a less systematic equity—direct and indirect—program than the IFC, its analog organization at the World Bank after which IDB Invest is modeled.[8]

More recently, *Corporacion Andina de Fomento* (CAF) also started to include some private capital into its portfolio. Given its mandate, it is targeted toward infrastructure-focused private equity funds. Moreover, it supports domestic public sector initiatives to enhance the involvement of the private sector in infrastructure. For example, CAF, together with the IFC, is a minority shareholder of Colombia's recently launched development bank, *Financiera de Desarrollo Nacional (FDN)*, and has also supported Mexico's government fund of funds.

Finally, outside of the multilateral space but still external to host countries, there are several mostly European DFIs that engage with the private sector in emerging economies mostly through PE funds. Among them are British CDC,[9] French Proparco, Dutch FMO, Norwegian Norfund, German KFW DEG, the European Investment Fund (EIF),[10] and US OPIC.[11] Mostly owned by their home-country development financial

[8] For a comparative study of equity investing strategies of DFIs, see IDB/IIC (2017).

[9] Actis and Aureos, two of the largest PE firms, specialized in emerging markets are spin-offs of CDC group, UK Government's development finance institution created in the second postwar to promote private investments in the former British colonies (McWilliam 2001).

[10] European Investment Fund, the investment arm of the European Investment Bank, is the largest provider of capital for risk capital (VC and growth equity) funds in Europe. See more in Chapter 6.

[11] OPIC (US Overseas Private Investment Corporation) was revamped in October 2018 by the Build Act. The bill that was approved with bipartisan support capitalized the agency with $60B and grant it with more flexibility, allowing it to take equity stakes in private companies. This reform intended to counteract Chinese influence in the emerging world. OPIC was merged with USAID into a new entity names DFC (U.S. International Development Finance Corporation).

institutions, in some cases they have participation from the private sector. They replicate in developing countries, especially in some of their former colonies, what they do in their home countries in order to promote the private capital industry. Engaging through PE funds is an easier way to maximize their private sector development impact in emerging economies, without large on-the-ground staff requirements. Even though they are much more active in the MENA region, these development agencies have also been core investors in many Latin American private equity funds. Interviewees repeatedly highlighted their role and stressed their importance, particularly in the case of first-time-funds. Together with funding, they also help formalize their practices and improve their reporting and governance standards.

Overall, multilateral development banks had an important incubating role for private equity in Latin America. MDFIs pioneered the asset class, and as repeatedly mentioned in the interviews, function as anchor investors of first-time funds, serve as a vector for the implementation of industry's best practices and disseminated the policy models to national development banks. While the total allocation of their portfolios to this asset class is not big since they are mostly concentrated in the loan business, given the absence of other institutional sources of equity financing in most countries in the region, multilaterals are still significant. Moreover, as Chapter 5 develops more thoroughly, the role of some of these multilateral institutions went beyond providing capital, and also supported promotional and regulatory initiatives. Crucially, they fostered private capital's industry collective action, both at the national and regional levels.

While MDFIs multilateral status fits well with a policy-based explanation of the origin of private capital markets, their role is less able to explain the cross-country differences. Their programs are conditional on the support they have from each national government. Ultimately, governments are their shareholders and usually through their finance ministries the ultimate principals of these multilateral institutions.[12] Moreover, multilateral's domestic counterparts have established financing programs

[12] Country representatives in each of these multilateral organizations monitor closely the transactions their country's private sector firms are involved in. Moreover, the bylaws that rules both the IFC (Section 3 (ii)) and IDB Invest (Article III—Section 4 (b)) operations grant each country veto powers over any operation within their territory. Ministries of Finance have to be formally informed of all transactions that involve a firm operating in their country and they have the right to object them.

on their own. The next sections analyze each country's local development financial institutions and examine their main initiatives with respect to the private capital markets, together with the investment regimes of local pension funds. As shown below, the strategies pushed by MDFIs are many times emulated at the local level, who are used explicitly as models. The rest of the chapter develops brief country case studies that review the main outcomes of each case, introduce the main institutional investors, and describe their most relevant initiatives related to venture capital, private equity, and infrastructure financing.

4.2 Country Case-Studies

4.2.1 Brazil

Brazil is the most developed private equity market in the region. It is the only Latin American country that appears systematically on the radar of global investors, and even after losing its investment grade, suffering its worst recession in history, and going through significant political turmoil, continues leading the region in terms of PE activity. Among industry participants throughout the region, there is no doubt about Brazil's leadership position. Tellingly, Brazilians do not benchmark themselves with their Latin American peers, but with Europe, the US, or Asia. The opposite happens in the other Latin American countries, where Brazil is the standard.

Related to this more institutionalized private equity industry, Brazil's stock market arguably exhibits relatively greater dynamism in terms of fundraising than its regional peers. And listed companies have relatively more dispersed shareholders, business executives in both board of directors and top executive positions more frequently have a financial background and fewer family ties between each other, as Chapter 3 shows.

In contrast to what it would be expected from the literature, the macro-variables emphasized by institutionalist hypothesis such as indexes of economic freedom and ease of doing business rank Brazil in the regional lower tier. Still, Brazilian judiciary exhibited substantial autonomy from politics. And in terms of its shareholder rights Brazil unquestionably made progress since the 1990s, particularly after the introduction of the Novo Mercado listing segment in the early 2000s (Nenova 2006). But this is still not that different from other countries in the region that, beyond this particular metric, are well known for being more open to trade, stable, and market friendly, in particular those in the Pacific Alliance (Chile, Peru, Colombia, and Mexico).

Of course, Brazil is the largest country in the region. Its market size attracts the attention of international investors. Global capital allocators, investing through local PE firms and more recently also directly, have certainly played an important role in the development of the private capital market in this country. But as discussed in previous chapters, demand-side factors are unlikely to drive the whole difference observed in the cross-country comparisons. Together with its size, another factor that also distinguishes Brazil from its regional peers is the longstanding participation of government-related investors together with—even if quite erratic—an early involvement of pension funds in private equity markets.[13] As discussed below, these local institutional investors helped grow the market, but also contributed to generate many of the challenges the sector faces today.

With all its ups and downs, Brazil is the only country in the region that can exhibit a significant number of complete investment cycles: from fundraising, to investment, holding period, and exit. The first formal PE funds started during the mid-1990s, in general led by some local bankers, many times in partnerships with international firms. These PE funds participated in some privatizations, and as mentioned below, had an early engagement with local state-related financial institutions. But still, this first initial phase had a more international flavor than what we observe after the turn of the century. As a senior businessman, former president of the local business association who started working in the industry during the 1990s describes, "*it was a US-centered model, with a ton of leverage. Completely different from when it resumed in the mid-2000s, based locally, with no leverage, and local teams.*"

Following the currency devaluation and crisis of the late 1990s paired with the dot-com crash, this incipient private equity industry experienced a slowdown. Fundraisings were paralyzed, as well as new investments, only to resume a couple of years later, in the mid-2000s. In this new phase, two public organizations played an active role: Brazil's well know

[13] For a great analysis of the ties among BNDES, state-related pension funds and business elites, see Lazzarini (2010).

development bank BNDES, through its investment arm, BNDESPAR[14] and FINEP (*Financiadora de Estudos e Projectos*), a federal level agency under the Ministry of Science and Technology devoted to funding science and technology.

BNDES's private equity arm, BNDESPAR is structured as a separate entity from the bank's core unit that is focused on the lending business. Even if the whole bank works under the same leadership, this internal division arguably enjoys higher status and more qualified professionals. Regarding private equity, it displayed two strategies. On the one side, it has injected massive amounts of capital directly into companies, mostly in the form of equity and convertible debt. And on the other, it participates as an investor in several independent PE firms who in turn invest in private companies. These two forms of investing sometimes work in tandem and on multiple occasions BNDESPAR participates directly in companies co-investing together with some of the funds they also participate in.

In terms of total amount of funding, BNDESPAR functions mostly as an independent investor, directly sourcing its deals and managing its own portfolio. Even when it operates across the broad spectrum of the private capital market, its direct operations are significantly larger than the ones of average PE funds operating in Brazil. From 2008 to 2016 alone it had made direct investments for more than $66 billion *reais*.[15] Importantly, when investing directly, BNDESPAR always took a minority role. But even without having control, the bank still achieved considerable participations, with up to around 30% of the companies' total equity. Through its direct equity investments, the bank channeled a substantial part of the more ambitious industrial policy of PT's administration, that

[14] *BNDES Participações S.A.* For other academic assessments of the bank, see Gomes Schapiro (2013), Hochstetler and Montero (2013), Lazzarini et al. (2015), Musacchio and Lazzarini (2014), and Bril-Mascarenhas (2016).

[15] This figure includes 2010's Petrobras massive recapitalization (~$25B *reais*). But even if not taking into consideration this transaction, the figure continues to be substantial. Importantly, these figures do not include the larger and more traditional activities of the bank specialized on commercial loans. Not all of these capital injections are made directly in equity, instead a big portion of them go into companies as convertible debt. This is a standard practice (Lerner and Schoar 2005) and is intended to protect the external investor from the downside. If the value of the company goes up, the debt holder can convert its contract into an equity stake, become a standard shareholder and participate in the upside. If the company gets in trouble, convertible debt is more senior creditors than standard equity holders.

helped consolidate some sectors and encouraged their internationalization, for example in the meat industry (Musacchio and Lazzarini 2014; Sierra 2017).

Through its indirect "funds" strategy, the bank intends to create a more complete small and mid-cap growth equity environment and is able to support smaller companies than what it would be able to achieve through direct investment. Even when the overall value of BNDESPARs indirect investment strategy is overshadowed by its massive direct investments, most primary and secondary sources, even those critical of the more recent role of BNDES, agree that the bank had an important role in the emerging funds industry. BNDES has been promoting the asset class since at least 1990, for example, by structuring and investing in the first private capital vehicle, FMIEE[16] (see, e.g., Viveiros 2017, 55:60).[17]

In contrast with Mexico, where the state has a minority participation in most of the funds operating in the country, the BNDES has a more selective approach. It periodically makes public calls for fund managers, specifying in advance the fund's term and mandate. These calls result in competitive public processes. Only between 2008 and 2016, the BNDES supported 50 different funds, all of them managed by Brazilian firms, with around $3.5 B *reais* (around $1.5B) in actual disbursements, and capital commitments for larger sums. In all cases, these funds got additional capital from other investors, including local pension funds.

Industry-wise, the allocation of BNDES' investments followed its focus in financing large infrastructure projects together with supporting core sectors of the economy such as large industrial, agribusiness, and mining firms. Beyond this more traditional focus, the BNDES has also advanced into earlier-stage funds that target smaller, innovation-oriented projects, as for example they do through the *Criatec* program. The program is composed by a series of VC funds—they are now in their third one—sponsored by BNDES, together with *Banco do Nordeste*, a regional development bank, who outsourced their management to third-party private firms (see Borsato da Silva and Biagini 2016).

[16] F*undo Mútuos* de Investimento em *Empresas Emergentes, a tax-incentivized private vehicle launched in the mid-1990s in order to promote the asset class. Now it is mostly replaced by FIPs.*

[17] For a concise story of private equity in Brazil, see Chapter 7 of Leeds (2015) book on private equity in emerging economies who repeatedly highlights the role of BNDES as a catalyst of the PE industry in Brazil.

Overall, most sources agree that BNDES, through its private equity arm, played an important role in the development of the sector (Leeds 2015, 214; Bril-Mascarenhas 2016). Notably, the more vigorous intervention in the region is also the most contested, and interviewees had strong opinions about it. For example, an interviewee who had worked at BNDESPAR, and at the moment was part of a local investment firm managing mostly international money, was critical about the banks and state-related pension funds when talking about the role of the development bank in the PE market:

> Indeed, maybe it was the case in the past that BNDES performed an important role to create the market. [...] I was working there when BNDESPAR was recreated, and helped it go into private equity. Back then we thought it had an important role to play in private markets, help companies to bridge their financing gap, plus the anchor-funding type of argument. But that role doesn't make sense any more. There are already too many managers and too much money!

It is important to highlight, beyond its equity arm, BNDES as a whole has far from uniformly supporting of the PE model. First, there is a tension between investing directly into companies and fostering an active market for private equities composed of private—independent—fund managers. And second, and most importantly, overall BNDES most likely discouraged equity financing through its core loans business with cheap—subsidized—loans targeted toward large "incumbent" SOEs, legacy industries, and construction companies that controlled the infrastructure business.[18]

Besides *Criatec*, during the early 2000s FINEP was the most relevant public institution in Brazil for the emerging venture capital segment. With a mandate related to science and technology, public initiatives led by FINEP and BNDES to support a nascent VC industry can be traced to at least the 1970s. Still, the VC segment has been a laggard in the industry's development that emerged during the 1990s focused on the more standard private equity type of deals. But as I argued, these categories are sometimes hard to distinguish in practice. Accordingly, beyond supporting this smaller and riskier segment of the market, FINEP played

[18] Moreover, investing in both the equity and the debt of a company, as BNDES often does, can create significant conflict of interests (e.g., Jiang et al. 2010).

a role in the institutionalization of the domestic industry and got involved with the broader PE ecosystem. Central to FINEP's performance was the *Inovar* program, developed with close support from IDB's MIF.[19]

FINEP played a central role promoting this new business model and coordinating the fundraising process among potential investors. It organized forums in which fund managers were connected with potential investors, in particular pension funds, and provided training and education for both prospective managers and investors. Besides contributing with capital to anchor a series of funds, FINEP coordinated the fundraising process. It led multiple public calls for funds in which they would function as an anchor investor but also facilitate the engagement of other potential investors by conducting "collective" due diligences. FINEP's screening and selection process provided an informal certification for prospective fund managers that helped them fundraise with pension funds and other potential investors, most of them government-related. Otherwise, and given the interest rate environment that characterized Brazil at least since the economic stabilization of the mid-1990s, these investors were used to follow passive investment strategies that allocated most of their portfolio to fixed income instruments.

The *Inovar* program evolved since it was launched in 1999, and even if among the policy literature on the topic it was considered to be a relatively successful initiative (e.g. Leamon and Lerner 2012), it also showcases how challenging it is to get private investors on-board of public initiatives, particularly for the smaller VC segment. The current boom in VC investment is led by funds that channel mostly international and private money. Beyond its focus on early-stage innovation-related funds, it also incorporated larger growth-equity type of funds, closer to standard private equity, in which it overlapped with BNDES. Besides making capital contributions, FINEP supports the industry through other measures. For example, it provided guarantees to individuals that invested in this asset class. And trying to appeal to corporate money, it was pushing to give the investment in some of these private funds the same tax benefits than the ones granted to R&D expenses. And, as Chapter 5 discusses more thoroughly,

[19] For a more detailed analysis of INOVAR and its policy lessons, see HBS case (Leamon and Lerner 2012) together with the IADB's reports on the program. I will come back to this program in Chapter 5.

it was as part of *Inovar's* project that FINEP played a leading role in the creation of the local PE/VC association, ABVCAP.

Brazil's pension system is one of the few in the region that was not part of a trend toward an individual-capitalization and privately-managed model. Instead it is still structured as a multi-tiered system. Its first two tiers are constituted as mandatory pay-as-you-go regimes that provide basic coverage to all formal workers. The first tier is oriented to private sector workers, and the second one is focused on government employees, with over 2,400 specific pension regimes managed by the federal, state, and municipal governments. Massively underfunded, this system is arguably responsible for a significant part of Brazil's chronic fiscal deficits.[20] On top of these two tiers, a third one is composed by closed pension funds that offer partially-funded individual and occupational plans through private pension entities. Their accumulated assets are legally segregated from their sponsoring entities and submitted to specific regulations from PREVIC.[21] Historically, this segment of the pension system grew based on the employees of large state-owned companies, but private enterprises also offer benefit plans to its employees.[22] Even if there are over 300 independent funds, the largest ones are related to state-owned enterprises. Previ, Funcef, and Petros, who, respectively represent employees at *Banco do Brasil*, *Caixa Economica Federal*, another state bank, and *Petrobras*, Brazil's national oil company, manage close to half of the total funds of the system.

Consequently, the government has substantial leverage over its investment decisions and its management is politicized.[23] This is not only because of political appointments from the company's management side, ultimately controlled by government, but also because unions representing workers/pensioners participate in each foundation's board of directors, with direct authority over the investment officers. In the case of the PT administrations (2002–2016), government had leverage both over the management appointments and over the union's representatives

[20] This tier of the pension system was the object of a long-awaited reform, approved in 2019.

[21] *Superintendência Nacional de Previdência Complementar.*

[22] For a summary of Brazil's pension system, see ABRAPP (2014).

[23] Among the largest funds, the case of Valia, Vale's pension fund, is often highlighted as a somewhat less politicized management.

(Dieguez 2009; Musacchio and Lazzarini 2014, Chapter 9).[24] A former director of PREVI, the largest pension fund in the region confirms their close relationship with government:

> We had direct relationship with Casa Civil [chief of staff], also with Fazenda [Treasury]. Ultimately, we depend on them (...) There is always pressure from government, in particular to go into infrastructure projects.

Pension funds participated in the privatization of state-owned enterprises.[25] They did so directly and still hold large blocks of former state-owned companies such as Vale and Embraer, companies with a quite dispersed shareholder base, whose stocks are among the most liquid in Brazil's exchange. Indirectly, pension funds also invested in some funds that also participated in privatizations. For example, some of the larger pension funds were investors in the CVC Opportunity Fund, managed locally by people related to Opportunity Bank, with support from Citicorp.[26] The fund participated in the privatized telecommunications sector. Even if they were the larger investors, pension funds had no control over the fund's decision-making. This became highly contentious, and ended up in court, with a long dispute around the governance of the fund and the rights and liabilities of its investors.[27]As most industry participants mention when asked about the involvement of local pension funds in the PE industry, this experience proved to be notorious for the pension funds. And their reaction arguably shaped the Brazilian private equity market in the following decade.

Once the fundraising market re-opened in the mid-2000s, and arguably as a reaction to the ongoing Opportunity Fund case, pension funds started requesting more governance rights and a tighter control over the investment process of the funds they would invest in. For example, they demanded a seat on the fund's investment committees. This

[24] See Anzia and Moe (2019) for an interesting analysis on the governance of public pension funds in the US. For the relationship between unions and pension funds also in the US, see McCarthy (2014).

[25] For a history of Brazil's private equity industry before the turn of the century, see Monteiro Ramalho (2013).

[26] Citibank's private equity arm.

[27] For a journalistic description of the conflict between Opportunity's manager and Previ, see Dieguez (2009).

is a departure from standard practices, where investment decisions are made by the funds general partners (GPs) and not by its investors. Moreover, they pushed for clauses that allowed investors the right to replace the GP under certain conditions and negotiated to pay lower management fees.

In part as a consequence of these governance issues, the industry basically separated in two. On the one side, some funds fundraised almost exclusively internationally; and on the other, funds managed resources that came mostly from Brazilian government-related institutional investors (A. M. A. F. Minardi and Bassani 2016; A. M. A. F. Minardi et al. 2014). There were only a handful of funds that combined local and foreign institutional sources of funding. Doing so is cumbersome. For example, to get local and foreign institutional investors, firms have to necessarily use separate investment vehicles, as it would be hard for any foreign institutional investor to accept participating in a fund where local pension funds have veto power.

Moreover, pension funds engagement with the asset class has not been as systematic as many industry participants would have hoped. Larger pension funds did not develop their own private equity strategies and teams,[28] but tended to invest together with other state-related large funds, and development financial institutions. Moreover, and as a result of these governance demands, pension funds arguably suffered from an adverse selection problem. More experienced managers with a more complete investment track-record and who were better connected to international investors were able to avoid fundraising locally and dealing with pension funds, even if they had been in business with them before. Instead, pension funds invested in funds without an easy access to international money that therefore had no alternative but to rely on local investors, even if that meant loosing their decision-making autonomy. Many of these funds ended up being over-exposed to oil and gas and infrastructure-related projects, arguably pushed by government. The end

[28] I reviewed the professional profiles of PREVIs executive leadership since the late 1990s. For the most of this period, the president had a union background. Otherwise, chief investment/planning officers came from Banco do Brasil (BB) and showed no asset-management experience outside Previ/ BB. This appears to be in line with the relatively low level of professionalization of most US public pension funds, but it is in sharp contrast with Canadian pension funds who are able to attract top financial talent (World Bank 2017). Regarding specialized private equity teams in large institutional investors, see Da Rin and Phalippou (2017).

of the commodity boom, paired with the economy's recession, translated into bad financial performance. The downturn in the economic cycle, together with the corruption scandals that involved pension funds,[29] made them withdraw from private capital markets.

Still, the market was quite active during the latest recession. The infrastructure sector appeared to be especially attractive. With local construction companies out of the game due to corruption scandals, and the BNDES no longer providing cheap subsidized loans, there were several large infrastructure-related transactions that involved private-equity-like financial investors. Since local fundraising was closed, the firms that could tap international investors were the most active. Among them, and notably, some large foreign institutional investors with a local footprint were sourcing deals directly (e.g. Canadian Pension Plan (CPPIB), Singapore's two sovereign wealth funds, GIC Temasek and Temasek, and Brookfield).[30] A similar dynamic is observed in the VC market, where the booming digital and fintech ecosystem was funded mostly by investors with access to international markets. So, fueled by firms with an international investor base but mostly local teams, the market showed dynamism after the last recession.

Following corruption scandals and the end of the PT administrations, BNDES appears to be revamping its business model, trending toward a less interventionist model. It has stopped providing massive amounts of cheap subsidized credit to insiders, which would arguably drive the need for more equity investments. Moreover, while it is shrinking its balance sheet, it is unlikely to continue making direct investments and will privatize part of their equity portfolio, generating further opportunities for financial investors. Still, it seems it will keep some of its indirect investment programs. Even during this period, BNDES participated in some new funds, accepting the more standard governance clauses that give fund managers more autonomy. And it also continues to push forward the

[29] Some private equity vehicles (FIPs) were part of a judicial (Greenfield) and congressional investigations (see CPI Fundos de Pensao—Relatorio Final 2016). The funds under investigation were mostly mono-company vehicles, used for tax purposes and managed directly by some state-institution (e.g. Caixa), and not standard private equity funds managed by an independent third-party pooling resources form a broad investor base. See Minardi and Bassani (2016) for a complete inquiry of pension funds' private capital investments.

[30] Also, Chinese investors and large local groups (e.g. Itausa) were also active in the infrastructure space.

introduction new financial products, for example, fostering private-debt funds.

The Brazilian PE market certainly exhibited a lot of problems. But with all its flaws, from which we can extract lessons and illustrate some of the trade-offs policymakers face, the Brazilian case is still particularly salient when contrasted with other cases in the region. Through significant support that began well before the PT administration and an early involvement of pension funds, it exhibits the most dynamic private capital industry in the region. Far from unique, these two characteristics are in different ways also present in the other cases explored below.

4.2.2 Mexico

With limited activity during the 1990s, mostly related to international investors, Mexico was more of a latecomer to private equity (Charvel and de Yeregui 2002). Still, the timing of events of this case supports my hypothesis and illustrates well the two stages of the emergence of a domestic private capital market. In a first stage, government-related financial institutions began investing in pioneering private equity funds. And following this early incubating phase, the entrance of pension funds was the key step that allowed the industry to take off.

The first steps of a Mexican proto-private equity industry can be traced back to the late eighties, with the creation of SINCAS.[31] SINCAS were a public investment vehicle that received strong support from *Nacional Financiera (NAFIN)*, Mexico's largest development bank, who automatically contributed with a minority portion of the capital of these public investment vehicles.[32] According to early industry participants, SINCAS were expensive vehicles, information requirements were onerous and, critically, pension funds could not engage with them. But it was from the legacy portfolio of SINCAS that in 2006 Nafin, together with other policy banks, created Fondo de Fondos (FdF). Registered as a corporation independent from its shareholders, state-owned banks, FdF is formally constituted as *Compañía Mexicana de Inversiones de Capital, S.A de CV*.

[31] *Sociedades de Inversión de Capitales.*

[32] SINCAS apparently provided finance to around a dozen companies that were listed in the Mexican stock exchange back in the nineties; other than that, there is not much information about them (EY 2015).

Led by NAFIN, who holds around 75% of the capital of this new investment company, other policy banks such as FOCIR, Banobras, and Bancomext also participated in this venture from the beginning. NAFIN's strategy is different from BNDES, where the bank invests either directly into companies or indirectly into funds. As the names indicated, Mexico followed a fund of funds approach (Lerner 2009, 133). Instead of investing directly into companies, as standard PE funds do, a fund of funds adds an additional layer of intermediation, and itself acts as an investor in multiple funds, that then capitalize companies. Therefore, a fund of funds holds a portfolio of quotas of other funds, rather than directly holding its underlying assets, the equity of private firms. This model adds an extra layer of intermediation in the flow of capital from its ultimate investor (e.g. the pensioner or taxpayer, in this case) to its recipient, a privately-held company. And in the case of Mexico, it moves the government-owned banks one step up in the financing chain, further away from the ultimate investment decision.

Most distinctively, the FdF is structured as a separate organization from its sponsors and has its own and potentially different pool of investors. At first, its main sponsors and owners were the same as its investors, but then it obtained investments from multilaterals, and later from local pension funds. Another key difference with the Brazilian case where fund managers have to participate in open competitive bid processes in order to receive funding, the FdF is permanently open for new applications. That is, as long as the fund has not run out of capital, a prospective fund manager can show up at any time with its business plan to be evaluated. Notably, the terms of the investment are negotiated individually and are not disclosed. Since its inception the FdF has sponsored most of the funds operating in the country, both local and international. As of the end of 2016, they have participated in 71 funds and have made capital commitments for close to one billion dollars.[33]

The FdF also aims to crowd-in private capital from other sources and maximizes the multiplier effect of its money. For example, as a rule, it never invests more than 35% of a fund, and their average participation is of around 15%. Their ticket size cannot exceed $30M per fund, nor $75M in a family of funds (i.e. funds operated by the same PE firm). Given these limits, it is a more significant investor for small and mid-sized funds. Even

[33] They reported, only through highly-aggregated and hard to verify data, average annual return in dollars of around 10% (as of 2018).

so, it also participates in larger international funds that invest in Mexico as part of their regional focus.[34] Given the importance of exhibiting the commitment of local investors when fundraising internationally, FdF was still considered a valuable resource for these funds, according to interviewees. Until pension funds entered the scene this was the only Mexican institutional investor that could possibly contribute resources to the asset class. As a senior fund manager who launched one of the first funds in Mexico as the local representative of an international firm told me:

> They are still now the only Mexican institutional investors that invests in PE, besides the AFORES that have to go through CKDs. Before that, they were the only ones. That makes them quite relevant. They participate in most funds, with a relatively small share of the total fund. They know they are the only Mexican investor, and therefore that they have an important catalyzing role […] this is their real value, the catalyzing effect they have by being the only local institutional investor that can go into the asset class.

Interestingly, this model allowed *Fondo de Fondos* to grow and become increasingly sophisticated with time, diversify its holdings and extend its reach. Following the first two "generalist" private equity fund of funds, they developed some more targeted initiatives. In order to enhance their venture capital strategy, they partnered with an American VC firm, with experience managing state-related fund of funds in the US. Also, as a way to support 2013's energy reform, they launched a separate fund dedicated to the energy industry. In terms of products, they diversified into more flexible quasi-equity type of securities such as private debt and mezzanine, as a way to also promote these more novel asset classes. Moreover, moving down the investment chain, they started to co-invest with some of the funds they participate in.

In terms of fundraising, besides obtaining resources from its original state-owned shareholders and multilateral institutions, the FdF has also

[34] As many of these larger funds are not country specific, but rather have a regional approach that does not bind them to invest a portion of their capital in a particular country, FdF has an informal agreement in which they require these funds to invest at least double the value of their commitment into Mexican companies. Still, the enforcement of this agreement relies basically on fund manager's trying to maintain their reputation and relationship with FdF and can only be eventually enforced during the fundraising of subsequent funds by these managers.

raised funds from the local capital markets. They have issued their own vehicles to raise financing from the pension system's resources. Through a subsidiary, *PMIC Latam*, FdF now manages its own CKDs,[35] through which they raise capital for smaller funds that would otherwise be below the minimum investment size that would be worth the attention of pension funds.

FdF is an example of an organizational model that combines public goals with private expertise, similar to Colombia's FDN case introduced below. Well known within the small private capital community, FdF is rarely noted outside of it. They function under the radar, and try to keep it that way, cultivating a low profile that protects their independence. The staff do not recognize themselves as public servants and operate with autonomy from bureaucracy and therefore appear to be more flexible in their recruitment and compensation policies. Consequently, their office with around 30 people is in an otherwise standard corporate location and is staffed with officials with career paths that interlink the private sector.

Given that the FdF is a private corporation separated from its state-owned shareholders and is not structured as a bank, they have no requirements to disclose information. They operate similarly to standard private industry players, typically quite secretive and hard to trace. They can invest through offshore vehicles—which allows them to engage with international investors more easily. And can participate in private placements, since they do not have the requirement of investing only in public securities. This is something unthinkable in other contexts where government-sponsored investment funds are restricted to operate through local vehicles or only participate in funds regulated by local authorities. Moreover, the governance of the fund of funds is also closer to private sector standards. For example, their board of directors is independent from the management of the firm and half of it is composed by private sector businesspeople. Importantly, this external board-members have a veto power in the firm's investment committee.

Although FdF is Mexico's main public initiative to develop the private capital industry, there were other more specific programs aimed to mobilize further private capital funds and help introduce new financial players into different sectors of the Mexican economy. Parallel to the FdF,

[35] *Certificado de Capital de Desarrollo*. A publicly-listed private capital vehicle through which the pension funds are allowed to invest in this asset class. Next chapter discusses CKDs more thoroughly.

although led by its same—state-owned—shareholders, these initiatives are more targeted toward specific sectors.

Banobras also manages the *Fondo Nacional de Infraestructura (Fonadin)*, who has its own initiatives to promote private capital investments in infrastructure. Since its inception in 2009, it has invested in 21 privately-managed PE funds that targeted infrastructure, energy, real-estate, and tourism projects.[36] For example, it was the cornerstone investor in *Fondo de Infraestructura de Macquarie Mexico* (FIMM), the first peso-denominated fund focused solely on investment opportunities in Mexican infrastructure projects, managed by Macquarie, a large Australian asset manager with extensive expertise in infrastructure finance. It is also the Mexican sponsor of the US$1.2 billion China-Mexico Fund managed by the IFC. Moreover, *Fonadin* also participated, together with local pension funds, in a US$2B peso-denominated infrastructure-oriented investment fund with CPDQ, one of the largest Canadian—publicly-managed—pension providers.[37]

Moreover, the now defunct *Instituto Nacional del Emprendedor (INADEM)* was involved in the venture capital segment. Created in 2013 during Peña Nieto's administration as an initiative of the *Secretaría de Economía*, it attempted to consolidate programs scattered throughout the federal government targeting entrepreneurship. It was not conceived as a financial institution, but has a decentralized status that grants it some autonomy. Its activities went beyond providing capital and were mandated to promote the broader entrepreneurial "ecosystem" in Mexico. It sponsored over 40 new VC funds, supports incubators, and accelerators, and organizes activities to promote entrepreneurship and innovation.[38]

In addition to these smaller public programs, the key catalytic role in the industry was played by pension system resources, through the entrance of AFORES[39] into the market. AFORES are private companies authorized to manage individual retirement accounts. They were

[36] Among this 21 different funds, 16 were CKDs, 4 private funds, and 1 Fibra-E.

[37] The private capital model was also attempted to be introduced to the agricultural sector. *Fondo de Capitalización e Inversión del Sector Rural (FOCIR)*, another of *Fondo de Fondos'* shareholders, created a series of smaller private capital initiatives targeted to the agribusiness. Resources were channeled through so-called FICA funds and are also experimenting with agro-related VCs.

[38] AMLOs administration discontinued most programs related to the institute.

[39] *Administradoras de Fondos para el Retiro.*

created in 1997, as a result of the pension reform that transformed the retirement system from a pay-as-you-go, defined-benefit scheme to a mandatory fully-funded, privately-managed defined-contribution scheme. The reform, as in other emerging economies, followed the Chilean model and generated a system at odds with the Brazilian one, where as described above, the largest pension funds are related to the state-owned enterprises. In Mexico, instead, the individual capitalization accounts are managed by specialized private organizations, in general related to international financial institutions.[40] Importantly, in order to increase the transparency of the system and protect retirees' savings, Afores are restricted by law to invest only in publicly traded securities. While they started with a portfolio composed almost exclusively by public debt, they became increasingly sophisticated and in 2009 began to invest in "structured" alternative assets through the introduction of CKDs. As an experienced asset manager working in the investment team of a pension fund summarized, "*if it wasn't for CKDs, we would still be just trading government bonds.*"

Until their entrance into the market, the only domestic institutional investor available to provide capital was the government through the FdF. Beyond these resources, fund managers depended almost exclusively on external sources of capital. The creation of CKDs, an idiosyncratic financial instrument denominated in local currency and listed in the local stock exchange, allowed Afores and other institutional investors to allocate part of their portfolio to private capital projects. Their introduction created an important source of domestic fundraising, and what is patent from both interviews and industry reports, allowed the sector to take off (see, e.g., EMPEA 2016; Leal and Del Sesto 2013).

As the next chapter explains more thoroughly, peso-denominated CKDs are far from being standard industry investment vehicles, but are the result of a "quiet politics" compromise that even if suboptimal for most players was successful in channeling pension resources into real assets. Since it is a listed security, CKDs are required to disclose information quarterly and to have a daily price, even though given the limited public that can access it (since they were tailor-made to pension funds), they show no liquidity. Moreover, CKDs are restrictive in terms of the uses of the funds and limited to investments in Mexico. For these reasons,

[40] There is still one publicly-managed pension fund, *Pensionissste*, which has around 6% of the market.

it is usually considered a "necessary evil" and referred to as a "Frankenstein." It nevertheless seems to have worked, and since its inception, 86 different CKDs have been issued, amounting to over $22B dollars in capital commitments by 2018. Not all of these resources are expected to be invested in general purpose corporate private equity, but also fund infrastructure, energy, and real-estate projects.

Launched in 2009, CKDs have been incrementally fine-tuned through regulations and consolidated into legislation. Moreover, to overcome some of their limitations, regulators further experimented with new vehicles such as Fibra's and CERPIs. Anyway, it seems clear that the capital constraint of the incipient local private capital industry was relaxed once it was able to tap into the resources of pension funds. Given Mexican demographic dynamics together with a trend toward increasing formalization, the pension system funds available for "alternative" investments are expected to grow. Interviewees suggested the more pressing bottleneck was no longer on the funding side but on human capital: there are not enough experienced fund managers with a reputation and track record that are able to absorb all that available liquidity.

Relatedly, the Mexican case is noticeable for the prevalence of fund managers whose professional careers also include senior positions at the federal bureaucracy. With technocratic profiles that in most cases include graduate studies in the US, some former officials' path into business includes being part of private capital fund management partnerships. This seems to be more often the case in infrastructure-related funds. Still, this "technocrats into business" dynamic does not appear to be specific of the Mexican case, but it is often observed in Brazil and more generally across the industry.[41] Of course, this raise concerns about political cronyism.

The Mexican private capital industry is not short of challenges. For example, industry participants repeatedly complain family groups keep the best deals for themselves: "*In Mexico the problem is that PE only gets the bad deals! The good deals, the 6/7 families that control everything keeps them for themselves.*" The dominant position exhibited by family-owned business group throughout Latin America, that seems to be particularly salient in the cases of Mexico and Chile, seems to further limit the expansion of more institutional forms of capital, such as private equity.

[41] For research about politically connected private equity in the US, see Faccio and Hsu (2017).

There is also a shortage of professionals within pension funds capable of evaluating and managing this new type of illiquid, long-term private equity investments.[42] Moreover, given the large size of pension funds and their limited staff, there is a scale issue that conditions smaller participants: you need to have large ticket sizes in order to be able to attract pension fund's attention. This signals the more structural trend, in Mexico and elsewhere, toward a consolidation and subsequent concentration of AFORES, and of pensions fund managers in general. It raises a question about the sustainability of a market where there are just a handful of players (five pension funds in Mexico, two in Colombia, etc.), with no incentives to differentiate from each other and pressed to reduce their fees and commissions.

Given the length of investment cycles, it is too soon to make conclusive evaluations of the outcomes. But at least in terms of fundraising, the resources from the pension funds play a decisive role, building on top of pre-existing public resources. Even if far from a financial revolution, it is clear, as another fund manager from a leading mid-market PE firm argues, that "*there is now a proven domestic fundraising channel that allowed for the emergence, in each segment of the private capital market, of at least a couple of competing firms*." Interestingly, the Mexican case also illustrates nicely the dynamics of institutional change. The institutional money that flowed into private capital found a much easier path into new ventures than to the buyout of already existing standard corporate assets. Capital flowed more smoothly into infrastructure, energy, and real-estate projects than into old closely-held family companies.

Not exempt from challenges, the Mexican case displays my two-step argument. First, a state-owned investment corporation anchored both local and international funds that wanted to operate in the country. Mexican *Fondo de Fondos* exemplifies a novel organizational form that combines policy goals and autonomy from formal bureaucracy and appears able to interact with private capital investors. And second, access to pension fund resources through the issuance of CKDs allowed the industry to consolidate. As the Chilean case will help make clear,

[42] It was common during my interviews for fund managers to complain about pension funds' investment teams profile, arguing "they are all traders," referring to their preference and knowledge trading short-term liquid assets, mostly public debt, and their lack of experience evaluating/managing illiquid portfolios, see Da Rin and Phalippou (2017).

government-funding alone is not enough, and engaging pension funds is a necessary step for the institutionalization of the private capital industry.

4.2.3 *Chile*

Chile is the richest country in the region. It is also the region's most stable and market-friendly economy with a vigorous private sector. It has maintained investment grade since the early 1990s, and it is usually praised as the poster child of pension reform, that resulted in the largest pension funds in the region, comparable in terms of GDP to those encountered in advanced economies. And indeed, under most metrics Chile is financially—and otherwise—the most developed country in the region. The size of its banking system is large, the market capitalization of firms as a proportion of GDP reaches the level of developed countries, the maturity of its corporate bond market is impressive, and the population's overall access to financial services is broad. Still, Chile's domestic private capital industry is relatively underdeveloped, and in part relatedly, there are comparatively few IPOs, and is rare to find large companies that are not controlled by a family or a group of families other than multinationals.

Notably, and in contrast to the free-market portrait of Chile's economy (e.g. Bril-Mascarenhas and Madariaga 2019), the country's nascent private capital industry is heavily dependent of government backing. Since the late 1990s there has been a sizable support for private "risk" capital funds by its longstanding development agency, CORFO (*Corporación de Fomento de la Producción*). Other institutional investors did not consistently follow this early-stage state impulse, and little to none pension fund resources currently go into the domestic private capital industry. As a result, the industry has, on the one side, a relatively large number of small PE/VC funds highly dependent on public money, and on the other, a few large international investors, that unmediated by local fund managers, have invested mostly in the infrastructure sector.

Constituted not formally as a bank, but as an agency dependent of the Ministry of Finance, CORFO, who had a central role during the import-substitution industrialization period, adapted its profile to accompany Chile's shifting development model (Musacchio et al. 2017; Rivas 2012). Regarding private capital, it started promoting the venture capital industry in 1998, with a pioneer program in the region, inspired by the—back then recent—Israel's well-renowned Yozma experience.[43] CORFOs funds program has grown and evolved over time, but exhibit a remarkable consistency since the early Lagos' administration. There are at least three overlapping programs that target funds that invest in companies at different stages of development, ranging from seed capital to growth equity strategies. But as a key difference with the Brazilian and Mexican cases laid out above, all of these programs promote comparatively "early-stage" funds. Industry-wise, they are not only oriented toward digital ventures but also include programs specific to sectors they want to promote, including agriculture, biotech, and mining.[44] As the next chapter on the politics of reform discusses more thoroughly, CORFO's lack of autonomy arguably limited the size and the type of its investments and may have limited the expansion of the asset class in Chile.

CORFO depends directly from the Ministry of Economy. Its risk capital unit is not structured as an independent organization nor has external investors, and therefore, CORFO has to get yearly budget approvals for each of its programs. Instead of making regular public calls in which funds have to make competitive bids for a specific investment mandate, such as in the case of Brazil's BNDES and FINEP funds programs, CORFO is permanently open for new applications, similar to the Mexican fund of funds. But in contrast to the Mexican case, the main contractual terms with each fund are fixed by the program and information about their investments transparent to the public. To incentivize the crowding-in of capital from private sources it has a matching funds approach: CORFO's contributions are set to be a fixed multiple of the resources obtained from third-party investors, capped at a maximum amount.[45]

[43] A government initiative to attract venture-capital investments in Israel, especially foreign, promising to double any investment with funds from the government. The program is considered to be very successful, triggering the creation of a VC industry in the country (Avnimelech 2009; Lerner 2009).

[44] For a more complete description of the different programs, its characteristics, and recipients, see CORFO (2018) and other similar reports from the same institution.

[45] The public to private ratios are calibrated according to the stage of development of the target firms. The smaller the target companies, the larger the proportion of public money invested in those VC funds, with CORFO to private-money ratios ranging from 1:1 to 3:1.

In terms of how the support is provided, CORFO's programs are from the fund managers' perspective quite beneficial. Since Chile's 1980's Constitution limits state's "entrepreneurial" role,[46] CORFO capacity to make equity investments is constrained. Therefore, it cannot participate in a fund as any other private sponsor, but instead contributes capital through a senior debt contract. CORFO basically gives the fund—not the companies—cheap leverage against no collateral. In this way, this scheme intends to promote risk-taking and benefit fund managers and their other private investors. If the target company fails, everyone loses their investments, including CORFO, who usually then writes off the debt. But if the funds do well, CORFO's upside is limited and it only gets a small mark-up over a baseline risk-free rate.[47] In terms of governance, it has a somehow more hands-off relationship with fund managers; for example, and contrary to Brazil, they do not get involved in firm's investment committees, and just demand the compliance of internal protocols. At least from a manager's perspective, some of requirements can be somewhat tedious:

> I personally raised two funds. Would those two funds have existed without CORFO? We didn't have a chance to raise those funds without CORFO's support [...] CORFO gets most of the risk, and if it goes well, we all win. Still, operating with CORFO is a pain, you have to deal with a lot of useless rules made by lawyers that know nothing about our business. You get their money just because you need them [...] without them all this industry wouldn't have existed. We suffer them, but we are also very grateful.

Since 1998 CORFO has made disbursements for over \$800M in more than 50 different funds and still has close to \$ 200M in outstanding commitments available for both early-stage and growth equity funds. But after 20 years, the private capital industry in Chile is still mostly dependent on the funding by CORFO (ACAFI 2018; CORFO 2018); pioneer funds have had a hard time scaling beyond the state support phase.

[46] See Article 19 N° 21 of Chile's Constitution: *"El Estado y sus organismos podrán desarrollar actividades empresariales o participar en ellas sólo si una ley de quórum calificado los autoriza."*

[47] In most programs LIBOR +2%.

The main problems, according to a fund manager active in the venture capital ecosystem, are two:

> First, CORFO requires its money to be only invested in Chile. The Chilean market may be good to do a proof a concept or act as a platform, but it is too small of a market. You need to go out of the country, but it's difficult to do so and comply with CORFOs rules [...] And second, and most importantly, there is a lack of financial sources to follow-up CORFO's investments and complete the financial "ladder" [incrementally larger rounds of funding]. Family offices and high net worth individuals are reluctant to invest through unrelated professional asset managers. And crucially, given how they are regulated and absent any initiative such as the Mexican fund-of-funds, it is very hard for fund managers to engage with pension funds and insurance companies. Therefore, different from other markets in which the whole financing chain is much better covered, in Chile there is an absolute lack of funds beyond the $40M size.

This is puzzling, since Chile has served as the poster child of successful pension reforms in the emerging world. By removing social security from the public balance sheet liabilities, the reform certainly helped create a stable macro-economy, in itself a remarkable achievement. And the resulting pension funds are the cornerstone of Chile's otherwise quite developed financial system. In terms of the assets under management of the system, Chile has by far the largest pension funds in the region relative to the size of its economy. Even in absolute terms they are larger than their Mexican peers and close to Brazilian pension funds. Chile's system has served as a model after which the pension regimes in many countries inside and outside the region have been designed (Weyland 2005).

But the pension funds investment strategies are regulated in a quite conservative way, and fund manager's incentive structures are arguably biased toward shorter term securities (Da et al. 2018; Opazo et al. 2014). Regarding private equity, at least during the last decade, they have not engaged systematically with local private capital fund managers. Even if they have been increasingly active in the asset class, they are discouraged to go domestic. Instead, they have gained exposure to "alternative" asset classes by investing mostly in large blue-chip international fund managers (e.g. KKR, Blackstone, Carlyle, etc.) that have global strategies and invest mostly in US, Europe, and Asia. This is in some way the opposite dynamic we observe in the other cases, where before engaging with the asset class internationally, pension funds start locally.

As I explain in more detail in Chapter 5, the regulations around the pension funds investment regime were updated in 2016/2017, granting some more flexibility for AFPs to allocate resources into the alternatives asset class. The reform facilitated investment in external PE funds and laid the ground for a more direct role of pension funds in the infrastructure space. But local VC/PE was mostly excluded from the reform, and absent more ambitious initiatives such as the one in Mexico's FdF that blends public resources with pension funds money, industry participants thought it was unlikely that the domestic private capital sector would grow.

Of course, if Brazil enjoyed being the largest market in the region, Chile is—even if the wealthier—the smallest among the countries analyzed. As discussed in Chapter 3, there are three main points that counteract the size argument. First, and more generally, there are several examples of small countries that in the last couple of decades have developed more dynamic equity markets (e.g. Singapore, Malaysia, and Israel).[48] Second, it is often argued that Chile's small size makes it an irrelevant market for large international investors, and that is what explains Chile's relative market void. Contrary to the implications of this argument, notwithstanding its size, some of the world's largest global private capital allocators are indeed present in Chile. For example, Canadian pension funds, global leaders in this sector, have several direct investments in the country. Unmediated by local fund managers, they made a couple of buy-hold infrastructure investments. Instead, there are few local firms operating in the mid-market private equity that combine foreign and local money. Third, given its size, Chile has a significant number of listed companies; still, after more than 30 years of Chile's economic transformation, their shareholding structure is unchanged and still highly concentrated (see, e.g., Larrain and Urzúa I. 2016), and there are few new listings.

In sum, Chile's case illustrates at least two key points. First, and somehow counter-intuitively, Chile's private capital industry received strong public support that included capital contributions to most of the funds operating in the country. But the industry could not consistently engage pension funds, the largest and more consolidated ones in the region. Arguably as a result of its lack access to institutional sources of

[48] Chile's GDP is ~15 times larger the minimum size of an economy required to develop a viable stock market, as considered by the World Bank's IFC (see Demekas and Nerlich 2020).

funding, the industry in the more stable and institutionalized country in the region is still small and highly dependent on government-related funding.

4.2.4 Colombia

The Colombian case exhibits a similar trajectory as the one sketched in the introduction to this chapter and observed in other countries. A latecomer to the PE industry, the first private capital funds appeared in Colombia in 2005 with initial support from development financial institutions, domestic, and international. During this period Colombia was able to attract international investors, but the involvement of local pension funds was also important for the growth of the sector. With a pacified country and a booming economy, the industry experienced momentum, even if it has not generated significant exits. Following the end of the commodity boom the prospects for the industry, even if now more institutionalized, were less optimistic.

Together with the recurring presence of multilateral and European DFIs as investors in each country's pioneer funds, we also observe in Colombia early government initiatives that helped establish some PE funds. For example, through *Ecopetrol*, Colombia's national oil company, and *Fiduagraria*, a rural-focused DFI, the government anchored a series of funds specialized on the oil and gas and timber sectors, respectively. These were managed by LAEF, one of the pioneer PE firms of the region. Beyond these more targeted early initiatives, Bancoldex was the instrument through which the national government channeled its efforts to promote the sector.

Bancoldex is a second-floor bank—meaning that it does not have direct commercial ties with companies but operates through financial intermediaries (mainly commercial banks)—specialized in financing exports. As a division within the same organization, Bancoldex Capital was created to provide support to the nascent PE industry. Their program combines some funding together with promotional initiatives. In terms of capital provision, Bancoldex interventions were, for the moment, limited. The ticket sizes they contributed were small and fund managers complained their investment process is too bureaucratic. It started by investing directly from the bank's balance sheet, with the expectation of then creating a separate fund of funds. Modeled after the Mexican fund of funds, it planned to initially invest around $100M from the bank and bring-in some outside investors (see Bancoldex 2015, 2016, 2017). This initiative did not take off and seems to have lost political momentum, although with the 2018's change in government, the initiative has resurfaced. Rather than its role in capital provision, Bancoldex's indirect "table-setting" (Lerner 2009) initiatives appear to be more relevant, as explained in the next chapter. The bank helped local pension funds connect with PE managers. And in a clear case of organizational public–private partnerships, they helped set-up ColCapital, the local association that groups industry participants.[49]

It is in infrastructure financing where the Colombian case is more revealing. In a first stage, the government promoted the creation of several infrastructure-oriented private equity funds, managed by well-recognized international asset managers. For example, in 2009 the government—through Bancoldex—pushed for a pioneer infrastructure fund that was managed by Ashmore, partnering with multilaterals and pension funds.

Moreover, as part of the 4G ambitious infrastructure plan of President Santos' administration, the government embarked in an ambitious institutional building process. On the regulatory side, they centralized all competencies concerning PPP contracts in one agency (ANI). But more related to the focus of this chapter, in order to secure the financial viability of private–public partnerships, the government built a new development bank basically from scratch: *Financiera de Desarrollo Nacional* (FDN). Re-launched after 2011, the government sold minority stakes in this new bank to World Bank's IFC, CAF, and Japan's Sumitomo. Notably, the FDN is the only case in which these international institutions participate as shareholders in an otherwise state-owned development financial institution. External multilateral and private investors arguably helped secure bank's autonomy from bureaucrats and politicians, and guarantee its "commercial" orientation.

Funded in part by the proceeds obtained by the privatization of *Isagen*, a power generation company acquired by Brookfield (a large Canadian PE investor) FDN redeployed these resources into the 4G

[49] Colombia has other agencies, federal and regional, to enhance private capital industry, mostly oriented towards smaller VCs (e.g. Impulsa and Ruta N). Besides their promotional role they provide some seed capital. But as it seems to be the case elsewhere in the region, it seems very hard for these small funds to obtain other sizable outside investors beyond the state.

highway projects.[50] Together with some direct loans and guarantees, they channeled significant amounts of capital through third-party private asset managers. Given the highly-levered nature of the infrastructure business, the equity part of the projects was already mostly covered prior to the PPP biddings. Instead, the market voids were in the longer-term portion of the debt financing and some mezzanine securities (hybrid debt-equity securities). FDN therefore first promoted the creation of private-debt funds, structured similarly to private equity funds. There are now several of these new type of vehicles, managed by international and local institutions.[51] Together with FDN's money, these funds also pool resources from other investors, mainly pension funds.[52]

Taking a step back, the Colombian case also indicates the role of local pension funds. They are the main local investor in the asset class, but also arguably one of the main limitations for the sector's continued growth. During the initial years, they indeed helped foster the market. Together with sizable external investments, the private capital industry grew fast and accumulated a substantial amount of assets. As of 2018, there were around 50 firms managing resources for around $13 billion. In terms of regulation, the environment is quite pro-investor. Different than for example in Mexico, pension funds are allowed to participate directly in private placements, avoiding the need to go through onerous listed investment vehicles (e.g. Mexican CKDs).

As in every other country, the end of the commodity cycle and the consequent depreciation of the exchange rate hit the financial returns of the funds denominated in dollars, therefore limiting the fundraising

[50] Besides its financing activities, the FDN also provides with advisory and investment banking services to the different levels of government (e.g. it coordinated Electrocaribe's restructuring effort).

[51] For example, Ashmore, that also manages a pure private equity fund, structured the first of these private-debt funds, together with CAF, the multilateral institution. And Blackrock, the world's largest asset manager, started investing locally in Colombia through another of these private capital funds, anchored by FDN. It is important to note, even if part of large international franchises, that these funds are managed locally. Among the Colombian asset managers, Credicorp and Sura also manage their own funds.

[52] More recently, FDN announced it had structured a US$1.1B fund, the largest of its kind in the country, targeted towards equity investment in infrastructure projects and companies. Similar to the arrangement in Mexico, half of the capital is contributed by CDQP, Canada's second largest institutional investor, who manages Quebec public employees' pensions. The rest of the capital commitments are granted by FDN and local pension funds.

of subsequent funds. Again, private capital flowed more easily into new companies, real-estate and infrastructure investments than to already mature corporate assets. Moreover, the problem of pension system concentration observed throughout the region finds in Colombia its maximum expression. There are only four pension funds, and two of them (*Porvenir* and *Proteccion*, part of *Grupo Aval* and *Grupo Sura*, respectively) hold close to 90% of the assets. As the managing director of a large international fund with a long history of investments in the region, and former president of the Colombian PE/VC association told me, about the Colombia case, but also more generally about the region:

> The main barrier for the development of the PE industry is that there are no investors. Each country has four pension funds. I can count institutional investors here in Colombia with only one hand. Pension funds concentration is the most perverse for the funds, and for the capital markets in general. It is really hard to create a market with such a few numbers of players.

Not optimistic about the fate of the industry, still, this last quote is in line with the argument about the centrality of institutional investors for the sustainability of the private capital industry. With just a few pension funds, the development of the industry is jeopardized. And it signals one of the structural limits for the country and region's capital markets growth.

Overall, the Colombian case seems to fit with my two arguments. We observe a pioneering role of different public agencies in each segment of the private capital industry, PE, VC, and infrastructure investment, which helped attract pension funds into the market. The infrastructure segment is especially interesting and exhibits more clearly the dynamics emphasized throughout the chapter. In order to promote private sector participation in infrastructure financing, Colombia created of a new development bank, FDN. In turn, this bank anchored a series of private capital funds that attracted external asset managers into the country and catalyzed local and external pension funds participation in the asset class.

4.2.5 Argentina

Argentina was the hottest private equity market in the region during the 1990s. Following macroeconomic stabilization and extensive liberalization, the country attracted considerable amounts of external capital. As part of the broader restructuring of the economy, Argentina saw the emergence of the first formal private equity firms in the region (Baltin and Bell 2001). Led by local executives managing mostly international funds, these pioneer PE firms emulated the American leveraged buyout model. While initially successful, the virulent economic crisis at the turn of the century, that included a massive sovereign default and a substantial devaluation, turned out deadly for the industry.

Following the crisis and the rise of a more leftist government, the sector did not recover, even if the economy grew quickly fueled by the commodity boom. Argentina did not take any of the steps toward a more institutionalized private capital market we observe, even if timidly, in all of its regional peers. Fund manager's attempt to follow the other countries' path during the early 2000, creating a manager's association to engage with local pension funds, did not work out. The pro-business government inaugurated in 2015 was urged to mobilize financial capital into the real economy. In order to do so, they embarked in a reformist agenda that included the passage of several pieces of legislation that would encourage this type of investor. But, together with macroeconomic turmoil, the lack of any local institutional investors arguably limited the impact of this reformist agenda.

As mentioned, the industry had an early start parallel to the process of economic liberalization and market reform. Similar to Brazil, PE during the nineties in Argentina had an international flavor. Even if there was some engagement of local business groups as well as some financing from local banks that helped leverage deals, most money raised by these funds came from institutional sources in the US. Also, similar to Brazil, some funds also participated in the privatizations of state-owned companies[53] and propped the transformation of the corporate sector that followed the

[53] Interestingly, the first private equity funds in Argentina grew, among others, by doing a particular type of debt-to-equity deals that involved the government. These firms acquired distressed debt of private companies from the portfolio of the government's development bank that was being liquidated. And then participated in the firms restructuring, swapped their debt contracts for equity participations, and took control of the restructured companies (see Naishtat and Maas 2000, 31).

market liberalization. But in contrast with Brazil, local pension funds did not participate in the business since they have been only recently created.

Overall, during the decade there were close to twenty PE country-focused funds plus a handful of regional players. They managed a combined asset pool of over $12 billion and funded more than 160 transactions (Pereiro 2001). These are impressive figures, even by today's standards. Success cases of Argentinian start-ups (e.g. Mercado Libre and Despegar), in general all related to international funding, were first funded as part of this boom. In the buyout segment, the star of the market was the Exxel Group, whose case is illustrative of this decade. Formed by former Citibank executives, Exxel became the leading and most admired private equity firm in Latin America.[54] Emulating US buyout funds, they were financially and operationally aggressive, which proved to be, at least initially, highly successful. They managed to raise six consecutive country-specific funds in less than ten years—a remarkable achievement—and invested close to $5 billion. By the end of the decade they were one of the largest private employers in the country. But the combination of a deep recession followed by a massive devaluation, ended up badly. Companies with revenues in local currency and hard-currency debts soon had no option but to default on their loans. And lenders ended up in control of most of their companies, many of whom were later re-sold to smaller, less institutional, PE investors.

The comparison between Argentina's *Exxel Group* and Brazil's *GP Investimentos* exemplifies the trajectory of the industry in each country. This parallelism was often made by the business press during the nineties,[55] while these two firms were the unquestionable leaders of their markets, and is now usually raised by most experienced industry participants. The original founders of GP ended up playing in the international "big leagues." After the turn of the century, GP raised new funds, sponsored several IPOs, and engendered a couple of spin-offs that dispersed their human capital throughout the industry. In contrast, Exxel, who is also often praised by its human capital, disappeared, damaging the local industry's reputation. Its former executives are, if at all, doing small, non-institutional private equity and mostly outside the country. Notably, and

[54] See, for example, an HBS case about the firm (Lerner and Ballve 2001).

[55] See notes in NY Times ("Where the Risk in Riskier Yet", December 16, 1999) and Bloomberg ("Juan Navarro: the Buyout King of Argentina", June 22, 1998) about Exxel Group being the "KKR of Latin America."

as legacy of the first booming decade, there is a handful of Argentinean managers working in the largest regional Latin America funds, investing mostly outside their home country.

Even if the economy recovered quickly following 2002's default and devaluation, Argentina could never re-develop a private capital industry. The government was not business friendly and did not engage extensively with international capital markets. But still, at first glance its leftist orientation was not so different from the PT administrations that governed Brazil since 2002 during which the local PE industry experienced major growth. Significantly, Argentina never had any local institutional capital sources available for fundraising. In contrast to all of its regional peers, it lacked a relevant development financial institution. Most importantly, pension funds were not allowed to invest in the asset class, and were nationalized in 2008. Consequently, with no possible local institutional fundraising and a poor business climate, during the 2003–2015 period there was minimal activity, no country-specific funds and investments were limited to a handful of opportunistic transactions.

Following the 2015 election, Macri's market-friendly government (2015–2019) gave Argentina some momentum within the international financial community. Several officers with a career path in finance were appointed to senior executive branch positions. With this model in mind, the government pushed a reformist agenda. Overly optimistic of international sources of capital, and managing a complex political and economic scenario, this pro-investment agenda had few tangible results. Still, some episodes may provide support to the main points of my argument, indicating that, beyond more fundamental macroeconomic and institutional stability, the lack of any local institutional investors are also an obstacle to the development of the industry.

Macri's government advanced with three key pieces of legislation. First, a new private–public partnerships (PPPs) law was sanctioned in November 2016, aimed at boosting the participation of the private sector in infrastructure. With the help of multilateral institutions, it incorporated into local legislation international best practices in infrastructure financing. Practitioners agreed the law is technically good, in line with international standards. Second, a new "Entrepreneurship Law"was passed on April 2017 that introduced a novel "simplified" legal entity and granted it tax incentives.[56] And most importantly it created FONDCE,[57] a *proto* fund of funds through which the state would be able to anchor private capital funds. Finally, after a rough passage through the legislature, a new capital markets law was sanctioned in May 2018. Among more general issues that for example limited the capacity of the regulator to intervene in listed firms, increased during the Kirchnerist period, it also created an investment vehicle more appropriate for private equity investments and granted it a favorable tax status. But regulatory reform, together with former businessmen with extensive career paths in international finance appointed to top government positions, were not enough to mobilize capital.

Even if there is a heavy presence of the state in the commercial banking sector,[58] Argentina lacks any kind of relevant development financial institution.[59] More importantly, there are virtually no active pension funds—either private or publicly managed. Following the 2008 nationalization, the former private capitalization regime was transformed back into a quasi-universalized pay-as-you-go system financed mostly by payroll taxes. The holdings of the formerly privately-managed pension funds (AFJP) were inherited by a so-called sustainability fund—*Fondo de Garantia para la Sustentabilidad (FGS)*. Among other assets,[60] it included minority equity participations in most of the companies listed in the local stock exchange. After the nationalization, the FGS resources were used in a political, non-commercial basis. Besides financing the federal treasury and funding some infrastructure projects in a rather opaque way, it devoted considerable resources to social programs (e.g. conditional cash transfers, one laptop per child program, heavily subsidized mortgage credit). It kept its considerable equity portfolio and occasionally used the board seats gained through its equity holdings politically to pressure companies (e.g. *Grupo Clarin*, a media conglomerate, or Techint).

Overall, the FGS had no new interactions with the private sector, for example, by providing new financing to private companies through

[56] *Ley de Apoyo al Capital Emprendedor N⁰ 27,349.*

[57] *Fondo Fiduciario para el Desarrollo del Capital Emprendedor (FONDCE).*

[58] Even after a wave of bank privatization during the 1990s, the federal government still owns the country's largest bank *(Banco Nacion)*. Buenos Aires' state-government owns another large bank *(Banco Provincia)*.

[59] Macri's administration tried to revamp BICE, a state-owned investment bank.

[60] AFJP's assets were composed mainly by public debt (see Datz 2012).

the capital markets, either through equity or debt. Intending to change this, the new administration inaugurated in late 2015 appointed a former investment banker with an extensive career path in finance as head of the FGS, with the idea to manage it more actively. But after one year in the position, the head of the FGS resigned, without any tangible results in terms of portfolio management. It was hard to sell sizable equity stakes in listed companies, inherited from the nationalized private pension funds, in order to invest the resources in other projects. The fund continues to be paralyzed and mostly just finances the Treasury.[61]

As mentioned, the new "entrepreneurship law" included a chapter focused on capital with the creation of FONDCE. Even if inspired in the Mexican fund of funds model, it was executed in a different way. It had the status of a program dependent of an undersecretary (a third-level unit within a ministry), rather than being structured as an independent corporation, or at least as a program dependent of a financial institution. An officer in the undersecretary that led the law and the implementation of the program identified their lack of autonomy and capacity as a key limitation:

> In an ideal situation we need to have an autonomous agency. We need FONDCE to be outside the bureaucracy of the ministry. You end up fighting all day with the ministry's bureaucracy, from human resources to IT issues. Being inside the ministry is a limitation. It is very difficult to bring people from outside. This sector needs a flexibility and technical expertise that you don't have inside the state, it's a niche market. Definitely, in the medium term we need to go towards a more independent structure. And the model we are most interested in is the Mexican fund of funds. Still, we would do their inverse path. They started with big funds and then went down to earlier stage, we started small and hopefully we can grow together with the industry.

[61] Illustrating this last point, Macri's government tried to establish an infrastructure-oriented private equity fund and obtained a sizable capital commitment from Qatar's Investment Authority (Qatar's sovereign wealth fund). Capital was going to be sourced mostly from QIA (~$1 billion) together with ANSES' FGS (~$300 million). And similar to the arrangements observed in other countries (e.g. Colombia and Mexico) the fund was going to be managed by an experienced international GP. But after the memorandum of understanding became public the project was immediately blocked in Congress by the opposition and sidelined. As I will discuss in more detail in the next chapter, with a lack of a financial bureaucracy used to interact with the private sector, Congress approval becomes an unsurmountable obstacle for these types of initiatives.

FONDCE it is not a source of permanent capital, nor it is committed to have several rounds of funding; it was endowed with resources for only one round. It lacked any dedicated personal or professional staff other than those in the undersecretary, and the invested fund managers were selected by an outside committee composed by industry participants.[62] Together with some accelerators and incubators, it granted capital commitments for $12M to each of the three winning funds. This amount could represent up to 40% of the fund: i.e. the winners had to get at least $18M from other sources. The small size of the program attracted only small funds oriented toward tech start-ups that may expect to get some additional funding from some multilateral institutions, and possibly other public and private sources. Unlike in all the other countries, the program is not oriented toward mid-market PE funds that could have a broader sectoral reach. FONDCE's low bureaucratic hierarchy together with its lack of autonomy and dedicated staff hinder the continuity of the program. Talking about this program, a member of the local association who was also involved in its design told me:

> I would have liked it to be at least 10 times the actual size, so it can really make a difference. This can only work from VC downwards. It is too small for PE, completely out of the range. [...] The law only approved the budget for one round of financing. Once it is invested, it is over, there is no more. You would have to go again and ask for a new item in the budget law.

Moreover, given the pension funds void, the government pressured to tap on insurance company's balance sheets as a source of institutional capital. In more developed markets insurance companies are a significant source of funds for the private capital industry. But they are often behind pension funds, who have a more natural fit to the asset class given their longer time horizons. In Argentina, the insurance market is small and atomized, fragmented between a lot of small—and some of them quite informal—companies. In August 2018, the same unit in government in

[62] The FONDCE trust is administrated (not managed) by BICE, a publicly-owned second-floor bank focused in financing import–export operations, that the Macri administration tried to re-haul into a development bank (with Colombia's FDN model in mind).

charge of FONDCE achieved a change in regulation that allowed insurance companies to invest up to 1% of their balance in the tax-incentivized entities introduced by the entrepreneurship law.[63]

Finally, the fate of PPP projects related to highways through which the government first launched this new contracting model is also telling. There was a lack of interest from financial players as sponsors of the projects, even if they were actively targeted. Instead, winners were closely-held incumbent construction companies that already managed some of those road concessions, most of them involved in the corruption scandals with the previous administration. This, together with the macroeconomic and financial volatility the country experienced since 2018 precluded the project's financial closing (except for the projects that had Chinese support). At last, the government tried to revive the projects by anchoring private investors with further public resources and pushing for heavy multilateral support and still could not achieve any success.

The Argentinean case illustrates well more standard institutional arguments: chronic experience of expropriation paired with macroeconomic instability are certainly not conducive toward development, financial, and all other. Still, two arguments can be made. First, the parallelism with Brazil is informative. Up to the extent that both countries experienced similar investment trends in the 1990s followed by a macroeconomic crisis and had governments with similar political orientations in the post-crisis, it is not that obvious Argentina's underdevelopment is only a function of its poor macro-political and economic environment. The lack of policy support both in terms of investments and regulations, paired with the absence of pension engagement with the incipient community of fund managers, also seem to be factors that explain the post-2000 divergence. Second, the 2015–2019 pro-business government who prioritized an investment agenda and embarked in institutional reform still had limited impact. The counterfactual is hard to make, but even before the mid-2018 currency crisis, there were no great results in terms of the participation

[63] If fully utilized, this would mount to a maximum of around $100 M, a scant sum, especially in an environment with virtually no other source of domestic institutional capital. As expressed in interviews with people from the industry that were trying to tap this money, these funds can at best be used to support a tax-incentivized corporate venture program targeted toward the insurance industry ("insurtech"), with a strategic (plus marketing and promotional) goal rather than with a stand-alone investment rationale. Furthermore, it is unclear whether this capital could be effectively mobilized, even for this more narrow purpose.

of new financial players, local or international. Beyond solving its more urgent macroeconomic issues, even with the political will to promote the sector, without any active domestic—public or private—relevant institutional investor, it is hard to foresee a more dynamic capital market going forward.

4.3 Discussion

After scratching the surface of each country's private capital ecosystem, it seems clear there is no policy-free path toward a more institutionalized private equity market. In each of the case studies presented above, together with multilaterals support, there are a set of policy-initiatives specifically aimed at promoting this asset class. As part of their role incubating the industry, these policies include the investment of public resources into privately-managed funds and companies. The supply of capital was the focus of this chapter, the next one explains how these same actors pushed for the regulations that institutionalized the sector.

As discussed throughout the cases (and in the Appendix below), these programs face many trade-offs, require non-abundant organizational capabilities, often suffer from adverse selection of fund managers, and indeed, many of them indeed fail and waste taxpayers money (Lerner 2009). Still, public support appears to be widespread.

Notwithstanding the many limitations of these policy programs, government's potential counter-productive role is unlikely to explain the overall region's relative capital market underdevelopment. The presence of government-related financial institutions in private equity markets is by no means a Latin American exceptionality. As Chapter 6 shows, what distinguishes Latin American cases from other regions is not that they exhibit public support, but its extent and form. In Asia and Europe, for example, public investment programs appear to be larger and more systematic.

The role of government-related financial institutions pushing for private capital investments is—when coming from the literature—somewhat counterintuitive. As discussed in the theory chapter, the literature on financial development sidelines the role of government and policymaking. It does not go deep into the role of financial intermediaries either and mostly focuses on the institutional features that protect external investors from being expropriated, both by the state and corporate insiders. Its policy implications, if any, are more related to legal and judiciary reform.

And the older literature on the state and finance connects public interventions in national financial systems to bank-based models and equates more active equity markets with less interventionist, more liberal political economies. Private equity, in turn, is often characterized as the ultimate expression of financial capitalism and the hegemony of the shareholder-value model (see, e.g., Appelbaum and Batt 2014; Hall and Soskice 2001), at odds with an active role of the state in the economy.

Still, by simply observing that the government recurrently participates as an investor in this emerging sector, yet suggestive and maybe even theoretically puzzling, is by no means conclusive evidence of the effectiveness of these programs. The cross-sectional evidence, even with the limited number of cases analyzed, is broadly in line with the hypothesis that emphasized, first the incubating role of development financial institutions, and then the engagement of local pension funds for developing a local private capital industry. After examining the trajectories of the main Latin American countries during the last two decades, the cases support the hypothesis that where there was an earlier and more intense involvement of institutional investors in the asset class, the—broadly defined—private equity market is also more developed (Brander et al. 2015). In Brazil, BNDES, together with FINEP and other state-related financial institutions, have been involved directly and indirectly in private equity for a relative long time. They have participated in every segment of the market and arguably encouraged pension funds to join them. And, with all its problems, and now successfully exhibiting a more internationalized and private sector led profile, Brazil is in this realm the most consolidated market.

This is of course not definitive evidence either. Policy often functions reactively, and government policy may simply bandwagon the emergence of the new actor. Still, the timing of the cases provides some further support to the institutional investor-based argument. By process tracing the main milestones of the institutionalization of each countries' domestic private capital industry, the development of the sector appears to roughly follow the policies to promote it. Moreover, it also points that public money cannot work alone (Brander et al. 2015). The engagement of pension funds seems to be a crucial step for the viability of the industry. Mexico is the clearest example of the two successive stages, where a government-owned fund of funds paved the way for the entrance of privately-managed pension funds. In Brazil, public-sector investors working in tandem with pension funds also arguably helped the industry grow, even if their involvement later generated serious governance challenges, introducing some unhealthy dynamics into the market. In Colombia, the industry grew with the involvement of the pension funds, although their small number jeopardize the sustainability of the industry. In Chile, despite the strong government support for the emergent funds industry, the limited engagement of pension funds has arguably limited its scale. And in Argentina, despite recent political will to promote the sector—and notwithstanding its serious institutional handicap that undoubtedly explains a big part of the insignificance of its financial markets—the lack of any active institutional investors also appears to limit the development of the sector structurally.

In order to access institutional sources of capital and operate smoothly, the nascent private capital industry also requires a specific set of regulations. The next chapter goes into the discussion about the politics behind the some key regulations that shaped the sector in each country. Doing so, it emphasizes the "quiet politics" role of a group of asset-specific industry associations.

Appendix: Discussion on Trade-Offs and Challenges

This chapter suggests the support of development financial institutions and the engagement of pension funds are part of the path toward more developed private capital markets. Still, both policy-oriented investors and pension funds face substantial challenges when investing in domestic private equity. And to encourage risk-taking from both pension funds and the state while maintaining investment discipline requires non-trivial capabilities.

When government-related money tries to anchor further external investment in private funds, the incentives of both types of investors may not be aligned. The state is not necessarily—in practice but also theoretical—interested in maximizing profitability but "social returns." The co-existence of commercial and non-commercial priorities can generate multitude of instances of potential conflict of interest between development financial institutions and its private co-investors.[64]

[64] An executive from a top Brazilian PE firm that had at some point on his career worked in BNDESPAR explained what he called the catch-22 of development banks:

For policy-oriented investors there is also a tension between direct and indirect investment strategies, in particular when the purpose of the intervention is to promote the capital markets and not just to incentivize a particular sector of the economy. Beyond the trade-off between good governance and control when deciding to invest directly or indirectly, direct strategies may crowd-out other private managers, in particular if the state invests directly in the same market segment than other private investments firms. Direct PE investment strategies can hinder the development of private fund managers and, in turn, inhibit the emergence of a more competitive asset manager's landscape. Moreover, if the same institution is providing a company with both equity and debt capital (as, for example, BNDES often does), the potential for conflict of interests increases.

The agency problems faced by the state when investing directly are well known.[65] Some of these issues can possibly be ameliorated when investing through third-party privately-managed fund that pair state-money with outside investors. Still, even when DFIs invest through outsourced managers, the organizational capabilities/ pre-requisites still seem to be significant. Investing through third-party funds still requires selecting the right managers, performing due-diligence of funds, and then monitoring their investments (Da Rin and Phalippou 2017). This may require fewer capabilities than investing directly and "picking winners," but still requires non-abundant private-capital-specific skills. It requires recruiting, promotion, and compensation structures that allow public servants to take investment risks but not go rogue. Arguably, competent state-related investors help prevent adverse selection in fund selection (i.e. "good" managers avoid to get involved with government-related investors, if possible), a pervasive problem of this type of policy initiatives, particularly acute in the venture capital realm. And most importantly, it requires autonomy from politicians. Similar challenge also applies to pension funds when engaging with this new asset class.

The involvement of pension funds and their regulation also faces its own trade-offs. First, and more fundamentally, it is not pension funds programmatic role to develop capital markets, but to secure pensioners

their only point is to make things the market won't do by itself, but then, they are evaluated on a market-basis.

[65] Brazil could illustrate how through state's involvement as an investor, public resources can be diverted for political benefits and the proliferation of cronies. Even more grotesquely, see the 1Malaysia Development Berhad scandal.

the best possible retirement. To avoid being used as government's captive investors and provide with financing below market conditions, expropriating pensioners, pension funds managers are often endowed with autonomy from politicians, at least *de-jure*. Beyond this more structural question around the autonomy of pension fund management from politicians, pension funds also face a trade-off between an inwards-oriented domestic focus, where local investors may have an informational advantage, and diversifying risk by investing internationally. Moreover, regulations that intend to protect pensioner's savings, many times do not generate incentives for differentiation across pension fund managers, limits competition, and disincentives risk taking. Pension funds are under pressure to reduce commissions, which determine pensioners' savings in a more direct and immediate way than the potential long-term benefit they could receive for allocating capital in a more risky—but also higher-fee—assets such as actively-managed investment funds. Passive "index" investing help economize fees. And pension fund consolidation, through scale economies, is another way to reduce commissions. At the same time, the increasing concentration of pension funds in just a few players in each country is problematic for the development of capital markets. There is no active market with just a handful of players.

The small size of the local markets, with a handful of participants, should drive a more integrated regional market. In Latin America there have been attempts in this direction, starting with the integration of formal stock exchanges. The MILA market intends to integrate stock markets in Chile, Peru, Colombia, and Mexico. But integrations efforts for the moment have achieved scant results, and it seems hard to harmonize complex regulations across these countries.

Private equity is, by definition, a risky asset class, and some investments are likely to fail. Fund of funds that diversifies across different funds—that in turn diversify across companies—can arguably help ameliorate risk and obfuscate some of the likely failures. Still, it is challenging for bureaucrats, as well as for pension fund managers, to stomach losing taxpayers' and pensioners' capital, respectively. Fear of failure often prevents policy experimentation (Mazzucato 2018). And headline risk is often mentioned as another important factor limiting risk-taking in contexts where trust in business and finance are low.

References

ABRAPP. 2014. *The Brazilian Pension System.*

ACAFI. 2018. *Reporte Venture Capital & Private Equity 2016–2017.*

Anzia, Sarah F., and Terry M. Moe. 2019. Interest Groups on the Inside: The Governance of Public Pension Funds. *Perspectives on Politics* 17 (4): 1059–1078.

Appelbaum, Eileen, and Rosemary Batt. 2014. *Private Equity at Work: When Wall Street Manages Main Street.* New York: Russell Sage Foundation.

Avnimelech, Gil. 2009. VC Policy: Yozma Program 15-Years Perspective. *SSRN Electronic Journal.*

Baltin, Matthias, and Philipp Bell. 2001. Venture Capital in South America: Unlocking the Potential for Venture Creation in an Emerging Market. WHU.

Bancoldex. 2015. *Informe de La Junta Directiva y Del Presidente a La Asamblea General de Accionistas.*

———. 2016. *Informe de La Junta Directiva y Del Presidente a La Asamblea General de Accionistas.*

———. 2017. *Informe de La Junta Directiva y Del Presidente a La Asamblea General de Accionistas.*

Borsato da Silva, Filipe, and Fabio Luiz Biagini. 2016. *Capital de Risco e o Desenvolvimento de Empresas de Base Tecnológica No Brasil – a Experiência Dos Fundos Criatec e Perspectivas.*

Brander, J.A., Q. Du, and T. Hellmann. 2015. The Effects of Government-Sponsored Venture Capital: International Evidence. *Review of Finance* 19 (2): 571–618.

Bril-Mascarenhas, Tomás. 2016. *How States Shape Markets in Latin America.* PhD dissertation, University of California, Berkeley.

Bril-Mascarenhas, Tomás, and Aldo Madariaga. 2019. Business Power and the Minimal State: The Defeat of Industrial Policy in Chile. *The Journal of Development Studies* 55 (6): 1047–1066.

Charvel, Roberto, and Juan Carlos de Yeregui. 2002. Private Equity in Latin America: The Mexican Case. *The Journal of Private Equity*: 1–12.

CORFO. 2018. *Informe Publico de Capital de Riesgo.*

Cornelius, Peter. 2011. *International Investments in Private Equity: Asset Allocation, Markets, and Industry Structure.* Amsterdam: Academic Press.

CPI Fundos de Pensao - Relatorio Final. 2016. Brasilia.

Da Rin, Marco, and Ludovic Phalippou. 2017. The Importance of Size in Private Equity: Evidence from a Survey of Limited Partners. *Journal of Financial Intermediation* 31: 64–76.

Da, Zhi, Borja Larrain, Clemens Sialm, and José Tessada. 2018. Destabilizing Financial Advice: Evidence from Pension Fund Reallocations. *The Review of Financial Studies* 31 (10): 3720–3755.

Datz, Giselle. 2012. The Inextricable Link Between Sovereign Debt and Pensions in Argentina, 1993–2010. *Latin American Politics and Society* 54 (01): 101–126.

Demekas, Dimitri, and Anica Nerlich. 2020. *Creating Domestic Capital Markets in Developing Countries: Perspectives from Market Participants.*

Dieguez, Consuelo. 2009. Sergio Rosa e o Mundo Dos Fundos. *Piaui.*

EMPEA. 2016. *Special Report: Private Equity in Mexico.*

EY. 2015. *Estudio Sobre La Industria de Capital Emprendedor En Mexico.*

Faccio, Mara, and Hung-Chia. Hsu. 2017. Politically Connected Private Equity and Employment. *The Journal of Finance* 72 (2): 539–574.

Gomes Schapiro, Mario. 2013. Rediscovering the Developmental Path? Development Bank, Law, and Innovation Financing in the Brazilian Economy. In *Law and the New Developmental State: The Brazilian Experience in Latin American Context*, ed. David M. Trubek, Helena Alviar Garcia, Diogo R. Coutinho, and Alvaro Santos. Cambridge: Cambridge University Press.

Hall, Peter A., and David W. Soskice. 2001. *Varieties of Capitalism: The Institutional Foundations of Comparative Advantage.* Oxford: Oxford University Press.

Hochstetler, Kathryn, and Alfred P. Montero. 2013. The Renewed Developmental State: The National Development Bank and the Brazil Model. *Journal of Development Studies* 49 (11): 1484–1499.

Ibanez, Fernan. 1989. *Venture Capital and Entrepreneurial Development.* Washington, DC.

IDB/IIC. 2017. *Comparative Study of Equity Investing in Development Finance Institutions.* Washington, DC.

Jiang, Wei, Kai Li, and Pei Shao. 2010. When Shareholders Are Creditors: Effects of the Simultaneous Holding of Equity and Debt by Non-Commercial Banking Institutions. *The Review of Financial Studies* 23 (10): 3595–3637.

Larrain, Borja, and Francisco Urzúa I. 2016. Do Business Groups Change with Market Development? *Journal of Economics & Management Strategy* 25 (3): 750–784.

Lavelle, Kathryn C. 1999. International Financial Institutions and Emerging Capital Markets in Africa. *Review of International Political Economy* 6 (2): 200–224.

Lazzarini, Sérgio G. 2010. *Capitalismo de Laços.* Elsevier.

Lazzarini, Sérgio G., Aldo Musacchio, Rodrigo Bandeira-de-Mello, and Rosilene Marcon. 2015. What Do State-Owned Development Banks Do? Evidence from BNDES, 2002–09. *World Development* 66: 237–253.

Leal, Antonio Martinez, and Pino Del Sesto. 2013. *Private Equity in Mexico: Primed for Significant Growth.*

Leamon, Ann, and Josh Lerner. 2012. *Creating a Venture Ecosystem in Brazil: FINEP's INOVAR Project.*

Leeds, Roger. 2015. *Private Equity Investing in Emerging Markets: Opportunities for Value Creation*. New York: Palgrave Macmillan US.

Lerner, Josh, and Alberto Ballve. 2001. The Exxel Group. *HBS Case Collection*.

Lerner, Josh. 2009. *Boulevard of Broken Dreams: Why Public Efforts to Boost Entrepreneurship and Venture Capital Have Failed, and What to Do About It*. Princeton: Princeton University Press.

Lerner, Josh, and Antoinette Schoar. 2005. Does Legal Enforcement Affect Financial Transactions? The Contractual Channel in Private Equity. *The Quarterly Journal of Economics* 120 (1): 223–246.

Márquez, Luis Antonio, and Fernando Sandoval-Arzaga. 2017. Myths and Realities of Family Offices in Mexico from an Investment Perspective. *Family Capital*.

Mazzucato, Mariana. 2018. Mission-Oriented Innovation Policies: Challenges and Opportunities. *Industrial and Corporate Change* 27 (5): 803–815. https://academic.oup.com/icc/article/27/5/803/5127692 (May 30, 2021).

McCarthy, Michael A. 2014. Turning Labor into Capital: Pension Funds and the Corporate Control of Finance. *Politics & Society* 42 (4): 455–487.

McWilliam, Micheal. 2001. *The Development Business: A History of the Commonwealth Development Corporation*. New York: Palgrave Macmillan.

Menaldo, Victor. 2016. The Fiscal Roots of Financial Underdevelopment. *American Journal of Political Science* 60 (2): 456–471.

Michelitsch, Roland, et al. 2017. *Comparative Study of Equity Investing in Development Finance Institutions*.

Minardi, Andrea Maria Accioly Fonseca, Ricardo Vinicius Kanitz, and Rafael Honório Bassani. 2014. Private Equity and Venture Capital Industry Performance in Brazil: 1990–2013. *The Journal of Private Equity* 17: 48–58.

Minardi, Andrea Maria Accioly Fonseca, and Rafael Honório Bassani. 2016. *Investimentos Em Private Equity Feitos Por Fundos de Pensao Brasileiros*.

Monteiro Ramalho, Caio Cesar. 2013. An Essay on Private Equity: The History and Fundamentals of Fundraising in Brazil. FGV-EPGE.

Musacchio, Aldo, and Sérgio G. Lazzarini. 2014. *Reinventing State Capitalism: Leviathan in Business, Brazil and Beyond*. Cambridge: Harvard University Press.

Musacchio, Aldo, Sérgio G. Lazzarini, Pedro Makhoul, and Emily Simmons. 2017. *The Role and Impact of Development Banks: A Review of Their Founding, Focus, and Influence*.

Naishtat, Silvia, and Pablo Maas. 2000. *El Cazador: La Historia Secreta de Los Negocios de Juan Navarro y El Grupo Exxel*. Planeta.

Nenova, Tatiana. 2006. Control Values and Changes in Corporate Law in Brazil. *Latin American Business Review* 6 (3): 1–37.

Opazo, Luis, Claudio Raddatz, and Sergio L. Schmukler. 2014. *Institutional Investors and Long-Term Investment: Evidence from Chile*. The World Bank.

Pereiro, Luis E. 2001. Tango and Cash: Entrepreneurial Finance and Venture Capital in Argentina. *Venture Capital* 3 (4): 291–308.

Rivas, Gonzalo. 2012. *La Experiencia de Corfo y La Transformación Productiva de Chile*.

Settel, Daniel, Abu Chowdhury, and Ryan Orr. 2009. The Rise of MDFI Investments in Private Equity Funds. *The Journal of Private Equity Spring* 200: 60–76.

Sierra, Jazmin. 2017. *Global Champions Are Made At Home: The Brazilian Development Bank and Domestic MNCs*.

Viveiros, Ricardo. 2017. *ABVCAP: A Força Da Indústria de Participações No Desenvolvimento Do Brasil*. Sao Paolo: AzulSol Editora.

Weyland, Kurt. 2005. Theories of Policy Diffusion Lessons from Latin American Pension Reform. *World Politics* 57 (2): 262–295.

World Bank. 1996. *Investment Funds in Emerging Markets*. Washington, DC.

———. 2017. *The Evolution of the Canadian Pension Model: Practical Lessons for Building World-Class Pension Organizations*.

CHAPTER 5

Industry Associations and the Politics of Regulatory Reform

Last chapter introduced the five country case studies from the investors' perspective. It highlighted the involvement of domestic and multilateral development financial institutions, followed in some cases by local pension funds. This chapter focuses on how the nascent industry organized and pushed for regulations that allowed fund managers to tap into pension fund resources, helped create tax-efficient investment vehicles, and claimed legitimacy for their investment activities.

In contrast to macro-coalitional arguments common to most of the political economy literature on corporate governance reform, this chapter advances a "quiet politics" explanation. It emphasizes the role of asset-class-specific industry associations and makes a two-step argument, outlined in Fig. 5.1 and developed throughout the chapter. First, it explains how, in most of cases, these industry associations were created through the public–private collaboration between industry participants, multilateral institutions, and public agencies. And then, shows how these associations lobby for the regulations that help the industry institutionalize.

Chapter 4 dealt with the policies that addressed directly the supply of capital into funds and companies. This chapter shows how development financial institutions (DFIs) also tried to advance a workable regulatory

I. Puente, *Private Equity and Financial Development in Latin America*, Latin American Political Economy,
https://doi.org/10.1007/978-3-030-88983-8_5

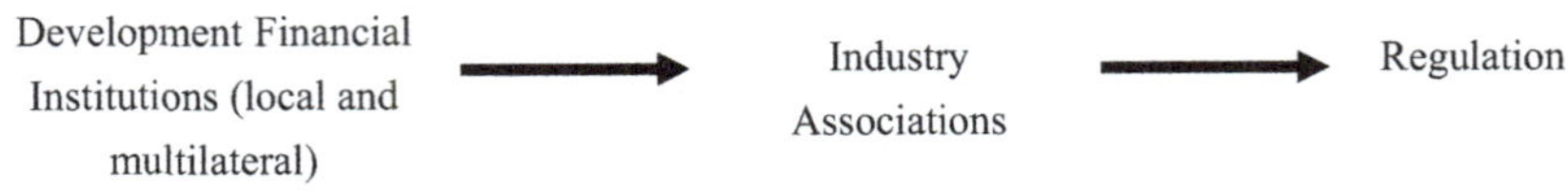

Fig. 5.1 Two-step argument

framework for the industry. Examining the organizational and regulatory side of the emergent private equity industry will make clear that "incubating" policies are not limited to providing capital but also include helping the industry organize and push for specific pieces of regulation. In contrast to arguments that forefront rules rather than actors, at least at the micro-level, the regulatory framework appears endogenous to the players, who try to mold the rules under which they play.

This chapter is organized in the following way. First, it briefly recaps the main theoretical discussions regarding the political economy of corporate governance reform. It contrasts the quiet politics hypothesis with alternative approaches prevalent in the literature. Then, it introduces the role of multilaterals and goes into each of my five country case studies to provide evidence on the two main empirical steps outlined in Fig. 5.1. The last section discusses the main findings and draws some conclusions.

5.1 Quiet Politics Agenda

In order to explain the regulatory process that enabled the institutionalization of a local private capital industry, this chapter takes a quiet politics approach (Culpepper 2010). In low saliency and technically opaque policy areas, such as those related to corporate governance, Culpepper argues that managerial organizations, given their superior knowledge and technical lobbying capacity, often have an advantage. In contrast to more visible policy domains such as taxation or pension system reforms where outcomes are more closely tied to the dynamics of electoral politics, corporate governance issues, while they stay under the public radar, would enjoy some autonomy from the electoral and legislative arenas. While my findings mostly agree with the description of Culpepper's policy domain, the key protagonists are different.

The main regulatory milestones that enable the institutionalization of a private equity industry indeed appear to follow a quiet politics dynamics. The type of reforms are technical and remain outside the scrutiny of the larger public. Lobbying is less centered on money than on expertise, and alignments do not appear to be related to big societal coalitions. Regulatory change usually comes through small, incremental, administrative-level reforms across different governments instead of through a salient public milestones, such as a law sanctioned by Congress backed by a well-defined societal or partisan coalition. Congress is purposefully avoided and is in general an insurmountable obstacle; when regulation goes through Congress, typically it makes it as a part of a larger legislative package pushed by the executive.

Culpepper's quiet politics approach, similar to the larger macro-coalitional literature on corporate governance reform, puts managers, together with labor, large shareholders, and institutional investors, at the core of the analysis. This seems reasonable to explain reform in already developed economies. In particular, the shift to a more active market for corporate control in Europe, where professional managers and powerful external shareholders already existed before the reforms they arguably lead. But it is less useful when trying to explain the emergence of a new industry. Managers' existence as an autonomous group cannot be taken for granted in the case of emerging economies such as those in Latin America, where most firms lack external investors and ownership is mostly concentrated in individuals and their families. There is, therefore, no clear separation between ownership and control, and less space for autonomous management. As discussed in the theory chapter, it is hard to make an argument in which managers are at the same time the main protagonists of reform and the outcome of this reform.

A common trend across my cases, fund managers' business associations emerge with public support. These associations, in turn, represent the industry to broader audiences, some of them outside the public sector, but most importantly, serve as the private sector counterparts to a variety of government agencies (e.g. securities and pension system regulators, tax authorities, development banks) and push for a regulatory framework that allows the industry to operate more smoothly.

Even taking into consideration the sector's small size and the technical nature of its main regulatory interests, the quiet politics arena is not always its natural setting. Keeping their policy working space "quiet" by, for example, circumventing Congress, is often an explicit strategy, actively chosen at a cost. This cost is illustrated, for example, by the case of Mexican CKDs,[1] a publicly-listed private capital vehicle described by many as a "Frankenstein," that nevertheless allowed the industry to fundraise from pension funds without changing the law that regulates the pension fund's investment regime. Similarly, Brazilian FIPs,[2] that even though having a weak legal standing and loosely-defined liabilities, have been incrementally upgraded through administrative-level regulations, while allowing the industry to avoid getting involved in larger and more partisan politics. These business associations, while more seasoned navigating the narrow technical arenas of financial regulation, have a harder time when addressing larger audiences and trying to go through Congress.

The institutional literature on stock market development has, at its core, minority shareholder protections (La Porta et al. 1998). Regarding the legal origins argument, that highlights the origins of each country's legal system as the key long-term determinant of the depth of its capital market, it is important to recall that given their common colonial past, all these countries share the same legal tradition. Currently, minority shareholders' protections are not that different across cases, as shown in Chapter 3. And even if relevant, the most important regulatory instances that helped the industry emerge dealt with issues other than minority shareholder rights. While minority investor's protections provisions are central from the perspective of an atomized and passive investor, they do not seem to be as relevant for private equity. Even when private equity investors go into companies by investing in minority stakes (i.e. without complete control, usually the case in VC and growth equity investments), they still acquire concentrated stakes, many times as part of the controlling groups,[3] and usually have the capacity and the incentives to monitor their portfolio firm's management and other shareholders. Moreover, important contracts between large shareholders are in general made under foreign jurisdiction, and therefore supersede national laws. Regarding property rights and "ease of doing business" more generally, again, they are certainly important drivers of investment, but can hardly explain all of the differences across the cases nor their timing.

[1] *Certificado de Capital de Desarrollo.*

[2] *Fundos de Investimento em Participações.*

[3] In most cases, shareholder agreements between shareholders are enacted under foreign law, therefore enforceable on a foreign jurisdiction with legal systems different from the one in the host country.

Different governments bring different flavors in their approach to the private capital sector, and more leftist and anti-business governments certainly do not promote this model. Still, in most countries policies were stable across administrations. Within my limited sample, variations in government partisanship or big societal interest groups coalitions, the actors behind societal hypotheses, do not have a good explanatory capacity either.

As showed below, the regulations and policies important for the private capital industry are far from the electoral arena and tend to remain outside of Congress. This dynamic is therefore hard to reconcile with the mechanisms behind arguments based on electoral rules and median voters (Pagano and Volpin 2005), nor more generally with arguments about the association between democracy and financial development (e.g. Girma and Shortland 2007; Menaldo and Yoo 2015). I could not find evidence on the direct involvement of labor in this type of arena. Labor is of course an important actor within corporations that can limit corporate decision-making and therefore inhibit the entrance of a particular type of external investors into companies. But the relative ordering of the countries under study is at odds with the hypothesis that could be extrapolated from labor-based arguments (Roe 2003). For example, in Brazil, where labor is comparatively stronger, it is where this model has evolved the furthest, at least with respect to its regional peers, which have weaker organized labor. Beyond class-based explanations, coalitional arguments (Gourevitch and Shinn 2005) are also problematic, since the main participants of these coalitions are either weak or inexistent. Labor is rarely aligned with advancing financial markets, nor capital-owning pensioners become "neoliberal" voters (Kerner 2018). As mentioned, managers, the main actor that could be pushing for reform, are, at least at the beginning, basically inexistent as a group. And institutional investors, particularly pension funds, are in several cases the recipients but not the initiators of many of these policy initiatives. As explained throughout the chapter, the development of the sector is better explained by the actions of fund managers organized into asset-specific industry associations, in most cases, aided by national and international bureaucrats.

5.2 Private Equity Industry Associations

Over the last two decades, a group of industry-specific industry associations that represent the nascent private capital industry emerged across Latin America; Table 5.1 summarizes their main characteristics. The similarity between these business associations across the cases is both empirically surprising and theoretically interesting.

Financial investors are expected to have ample structural power, lack sectoral embeddedness, and enjoy high mobility. They are expected to "exit" more often that exercise their voice (Campello 2015; Fairfield 2015). Therefore, business associations in finance are often overlooked. If business associations in finance are—at first glance—theoretically disregarded compared to other sectors, they are more so in the private capital segment. In order to protect retail investors and reduce information asymmetries, public capital markets and banks are much more extensively regulated than private capital market. As a response, participants in these two segments are expected to develop strong business organizations. As its name indicates, the private capital segment is defined in opposition to public markets, it is outside the reach of retail investors and therefore tends to operate at the margins of regulator's oversight. But even though substantially less regulated than other financial activities, to operate smoothly it still requires a sound regulatory framework. For example, it requires specific types of investment vehicles, friendly liability and tax provisions in line with international standards, and rules granting fund managers access to institutional investor's investment regimes, among others.

Table 5.1 Asset-specific private capital business associations

Country	*Association*	*Year founded*	*IDB program*	*Members (#)*	*Staff (#)*
Brazil	ABVCAP	2000	Yes	150	14
Mexico	AMEXCAP	2003	Yes	110	13
Colombia	COLCAPITAL	2012	Yes	46	6
Argentina	ARCAP	2004/2015	No	27	1
Chile	ACVC	2017	No	14	1
Regional	LAVCA	2002	Yes	150	9

Source Association's webpages, IDB Lab, interviews; approximate information (as of 2018)

Even if the sector is small and participants many times know each other (Pandya and Leblang 2017), collective action is not spontaneous nor obvious to emerge. It is an industry that until recently barely existed, local managers are small and compete for scarce funding sources, and foreign investors, who usually pioneer the industry, have little incentives to participate in local associations. As exemplified throughout this chapter, the emergence of new industry-specific associations of fund managers is often explained as an instance of public–private collaboration. As part of the policies to promote this new financial player, and in order to advance their agendas, government agencies and multilaterals helped business organize.

While insufficient public sector capabilities are a major obstacle for effective productive policymaking, strong industry associations are also usually thought as key necessary partners to successfully implement sector-specific policies (Fernández-Arias et al. 2016). Organized private counterparts can bring both technical expertise and legitimacy. Though promoting business associations is not in general openly recognized as an explicit policy goal, public–private collaboration in productive development policies also consists of more political and organizational tasks that can include solving the industry's collective action problems. This is clear in most case studies, where some of the public agencies introduced in Chapter 4, together with IDB's MIF, had an important role helping organize the nascent fund management industry.

State involvement in the private sector's organization resonates with the literature about business association in Latin America, in particular with Schneider (2004). Offering a much broader historical approach, the focus of this book is on large, encompassing business associations that emerged throughout the last century. Crucially, it shows that state actors are the ones who sought to organize business in periods of economic and political crisis. They do it by providing selective benefits to the participants, sometimes in the form of material resources, but usually as privileged access.

While the type of associations this chapter focuses on is much narrower—specific to the fund managers of a particular yet-to-be-developed asset class—the evidence is remarkably in line with Schneider's key insight about the role of the state behind business associations. Still, the cases contrast with the broader macro-level evidence about business associations' strength in Latin America (Durand and Silva 1998; Schneider 2004). For example, while Brazil is characterized as a case where big business is weak, and Chile as a country with powerful and well-organized business (Fairfield 2015; Salvaj and Couyoumdjian 2016), the opposite seems to be true in the industry-specific business associations that are the main objects of this chapter. Brazil has the most institutionalized private equity association in the region, while in Chile, the representation of the sector is fragmented.

The main goals of these associations are consistent across cases. Access to institutional money from both the state and pension funds is typically their number-one priority. These associations also lobby for more specific pieces of regulation. For example, to introduce investment vehicles appropriate for private equity investing into local legislation, to make those vehicles tax transparent, and to relieve investors from different types of liabilities (e.g. tax, labor, environmental). Last, they promote their industry and help legitimize it among the business community and the broader public.

Regarding their operations, these associations in general have a full-time executive director who coordinates the organization's work and manages the relationship with its members and external stakeholders. As indicated in Table 5.1, in some cases, executive directors are supported by other staff. They are usually involved in research, PR and communications roles, and among other activities, coordinate events, manage partnerships, and generate publications. For more technical work and lobbying activities, associations have different thematic working commissions that involve the direct participation of the members of the association, both the fund managers and the industry's service providers (e.g. law and accounting firms). Operating under an organizational umbrella grants them access and legitimizes their interaction with policymakers and regulators.

These associations provide a combination of public goods for the industry (e.g. regulations, fundraising channels) and private benefits to their more active participants. There are many reasons why it makes sense for individuals to participate, such as networking and socialization. Associations can also allow their participants to have a more fluent access to the agencies that are the gatekeepers of funding sources, as the ones described in Chapter 4. Besides facilitating access to capital, being closer to rule-making can also provide benefits. While local and smaller investors with less funding alternatives have more incentives to participate, the local management teams of international firms are many times also involved in these associations. There is a lot of turnover of executives between firms, and it is frequent that those working for an international firm later join a local firm, or open their own shop. Therefore, staying close to rule-making can also boost their career paths.

The rest of the chapter provides evidence about the two-step argument focused on the origin and role of these business associations, relying mostly on primary research. To do so, next section introduces the role of multilateral development banks. And then, it dives into the five country case studies and explains how the organizational dimension is related to the outcomes described in the previous chapters.

5.3 Multilateral DFIs

Chapter 4 showed how a group of multilateral development financial institutions (MDFIs) contributed to the emergence of private equity across the emerging world, acting as core investors in multiple funds. Some of these multilaterals also played an important institutional-building role. In Latin America, this is particularly the case of IDB's MIF.[4] While its equity investments are small and focused mostly on early-stage funds, it had a key environment-building role across all segments of the industry. Importantly, MIF sponsored the creation of the regional private capital business association, LAVCA,[5] as well as most of its analogous associations at the national level.[6]

MIF's was created during the 1990s at a time when multilateral financial institutions were sponsoring market reforms. In this spirit, MIF aimed to expand access to financial markets. Their pioneering support to private capital ecosystems was framed around broadening access of equity capital to SMEs and promoting entrepreneurship and innovation. As part of their activities to promote the risk capital industry, in several of the countries they got involved, they tried to organize the sector. While MIF's and the

[4] IDB Multilateral Investment Fund (MIF), renamed as IDB Lab. For technical cooperation grants to enable a private capital ecosystem, see IDB's portal.

[5] Latin American Venture Capital Association, now renamed to the Association for Private Capital Investment in Latin America.

[6] As discussed in Chapter 6, other regional-level associations analogous to LAVCA also appear to have its origin close to multilateral organizations. For example, in Europe (Invest Europe) and in Africa (AVCA). Most importantly, World Bank's IFC together with other multilateral financial institutions sponsored EMPEA, who groups the largest and most prestigious fund managers operating throughout the emerging world.

association's narrative is more focused on entrepreneurship and innovation, and therefore more related to venture capital, as explained, policy requirements are similar across the different private capital segments. Private equity, venture capital, real estate and even infrastructure funds, while distinct in their underlying assets, often have similar legal architectures and fundraising channels. Therefore, their managers share some common policy goals.

The first of several environment-building programs were in Brazil. As part of the *Inovar* program in the late 1990's, where IDB partnered with FINEP, these two organizations sponsored the creation of ABVCAP, the Brazilian private capital association (Leamon and Lerner 2012; Viveiros 2017). An officer from MIF, speaking about the rationale behind their support for business associations:

> When entering a country, as one of the first actions to help develop the local ecosystem, we decided to support the creation of a local association. Our idea is to go in, develop and exit. Our support is transitory, and business associations are important to make the market self-sustainable, they can play a key role in that. For example in Brazil, ABVCAP was from the beginning thought of as part of our exit strategy; so they could develop the market by themselves. LAVCA was created with the same mindset.

Even though MIF partnered with the associations by providing funding and advice, they arguably kept a hands-off approach and did not participate in them directly as members. Instead, they prioritized the role of fund managers, above other industry participants such as service providers or investors. In words of the same MIF official:

> We don't tell ABVCAP or any other organization we sponsor what they have to do, never. We are not members of the association. Of course we can give some advice on specific topics, but it's an organization of funds managers. That has to be clear!

Following the Brazilian experience in the early 2000s, IDB's MIF also sponsored the creation of a regional-level industry organization, LAVCA. Based in New York, its role is less lobbying local regulators directly, and more about representing the Latin American PE industry with global institutional investors. In order to do so, for example, they organize several events where they bring together potential investors, fund managers, and service providers. They also help with policy advocacy and collaborate with local associations. They generate guidelines and recommendations on a variety of regulatory issues, organize trainings, and consolidate data on the industry.

While still under the umbrella of IDB's MIF brand, LAVCA has gained considerable autonomy since its founding, when, just to illustrate its closeness with IDB, its flagship annual meeting was part of IDB's annual meeting. LAVCA's most active members are regional funds and have representation of each asset sub-class (e.g. venture capital, growth, real estate, buyout, and infrastructure). The stability of multilateral's staff and programs, less impacted by changes in each country's administration, allows them to function as a more permanent counterpart for the emerging industry. Its more detached status, arguably made its support for industry's collective action also more legitimate.

Support from IDB's MIF was typically in the form of non-reimbursable grants for technical cooperation under a matching scheme. For each dollar the multilateral fund contributed, the association needed to obtain a proportional amount of funding from a third-party. These programs' local counterparts were many times public agencies, suggesting that the support from local governments was a necessary condition for their implementation. This is also clear from the conversation with the MIF official:

> The support of the government to all these programs is key. We can only be successful when they are on board. Their strong support is a necessary condition!

Therefore, while multilateral development financial institutions were key sponsors of local organizations across the region, there is a lot to be learned from the country case studies. Each of them explains the origin of the local private capital business association. And then, they provide evidence about the role they played in pushing for specific pieces of regulation, illustrating the quiet politics dynamics.

5.4 Country Case-Studies

5.4.1 Brazil

Brazil's private equity industry is the oldest and most institutionalized in the region. Beyond the country's economic and political crises and the controversies around the role of state-related pension funds discussed in the previous chapter, most players involved in the industry agree that the regulatory framework under which they operate works fairly well. This section explains how fund managers organized into an association and advocated for this working regulatory framework.[7]

As mentioned in Chapter 4, the late nineties' *Inovar* program was central to the institutionalization of Brazil's private equity industry. Led by FINEP and sponsored by IDB's MIF,[8] the program aimed to develop the risk capital markets in Brazil, in order to facilitate the access of new firms to equity financing. To achieve this goal, "the country needed entrepreneurs who understood how to raise funds and work with equity-owning investment partners, limited partners (LPs) who knew how to evaluate funds and what was involved in such vehicles; and general partners (GPs) who were familiar with selecting and managing companies and funds. In addition, an infrastructure had to be developed that included favorable tax regulations, a national private equity practitioners' organization, information sources on the industry and its performance in Brazil and globally, and a method to establish relationships between Brazilian and international private equity actors" (Leamon and Lerner 2012: 1). Remarkably, one of the first "infrastructure-building" projects of the program was supporting the foundation of a local private equity/ venture capital association, ABVCAP.[9]

Founded in June of 2000 by a group of pioneer fund managers of local and international firms together with other public and private entities, ABVCAP was the first association of its kind in the region. It was created even before the regional association, LAVCA, which was modeled after the Brazilian experience. ABVCAP has served as a model for the rest of the associations in the region and collaborated with policymakers and fund managers across the region that intended to replicate the experience. It has the most numerous staff and resources, offices in both Rio and São Paulo, gathers proprietary data, and organizes the region's largest industry meetings. It has become increasingly self-sustaining, in

[7] Probably as a consequence of its longer existence and its higher level of institutionalization, there are some secondary data sources available that I used to complement my primary research (e.g. Leamon and Lerner 2012; Viveiros 2017).

[8] Sebrae, a public–private partnership focused on supporting SMEs, and Petros, the pension fund of Petrobras, Brazil's national oil company, also joined the program.

[9] Originally called ABCR—*Associação Brasileira do Capital de Risco.*

particular after the more active involvement in the association of large international firms. Most importantly, as shown below, it has established a close working relationship with the key public agencies of its main areas of interest, in particular with the securities regulator, CVM.[10] And it even holds some self-regulatory capacities, as it issues governance best practices guidelines among its members.

Managers from global PE firms who source their capital outside the country are less interested in participating in business associations. This is also the case for investment firms with a broader focus that also offer asset-management services for other asset classes (e.g. hedge funds and mutual funds). Yet, many of them are involved in the association and the cleavages between VC and PE managers, and international and locals firms are patent. The internal equilibrium, reflected, for example, in the composition of the board, has changed over the years, following the economic and political cycle as well as the availability of local funding. Leadership roles have shifted from managers of smaller local funds to managers of larger international firms. Still, the association has been able to bringing on board all type of investors and has bridged the gap that separates the "two worlds" of fund managers (i.e. those who fundraise internally and externally) that as Chapter 4 explained, characterized the PE industry in Brazil during the PT administrations. As a manager of a smaller fund argued:

> Before ABVCAP, private equity and venture capital, as an asset class was only available to the ultra-high net-worth individuals that could take the risks, navigate regulations, now it is a much more institutionalized and democratic industry.

In this line, a former leader of the association, and managing partner of an international PE firm, also highlights ABVCAP's role in institutionalizing the local industry:

> It started mostly with smaller GPs that needed local pension funds since they had no access to international investors. They successfully achieved representation with local investors and the CVM. And they created an industry's regulatory framework that actually worked! All the regulation

[10] *Comissão de Valores Mobiliários*, Brazil's equivalent of US's Securities and Exchange Commission (SEC).

> we have is because of ABVCAP: FIPs, tax incentives, capital gains that favor GPs, and many others.

He also describes the changing profile of ABVCAP's leadership:

> At first it was mostly about local investors, big international firms didn't clearly see the benefit of participating. There were, of course, some exceptions. For example, Advent [the largest international PE firm in the region] was always active and supportive. [...][A former president of the association and manager of a local fund] approached me in 2010, and told me that the large international PE firms needed to speak up and participate more actively. He was right, we were free riding the benefits of the association. For example, there was this big dispute about a 6% IOF [Imposto sobre Operações Financeiras] tax that would have killed the industry: they managed to reverse it very fast and effectively! We started to see the benefits of participating and got more actively involved in the association. And the organization gained sponsors, size, and legitimacy across the whole business community.

ABVCAP fulfills multiple roles, representing the industry with its stakeholders. It functions both reactively and proactively, lobbies government agencies, and leads PR activities. On the reactive side, its role can range from testifying in Congress during an investigation of corruption schemes that involved local pension funds to protect the industry's reputation,[11] to helping spin the interpretation of the tax code in their favor. The section below briefly reviews three examples where the associations proactively pushed for specific pieces of regulation, illustrating its role in helping institutionalize the industry: the creation of FIPs in 2003, their reform in 2016, and its self-regulatory competences.

The first investment vehicle created specifically to facilitate the development of the private capital industry were the FMIEEs.[12] Pushed by BNDES, they were launched in 1994 through CVM's *Instrução 209*. Aimed at smaller VC funds, they were not useful to structure more standard PE operations through them (Baltin and Bell 2001). Therefore, during its early years, the industry operated through offshore vehicles and/or more "expensive" local holding companies. A key milestone for the industry's development was 2003's *Instrução CVM 391* that

[11] *Comissão Parlamentar de Inquérito (CPI) - Fundos de Pensão.*

[12] *Fundos Mútuos de Investimento em Empresas Emergentes.*

created FIPs, *Fundos de Investimento em Participações*. Besides pushing for the creation of this new investment vehicle, several sources agree on ABVCAP's role providing input on the technical details of the regulation was vital (Viveiros 2017:81).

Among many other provisions,[13] FIPs are fiscally transparent[14] investment vehicles that can be used to acquire a set of eligible securities (e.g. common and preferred shares, convertible debt) of companies of which they require to participate with effective influence on its decision-making process. Restricted to "qualified" investment professionals, they were designed to allow the participation of local institutional investors in the asset class, who were otherwise restricted to invest in listed securities. Moreover, they confer some tax benefits to investors. While they encourage the participation of foreign investors by also granting them tax benefits, the portion of assets a FIP can have outside of Brazil is restricted to 20%.

FIPs proved to be efficient and flexible investment vehicles to support the expansion of the Brazilian PE industry that began in the mid-2000s.[15] And it enabled the Brazilian private equity industry to operate mostly through "onshore" vehicles.[16] FIPs are registered and supervised by the CVM and are required to disclose financial information to the public regularly.

In 2016, the regulation concerning the functioning of FIPs was revamped through *Instrução CVM 578/9* that updated the 2003s rules. Among many changes, these two new administrative rulings clarified the distinct roles of fund managers and fund administrators, strengthened the corporate governance requirements for invested companies, classified different type of FIPs, defined valuation methods for financial disclosure, and arguably discouraged the utilization of FIPs as wealth management trusts.

Beyond its specific content, the process through which change was introduced illustrates ABVCAP's role. The update on FIPs regulation

[13] For details of the legal framework see, for example, ABVCAP's and LAVCA's reports on this topic.

[14] Flow-through legal entities considered "non-entities" for tax purposes.

[15] As of mid-2017, FIPs hold assets with a book-value worth more than $200 billion *reais*.

[16] Even if in many cases an international "offshore" fund functions as a feeder to local FIPs.

was, again, mainly mobilized by ABVCAP. This is evident from the public hearings documentation available at CVM website[17] as well as from interviews with people from both the association and the CVM. Recognizing ABVCAP as CVM's private sector counterpart for the purpose of private investment funds, the regulators' structured investments division manager (who oversees FIPs), told me:

> ABVCAP is very important for us. They led the initiative to change the regulation and modernize the management of FIPs. Before the public hearings, we had meetings with both ABVCAP and ANBIMA. There were some issues we disagreed on, but they were minor. ABVCAP raised many points in the public hearings, we accepted most of them. You can see the documents they presented, the end document and compare!

Beyond CVM's regulations, ABVCAP, partnering with ANBIMA, has also achieved some self-regulatory powers over its members. ANBIMA is a larger association that reunites all type of asset managers, mostly of listed securities. Dominated by larger banks, their relationship with ABVCAP swings from competition to cooperation. In this case, they agreed in a set of standards for the industry and incorporated them into a code of best practices with which all FIPs managed by members of the associations must comply with. For example, the FIP's prospectus and the disclosure of financial information have to follow a common standard, and fund managers have to abide with certain corporate governance provisions. The code also provides the associations with a supervisory role and the capacity to sanction wrongdoing, and there is some evidence that they exercise it. While CVM acknowledges the self-regulatory code, it has not delegated its supervisory authority, therefore in practice they both tend to overlap.

Even if the regulatory framework indeed appears to work, there are limits to the type of reforms that can be introduced through administrative-level rulings or self-regulatory codes that do not require going through Congress. In particular, after nearly two decades of growth, the whole Brazilian private equity industry is based on FIPs regulations that have the legal hierarchy of an administrative act. FIPs, in turn, are based on the condominium law. Their structure is hard to interpret by unexperienced judges, and a key question regarding the liabilities

[17] See the registries of the public hearings from ICVM 578/9, where ABVCAP was the main input provider for the change in regulation.

investors face when their ventures go under remains unclear. Even if a law would give a much stronger legal sustenance, industry participants agreed that trying to go through Congress was either pointless or too risky. For example, while talking about the controversy around local pension funds asking for a seat in the fund's investment committees discussed in Chapter 4, a public official from a development agency argued:

> What would be more important is to pass a law! That would have prevented us from going into all these investment committee issues that damaged the industry. It would clarify who is liable for what. Given funds have no legal status of their own, if the company goes bankrupt, the creditors would try to go after the funds investors. This is why pension funds started to ask to participate in fund's investment committees in the first place. As you know, this became a big problem. I think we should have a law. While it has been in discussion forever, and everyone mostly agrees, it is impossible to pass a law.

On the private side, a corporate lawyer, active in the regulatory discussion agreed on the desirability of a law for investment funds:

> In Brazil we need a law on investment funds, we need a law that gives the industry a more secure standing, now we are based on an administrative ruling!! It is not a very powerful instrument when you go to court. [...]

He also highlighted the risks of trying to push for an investment fund law and the reasons why they are more comfortable working directly with the regulator:

> The quality of the guys in Congress is a big problem. We are not able to trust the legislative process. Once it starts as a law for investment funds, you don't know when nor where it will end up going. You start the process with a law regulating investment funds and end up declaring some holiday or a national festivity. Therefore from both ABVCAP and ANBIMA we prefer to deal only with the CVM. CVM can amend their own instructions, even if they are slow, it has a better speed. You have public hearings, and CVM is a good competent authority. Actually, CVM is one of the best public authorities we have here in Brazil. It has very good employees, they are democratic and open. Instead, in Congress we would completely miss it. The level of interests that interfere with this process would be uncontrollable and unpredictable. One single law has the capacity to destroy a market, CVM doesn't. But still, we need a Federal law that states two and

> only two things: what is the legal nature of investment funds and who answers in each scenario. After having those two things clear, CVM should then take care of all further regulations.

The CVM official in charge of the division that oversees FIPs agreed:

> Sure, a law would be more than welcomed. We need funds to have their own legal structure, they can't be based on a condominium. There are lots of things today you can't do with a FIP, questions around liability and governance, many of them key when going into bankruptcy. [...] It should be feasible to pass a law, ANBIMA and ABVCAP try to push for it, but it never moves forward. We would help, for sure. But it is way beyond us, this also involves the tax authority [receita federal], and the ministry of finance [fazenda]. I do not expect to see any progress in the medium term.

As well as showcasing the limits of quiet politics, Brazil's case fits well with this chapter's two main arguments. First, ABVCAP, the region's oldest private capital association, is a good example of how this type of industry-specific business associations were created through public–private collaboration. FINEP together with IDB's MIF was key for the organization's foundation, which still keeps working ties with several public agencies. Second, the case explains how the association pushed for a working regulatory framework that helped institutionalize the industry, even if bounded by the limits of quiet politics. The private capital industry experienced numerous changes since the early 2000s, reflected in the profiles of the association's leadership, still the association helped bridge the industry's different cleavages and functioned as the private sector counterpart for the industry's stakeholders.

5.4.2 *Mexico*

Absent Brazil's statist configuration, the role of government-related financial institutions funding private equity in Mexico make the case more interesting. The Mexican case provides some leverage to the argument about the incubating role of the development financial institutions described in Chapter 4. On the regulatory side, it also illustrates the book's arguments well. As in several of the other cases, we observe an industry association that groups PE investors, supported by both government-related investors and multilateral institutions. In turn, this association plays a "quiet politics" role as the private sector counterpart for key regulations that allowed the private capital industry to take off. For example, in the creation and update of CKDs, the instrument that allowed pension funds to allocate capital to private capital funds.

Officially founded in the early 2000s, sources agree that the Mexican private capital association, AMEXCAP, took off with the support of *Fondo de Fondos* (FdF), Mexico's fund of funds owned by several of the country's state-owned financial institutions. While I could not find any public information about the relationship between FdF and AMEXCAP, since both of them operate as private entities with no disclosure requirements, from the AMEXCAP side, they agree that "*as the only institutional investor in Mexico's industry, it was for sure, one of our most important sponsor.*" Another senior interviewee, knowledgeable about the private equity's organizational landscape across the whole region confirms: "*FdF put a lot of money in AMEXCAP.*"[18] Besides FdF, AMEXCAP also received multilateral support from IDB's MIF and other state entities such as INADEM.[19]

Starting as a gathering mostly for mid-market PE fund managers, the association has grown together with the industry. It was staffed with around a dozen employees and organized around the different asset subclasses (e.g. VC, mezzanine, PE, real estate, and infrastructure). Besides organizing events, gathering information, and creating promotional materials to socialize the private capital model, AMEXCAP most importantly represents the industry and coordinates its lobbying efforts in front of different governmental authorities. As a senior fund manager while complaining about the regulatory framework, expressed:

> Amexcap role is to put forward all the frustrations that we have as fund managers to authorities and regulators and push for solutions. So far, even if progress has been slower than I could hope for, it had a positive impact.

[18] AMEXCAP started taking care of certain promotional events previously organized by FdF directly. Interestingly, FdF and AMEXCAP were, at least as some point, located in the same building, with just one floor of separation between them.

[19] *Instituto Nacional del Emprendedor*, a decentralized agency created in 2013 and dependent on the *Secretaria de Economía*, closed by AMLOs government. Tellingly, one of AMEXCAP's executive director was formerly INADEM's director for VC funding.

The logic behind the introduction of CKDs exemplifies the quiet politics dynamic of financial regulation. As argued in last chapter, the introduction of CKDs granted fund managers access to pension system resources and was repeatedly identified as the industry's key milestone (Leal and Del Sesto 2013). Talking to a senior fund manager, he highlighted the role of the association among the main actors involved in the creation of CKDs:

> It was a shared effort between AMOFORE [pension funds'' association], CONSAR [the pension system regulator] and the finance ministry, with, of course, lobbying from AMEXCAP.

Unable to change the law that legislates on the pension system's investment regime, CKDs were first introduced through administrative-level regulations. When discussing with one of the private-practice lawyers who designed this new vehicle, he explained they were an alternative to bypass Congress. Himself being a former public official, and involved in AMEXCAP's leadership, he explains the reason for taking the "quiet" path:

> At first, from AMEXCAP we tried to modify the law so that Afores, as well as the insurance companies could invest in PE funds directly, through a more standard private placement, as it is done everywhere else. But this won't happen, at least for some time. Because the law that regulates Afores, the pension law, is too sensitive politically. Trade union representatives are part of the executive committee of CONSAR, the regulatory body. These are people that don't understand and don't want to understand structured finance, they will turn down everything that is not very conservative. And Congress is even worse, the chance that a law can be modified is close to zero. Therefore, at the time, I recommended we looked for a public instrument that could serve as a fundraising vehicle, since that didn't require modifying the law. And then is when we started working towards CKDs.

But circumventing Congress is not free. In the case of CKDs, for example, having to channel investments through a public vehicle, at odds with industry norms, is indeed costly and creates a variety of complications when structuring a fund. Besides its listing costs, CKDs have a number of additional troublesome features, some of them adjusted through subsequent regulations. For example, the mechanisms to make capital calls[20] is not straightforward, the governance provisions of a listed vehicle have to be adjusted to the requirements of a closed fund, and the clauses that allow the CKD to co-invest in equal terms in the fund with non-pensioners money have to be carefully designed. As another senior fund manager told me, complaining about the way these investment vehicles are structured:

> CKDs were specifically designed for Afores. They are the channel through which they can go into funds as LPs. They are some sort of Frankenstein, an odd private capital vehicle that is listed in the stock exchange. A public vehicle to invest in private capital. The reason Afores cannot invest directly in a private fund is because they cannot invest in illiquid securities. If private capital investments are not liquid, they have to be structured as a security that looks liquid. But this is complete nonsense, because they don't have any liquidity. The fact that there is a daily price for a CKD doesn't mean there is liquidity. At best, companies disclose information quarterly, so they then having a super complicated process to reach a price that makes no sense.

With an active participation of AMEXCAP, regulators successively fine-tuned CKDs to address part of these problems. In 2014, their legal status was upgraded, as they were included as a small part of a much broader financial reform law. However, for the moment, pension system regulation has remained unchanged. Beyond CKDs, AMEXCAP also functioned as the private sector counterpart of regulators and advocated for the introduction of further investment vehicles such as CERPIs, that helped attract larger international funds into the country, and FIBRAs, related to infrastructure investing.

Under many important dimensions, Mexico and Brazil, Latin America's two largest countries, are significantly different. Mexico had a much more pronounced shift toward a market-based economy that included privatizing its pension system. But regarding the development of their private equity industry, they exhibit some similarities. As the last chapter shows, in both cases, their development banks functioned as pioneer institutional investors in the asset class, followed by their pension funds. With

[20] The process through which investors who have committed money to a fund transfer the money to the fund managers, in general before the closing of a transaction.

respect to the institutionalization of their private capital industry, Brazil and Mexico also share some key features. The business associations that represented fund managers received extensive support from domestic and multilateral entities, both in terms of resources as well as access to policymaking. And, ABVCAP and AMEXCAP, respectively, played an important role pushing for the reforms that allowed the growth and institutionalization of the industry in their respective countries. Importantly, as Chile's case shows, these two steps are not just part of the natural development of the industry. With no direct public support for its organization, the industry remained fragmented and regulations, in particular those governing access to pension funds resources, elusive.

5.4.3 Chile

Chile's development agency, CORFO, started investing in private "risk" capital funds in the late 1990s and has continued to do so in a consistent way. Still, as discussed in Chapter 4, the sector is still dependent on public funding and it is hard for local funds to fundraise with other institutional investors such as pension funds.

While Chile is by far the most stable and institutionalized country in the region with a massive privately-managed pension system, there are multiple factors that may help explain why the local private capital environment remains comparatively weak, especially given its level of development. Beyond the smaller size of its economy, CORFO's investments are targeted mostly toward smaller funds. It is not organized as an agency independent from bureaucracy, and the budget for its investments has to be approved by Congress on a yearly basis. Pension funds, the largest of their kind in the region, are discouraged to invest in domestic private equity funds. After some failed experiences during the late nineties/early 2000s investing in domestic PE, they have not been involved with local private capital investors. Still, analyzing the organizational side of the sector can help better explain some of these issues and introduce an interesting contrast with the others cases in this chapter.

In spite of CORFO's longstanding support of the sector, the industry is weakly organized. Until late 2017, some private capital funds were part of a larger association, ACAFI,[21] who represents all types of investment

[21] *Asociación Chilena de Administradores de Fondos de Inversión.*

funds. ACAFI is dominated by larger asset managers, mostly mutual funds that invest in public securities both in Chile and externally. Similar to Brazil's ANBIMA, ACAFI is dominated by larger financial institutions, whose priorities are not always in line with those of local private capital managers.[22] Noteworthy, ACAFI is mostly unrelated to the network formed between the PE/VC associations in the other countries such as ABVCAP in Brazil, AMEXCAP in Mexico, ColCapital in Colombia, and more recently ARCAP in Argentina.

Talking about the Chilean case with an executive from LAVCA, the regional association, he mentioned:

> I do talk with the people from ACAFI, but the focus they have is very different from ours. They have a much more generalist approach, and they are only concerned about the assets under management of their fund managers. Their measure of success is the assets under management, I completely disagree with that. Because it is not necessarily the case that if the Chilean asset manager has $100M to manage that is good for the local private capital industry. Because their managers have their pockets full of money, but all this capital is invested outside of Chile. [...] I am not sure about what happened in Chile, but a group of eight or nine venture capital managers decided to form their own association, my reading is because these managers were not identified with ACAFI.

Effectively, led by a group of venture capital fund managers, ACVC,[23] a new VC association was founded in 2017. Until then, Chile was the only country with no business association with the specific mandate of promoting the PE/VC segment of the fund management industry. The president of the newly-funded VC association explains the reason they decided to launch a new entity:

> 95% or more of ACAFI's members are large mutual funds, debt funds, all of the feeder funds.[24] There is no place for VCs, we were the poor brothers. We used to participate, and we have a pretty good relationship with them, but we decided to spin-off to have just one voice focused on

[22] For example, they were much more focused on *Ley Unica de Fondos* that on the reform that made alternatives assets eligible investments for pension funds.

[23] *Asociación Chilena de Venture Capital.*

[24] Investment vehicles through which the pension funds access large international private equity firms.

> this specific asset class. This is why we founded this new association, to give relevance to this asset class. To engage with more LPs, with CORFO, with potential institutional investors, with other business associations and to go out and connect our industry to the world.

Following the other countries' trajectory, ACVC has engaged IDB more systematically. But as opposed to other experiences, as far as I understand, none of the two business associations in Chile appear to have direct support from government agencies. Relatedly, ACVC is comparatively weaker, with a less fluid access to regulators or pension funds.

Their limited access to regulators was manifested during the change in the pension fund's investment regime regulation, in 2017, that followed a 2016 approval of *Ley de Productividad*. This miscellaneous law, which legislated over completely unrelated topics, among others, amended the 1980s law that regulates the pension funds' investment regime (*Decreto Ley N° 3.500*) to include alternative assets among the eligible securities. This reform, again, illustrates well the quiet politics nature of this policy area. The requirement of going through Congress often blocks reforms. In the cases when the reform finds a window of opportunity to go through Congress, the new legislation mostly ratifies what has been previously agreed among technical regulators and the private sector. Moreover, most of the technical fine-tuning of the regulatory change is made after the law is passed by the same agencies who pushed for the modification of the law. Talking with one of the leaders of the initiative from the pension funds side, he agrees Chilean's pension funds lag behind in terms of investing in alternative assets:

> We are laggards. Of course, you have the Canadian pension funds. But also the Mexican and the Colombian examples. Even Brazil, who has a different model than us, but still, they are more advanced that we are. We are way behind.

In order to explain the situation, he mentions how hard it is to go through Congress. The way the 2016's law was handled also illustrates the quiet dynamics of this type of legislation:

> You know, AFP were created in the early 80s by the DL 3,500. This alone explains the whole development of our capital markets. But AFP's investment regime is regulated by DL 3,500, and any change to it has to be necessarily by law. And you know, when you need to go to Congress

> "es todo una joda" [it's a big deal]. It was only modified in 2002, with the inclusion of multi-funds that allowed AFP's to diversify their portfolios a little bit more. Between 2002 and 2016 there were no changes to the investment regime at all. It is a long time! This was until 2016, with the introduction of the Productivity Law. The name doesn't make any sense. [...]This was a joint work with the SP [pension regulator]. The strategy was, "we need to have this ready just in case there is a window that opens and we can pass this law." And that was how it was passed. As a completely miscellaneous law. If we had introduced a law just to change the pension's investment regime, there was no chance of getting it through Congress, not even one!

Following the change in law, the pension regulator had a year to fine-tune regulations and implement it. ACVC had a hard time approaching the pension regulators and was not involved in defining new regulations regarding eligible investment instruments. In the end, even if the flexibility of pension funds to invest in alternative assets was enlarged, local private capital funds were excluded from the authorized instruments. As one of ACVC's leaders told me, regarding the law's implementation phase:

> We did present a memorandum to the Superintendencia de Pensiones [the pension fund regulator who implemented the law], sharing our point of view. But we were not considered, we were left out of the new regime. AFPs can now invest directly into a company, directly into foreign funds, but they still cannot invest in FIPs [private local funds].

Given its larger membership base mostly composed by managers who invest through public funds, ACAFI appears to be less focused on this narrow private local funds issues. Still, both associations are aligned in their policy agenda. Tapping into the pension fund's resources is still their top priority, and creating a fund of funds involving CORFO is the way to achieve it. This is expressed in ACVC's memo[25] presented to the Capital Markets Commission that explicitly cites the Mexican *Fondo de Fondos* and CKDs as a model. While both associations, ACAFI and ACVC, have

[25] While getting access to pension funds money is the central point of the proposal, they raise other issues. Among others, they request: an increase in the size limits of the companies funds can invest using CORFO's funding, an easier path to write-off of failed investments done with public money, tax benefits, and institutional support from other government-related agencies.

been pushing for the fund of funds proposal for some time, and CORFO is on board with the idea, they have not yet been able to make it happen. As CORFO's official in charge of risk capital investments, who had an extensive prior trajectory is the asset management industry, diagnosed:

> The experience from the US and from everywhere is clear, the [PE/VC] industry will only develop if the pension funds are in. This is our main goal! To lead that process. Clearly, there is a market failure, someone needs to structure the market, it won't happen if pension funds are left by themselves!

This diagnostic coincides with one of the main insights from Chapter 4 regarding the key role of pension funds for the development of the industry and the need to encourage them through public support. And regarding the politics behind these changes, he also points to Congress' as the main bottleneck:

> There is consensus in the fund industry that we need to have the fund of funds, we know it is the right path, it's clear from the international experience. But as CORFO would have to participate as an equity investor, not just in the debt trench, we need to go through Congress. We have a law project, it entered Congress in January 2018, but it has lost parliamentary status. It is not that the government don't want to do it, but they need to complement it with other initiatives so it can go through Congress, so we are still waiting.

In the meantime while the pension funds are making the headlines every day and their public scrutiny is high, their priority seems to be avoiding further headline risks. As explained by an executive of the AFP's industry association:

> All this external noises around the "No + AFP"[26] movement go against investing in alternative assets [...] First, you have the regulatory part, that doesn't give fund managers any incentives to deviate from what the other funds are doing. That profitability is measured on a monthly basis, and every month everyone has to know if you are up or down, that doesn't help either for illiquid investments. Even after the commissions question

[26] A social movement whose main goal is to nationalize the pension system.

> is resolved,[27] we'll keep doing international PE, and then we'll see. For AFPs in Chile, today it is much easier to invest outside the country. Given the level of rejection that AFPs have, and how closely we are scrutinized, investing down the capital structure (i.e. equity) and here in Chile is simply too risky.

While this quote is in line with the quiet dynamic of financial regulation common to all cases, overall, the Chilean case provides some insightful contrast with the rest of the cases. With a hands-off government, the private capital industry representation is weak and fragmented. In turn, they had a more limited capacity to access regulators and lobby effectively for access to pension fund's capital. Exhibiting by far the largest privately-managed pension system in the region, it is still hard for their local private investors to fundraise from them.

5.4.4 Colombia

Colombia exhibits a similar dynamic than the Brazil and Mexican cases described above and illustrates well this chapter's two main arguments. First, a local development bank had a key role helping the incipient community of fund managers get together, providing another example in where the industry association is created as an instance of public–private collaboration. Second, following its creation, the association lobbies for specific pieces of regulation that contribute to further institutionalize the industry.

As mentioned in Chapter 4, Bancoldex, one of Colombia's development banks, had a dedicated private capital unit. Officially launched in 2009, Bancoldex Capital, Bancoldex's private capital program, had two roles: one of them financial, and the other one non-financial. On the financial side, as Chapter 4 reviewed briefly, Bancoldex made several capital commitments to a handful of funds (it had $100M allocated to the program), but had a hard time formalizing a fund of funds. But beyond this financing role, Bancoldex was particularly active in promoting the nascent industry. In collaboration with IDB's MIF, they sponsored industry events, invited external speakers, organized trainings, and other

[27] The discussion over who pays (pensioners or AFPs) the commissions charged by third-party fund managers such a PE fund. This was a salient issue during the discussions around the pension system reform.

promotional activities targeted mainly toward potential investors. In order to further institutionalize the industry, in 2012 they helped found a local private capital association. Born as a spin-off of Bancoldex private capital department, Colombia Capital (ColCapital) started taking care of all the promotional activities and representing the fund industry before government and the business community more generally.

When asked about the origin of the association, ColCapital's managing director—whose previous job was, tellingly, in Bancoldex Capital—told me:

> In 2012, with resources from Bancoldex, ColCapital was launched. We told the fund managers: "Gentlemen, get together and decide what you want to do," and that's how we created this entity. It was then when they called me. We were born as a private association, at first we also had multilateral funding, but today it is mostly self-funded from member fees and events. This is how we were born as an institution.

Beyond its promotional activities, ColCapital's main role is to push for new resources into the industry, enlarging the base of investors. In order to do so, it brokers the industry's relationship with pension funds and regulators to increase the amounts they can allocate to alternative assets and pushes for Bancoldex's fund of funds. In this vein, when asked about the main purpose of the local association, the managing partner of a large international fund and a former president of the association, explained:

> The main thing we do is to make sure that the AFPs and every state pocket that is around is allowed to invest in private equity. Then you have a regulatory component: that the regulatory authorities don't go crazy with reporting requirements. And third, education, we promote industry best practices, so we can avoid problems such as the one of Abraaj[28] is having right now that taints the whole industry.

For example, regarding regulation, ColCapital has arguably functioned as the private sector counterpart behind the reform that helped update the type of investment vehicles and their management. In particular, through

[28] A large Dubai-based emerging markets PE firm that collapsed after getting involved in an accounting and governance scandal.

an executive-level decree,[29] it regulates a specific vehicle tailor-made for private capital funds and clarifies their management role.

While briefer in the analysis, the Colombian case confirms the chapter's main arguments: as part of its environment-building agenda, the collaboration from a local development bank was key to form an asset-class-specific association. ColCapital is basically a spin-off from Bacoldex's—a state-owned policy banks—private capital unit. And once organized, the association's priorities and main activities are in line the other cases.

5.4.5 Argentina

The organization of Argentina's private capital industry tracks the history of the sector and provides further evidence supporting two of the chapter's main arguments. First, the contrast between the association's failed experience during the early 2000s, and the post-2015 re-birth showcases the importance of government support for the organization of the sector; multilateral support is not enough. And second, regarding the priorities of the associations, it is clear from both these experiences how central it is for their mission—and more broadly for the fate of the industry—to get access to local institutional funding.

In contrast to what we observe in Brazil, where the sector began organizing in the late nineties, in Argentina, during its early—and booming—stage, the private equity industry was mostly internationally oriented, unorganized, and thinly regulated. In words of a corporate lawyer active at the time, talking about the novelty of the model and the absence of a regulatory framework:

> KKR's LBO[30] model that Navarro[31] brought into Argentina didn't have any precedent. There was no experience in the country for this type of operations. Just as an example, it was not even clear something as basic as whether you could deduct from taxes the interest paid to serve the debt used to fund an acquisition. There were no rules, Navarro was trying

[29] *Decreto 1984—Ministerio de Hacienda y Crédito Público* (October 30, 2018).

[30] KKR refers to the US-based PE firm most famous for pioneering the leveraged buyout (LBO) model.

[31] The head of the Exxel Group, the largest PE fund in Argentina during the 1990s.

to make the rules by himself. And when AFIP[32] said interest payments weren't deductible from taxes, the liability was huge.

While recovering from the 2001 crisis that ended with the convertibility system and struck a big hit to most of the funds operating in the country, we observe in Argentina some of the incipient steps also observed in the other cases. With the idea to replicate ABVCAP's—Brazil's pioneer association—model, a group of fund managers founded ARCAP.[33] Their key goal, as in all the other cases, was to tap pension funds money, at that time privately managed. As stated by one of the founding members of the association:

> Everyone agreed the goal was that AFJPs [Argentinean pension funds] could invest in private equity, and that was the reason the association was founded: to convince the Superintendencia de Pensiones [pension's regulator] that this was the right thing to do.

Some fund managers contributed with resources, and they counted with the initial institutional support from IDB's MIF. But without support from the local government, they had trouble advancing in a more formal program with MIF, as the ones in Brazil, Mexico, and Colombia. It was hard for them even to register as a formal civil-society organization. This anecdote shared by an ARCAP's founding member showcases the association limited access to policymakers:

> The idea was always to engage with the public sector. It is better that our activity is regulated in the correct way, than in no way or incorrectly. We constantly tried to meet officials, but we were not successful. It took us more than three years to get access to the finance minister. After Cristina took office,[34] we could finally meet Lousteau, who at the moment was the finance minister, at IDB's 2008 annual conference in Miami. He didn't know much about the sector. We had to explain to him that we were not

[32] Argentina's tax agency.

[33] *Asociación Argentina de Capital Privado.*

[34] Cristina Fernandez de Kirchner, who took office on December 2007 and was President until 2015.

> vulture funds[35]; that we made long-term genuine investments and brought in external capital into the real economy. We presented our proposal. They told us they had some new ideas regarding the pension system. We thought they were aligned. A couple of weeks later, they nationalized the pension funds.

ARCAP's demise, following the nationalization of the privately-managed pension funds confirms how central pension funds are for their organizational mission. After the nationalization in late 2008, it made less sense to continue with the association, and it slowly faded away:

> Following the nationalization, even scheduling internal meetings was much more difficult. There was no interest. Besides, who were you going to talk to in government? In 2011, we finally made the formal decision to keep the association dormant. You have fiduciary rights with your LPs, you can't tell them to put their money in a place where you wouldn't put your own money.

The association was re-launched at the end of Kirchner's administration in late 2015, discounting that whatever the outcome of the presidential election, the new administration would be friendlier to business than its predecessors. There was some change in the profile of the association's members, with more active membership from managers closer to the new entrepreneurial ecosystem rather than to traditional PE. As another member of the association explained:

> If you need to talk with a government official or a legislator, the message that is always more welcomed is "we are going to create jobs." And from all the type of funds, it is easier to argue that point with venture capital and entrepreneurship. But in the end, the investment mechanism is the same for all funds, you just scale the model.

Following Macri's victory, the association followed a similar dynamic to the one we also observed in the other country case studies. It was supported by some of their peer associations and established a fluid working relationship with LAVCA, the regional organization. It also

[35] Investors specialized in distressed assets that had an important—and highly contentious—role during Argentina's sovereign debt restructuring that followed the 2001/2 default.

developed close ties with the incoming government, in particular with *Secretaría de Emprendedores y PYMES,* an undersecretary part of the Ministry of Production.

Still, the association is small—it only has one full-time employee—and, given the underdevelopment of the local industry in the country, has little resources. At least until the end of 2019 when the national administration changed again, for most of their activities they relied on the support from this government agency, the undersecretary for SMEs and entrepreneurship. As one officer from this undersecretary described when asked about how they supported the association:

> We support them with money and with people. For example, we organize together the Foro Argentino de Inversiones [the association's flagship events]. Our relationship is strong and very good. They are key for what we aim to do.

ARCAP helped the government agency write the new *Ley de Emprendedores* and cooperated closely with the government in order to implement the new "fund of funds" the government was trying to launch. As this same government official explains:

> After the Ley de Emprendedores and FONDCE's first phase, we are now working to farther improve the regulatory framework, always with both ARCAP and LAVCA. The input from the private sector is key for us.

As elsewhere, in addition to government-funded programs, the association also pushed for more institutional money into the ecosystem. As mentioned in Chapter 4, insurance companies were allowed to invest a small part of their reserves through private capital funds.[36] This change, which did not require an act of Congress but just a modification in an administrative regulation was also promoted by ARCAP through the *Subsecretaria PYME* who brokered the relationship with the *Superintendencia de Seguros* (the insurance regulatory agency):

> ARCAP gave us their input, they told us: "if you want to change the market all these guys [referring to insurance companies] have to be in,"

[36] Even in the unlikely case they reach the upper threshold allowed by regulation, given the small size of the insurance industry in Argentina, this wouldn't represent much more than $100M.

> they presented the need and gave us input. We thought it was going to be really hard, but we could change the Superintendencia's regulation. Now we have to evangelize the insurance industry, it's a hard task, it will take time.

But regarding the possibility of getting access to Argentina's state-managed pension fund resources (FGS), all actors agreed that this is not an option. For example, a member of the association active during its two phases reflected:

> Is it possible? Today, politically, it is not. It is not that we don't want to do it. But you would have to go through Congress, and we have no chance. Still, it is really hard to think about the development of a local private capital industry without local institutional investors.

From the government side, they mostly agreed:

> Today, forget about ANSES [social security]. Maybe in a couple more years. They don't even have the money. Still you would have to go through Congress. That's a no go, you would have to face all this discourse about pensioners' money, and you would have to go there and propose investment funds that go through the Cayman Islands? For the moment, we are not even trying.

In sum, analyzing Argentina's case from the organizational and regulatory side supports at least two points. First, the sharp contrast between the association's lack of access to policymakers during the Kirchner's administration and the relationship it developed with the new government after 2015 confirms the importance for these associations of partnering with an agency aligned with its policy goals. Second, the Argentinean case also makes clear that tapping institutional fundraising sources is the key goal behind the industry's organization. The main objective behind the first attempt to form an association in the mid-2000s was accessing pension funds resources; their nationalization made the organization pointless. During Macri's administration (2015–2019), although the results were meager, most efforts were devoted on developing fundraising sources. But as argued more extensively in Chapter 4, beyond its macroeconomic instability and anti-business administrations, Argentina's lack of institutional pools of capital—or its inaccessibility—also limits the development of the industry structurally.

5.5 Discussion

The private capital industry is by definition one of the most deregulated segments of the capital markets. Still, in order to develop, the industry requires a working regulatory framework. For example, some of the issues central for the development of the asset class are the creation of tax-neutral investment vehicles and of regular channels to access institutional funding. While these issues are quite technical and rarely salient for the larger public, someone has to push for them.

This chapter stressed the role of asset-specific business associations working together with public agencies to advance the industry's regulatory framework. It made a two-step argument. First, multilateral development banks, together with some public agencies, support the creation of a local private capital association. Second, these associations push for to specific regulatory outcomes that help formalize the private capital industry.

The origin of these business associations is in itself noteworthy and exemplifies how a public–private approach to development policymaking can include solving the collective action problems of the private sector. Fund manager's organizations grew by developing close ties with different public agencies, some of which were also acting as investors in the nascent industry. Their support consisted not only on facilitating access to policymakers, but included direct funding. This dynamic is common to all the countries under study, with the exception of Chile where the new association appears to have a more arms-length relationship with CORFO. In Brazil, FINEP working in tandem with IDB's MIF supported the creation of ABVCAP, the Mexican association was, apparently, linked to *Fondo de Fondos*; in Colombia, the local association was created basically as a spin-off of Bancoldex; and more recently in Argentina, the association was re-founded and developed close working ties with the government's (2015–2019) undersecretary in charge of promoting SMEs and entrepreneurship. Moreover, these associations are integrated into a regional network that has at its center a regional-level association, LAVCA, also founded with strong multilateral support.

These business associations are at the same time a consequence and an actor pushing for the broader institutionalization of the sector. Within the narrow policy domains, they function as the voice of the industry that pushes for reform. From the public agencies' perspective, having a private sector counterpart provides them with technical input and information and legitimizes their agendas as well as their interactions with the private sector. Associations generate both some public (club?) goods for the industry and probably also some private benefits (e.g. status and connections) for their more active members. Obtaining institutionalized channels of access to capital from both government-related sources and pension funds seems to be their top priority. They also unify the private sector's voice regarding the industry's regulatory architecture, and through their working relationships with regulators, participate in updating the rules that shape the functioning of the industry.

The claim is not that these associations are distinctly capable or always successful implementing their preferred policies, but more simply, that they contributed to building the rules under which the sector operates. Even if a counterfactual to the role of associations is hard to grasp, given the evidence provided above it is plausible to expect it would include a somewhat less institutionalized private capital industry. The case studies show the association's role in providing the inputs for reforms and lobbying for their implementation. Moreover, these associations are formed prior to major regulatory milestones as part of a plan to strengthen the sector. The timing of events in each case supports the argument about associations participating in reforms. Cross-country comparisons also support this point. Without direct government support, Chile's associations are comparatively weaker. And at least partly related to this, Chile arguably has a less developed domestic private capital industry, particularly with respect to the overall large size of its financial markets. Finally, within-country variation in the Argentinean case, where I contrast two administrations, also shows the importance of developing close ties with government agencies for the industry's organization.

Cases outside Latin America provide further external validity to my arguments about the origin and role of asset-specific business associations, as discussed more thoroughly in the next chapter. The European case, for example, is telling. Regarding its origin, Europe's private equity association, formerly known as EVCA[37] and recently rebranded as Invest Europe, was founded in 1983 as an initiative of the European Commission (Ooghe et al. 1989). Based in Brussels, Invest Europe groups all sub-classes of private capital fund managers and has pushed for access to

[37] European Venture Capital Association.

state and institutional fundraising sources, lobbied for harmonized regulations across the EU, and introduced corporate governance guidelines for its members. While it now appears to mostly self-finance and therefore it is somewhat more detached from the EU, it continues to have a key role as the private sector voice of the industry.

Returning to the larger theoretical discussion regarding corporate governance reform, investment funds' regulation appears to serve as an example of a topic better understood through the quiet politics lens. Most regulatory initiatives are not involved in larger partisan politics, but restricted to bureaucratic domains. The evidence described throughout this chapter as well as the overall configuration of cases does not seem to follow some of the main hypothesis about corporate governance reform. Explanations based on property rights that focus on minority shareholders' protections are probably not wrong, but have limited capacity explaining the variation, at least among the cases analyzed here. And regarding societal arguments, both in its macro and micro-politics versions, the configuration of actors is different in emerging economies from the ones that would lead corporate governance reform according to this literature. As showed above, managers are an actor that have to be "created," rather than the ones initiating reforms. Institutional investors, in particular pension funds, are still new to more active forms of investing and creating the market that can put part of their funds to work is actually a key policy goal. Labor is mostly absent from the micro-level discussion, and its strength does not appear to be directly related to the variations observed across the cases.

In line with a quiet politics approach, associations try to establish fluid working ties with regulators, particularly from the executive branch and decentralized agencies. Congress and "big politics" seem to be outside their repertoire, and when possible, purposefully avoided. These findings, therefore, raise doubts on the mechanisms through which democracy is a force that promotes the deepening of financial markets. Of course, they can also raise normative concerns. That relevant issues are resolved outside of public scrutiny could be problematic from a democratic accountability stand-point. But it also signals the practical limits of quiet politics both as a strategy and as an explanation. To advance broader more structural change requires to go beyond regulators and appeal to larger audiences, pushing the limits of what can be achieved through quiet politics.

References

Baltin, Matthias, and Philipp Bell. 2001. Venture Capital in South America: Unlocking the Potential for Venture Creation in an Emerging Market. WHU.

Campello, Daniela. 2015. *The Politics of Market Discipline in Latin America: Globalization and Democracy*. Cambridge: Cambridge University Press.

Culpepper, Pepper D. 2010. *Quiet Politics and Business Power: Corporate Control in Europe and Japan*. Cambridge: Cambridge University Press.

Durand, Francisco, and Eduardo Silva. 1998. *Organized Business, Economic Change, and Democracy in Latin America*. Coral Gables: North-South Center Press.

Fairfield, Tasha. 2015. *Private Wealth and Public Revenue in Latin America: Business Power and Tax Politics*. New York: Cambridge University Press.

Fernández-Arias, Eduardo, Charles F. Sabel, Ernesto Stein, and Alberto Trejos. 2016. *Two to Tango: Public-Private Collaboration for Productive Development Policies*. Washington, DC: Inter-American Development Bank.

Girma, S., and A. Shortland. 2007. The Political Economy of Financial Development. *Oxford Economic Papers* 60 (4): 567–596.

Gourevitch, Peter, and James Shinn. 2005. *Political Power and Corporate Control: The New Global Politics of Corporate Governance*. Princeton: Princeton University Press.

Kerner, Andrew. 2018. Pension Returns and Popular Support for Neoliberalism in Post-Pension Reform Latin America. *British Journal of Political Science* 50(2): 1–36.

La Porta, Rafael, Florencio Lopez-de-Silanes, Andrei Shleifer, and Robert W. Vishny. 1998. Law and Finance. *Journal of Political Economy* 106 (6): 1113–1155.

Leal, Antonio Martinez, and Pino Del Sesto. 2013. *Private Equity in Mexico: Primed for Significant Growth*.

Leamon, Ann, and Josh Lerner. 2012. *Creating a Venture Ecosystem in Brazil: FINEP's INOVAR Project*.

Menaldo, Victor, and Daniel Yoo. 2015. Democracy, Elite Bias, and Financial Development in Latin America. *World Politics* 67 (04): 726–759.

Ooghe, Herbert, Ann Bekaert, and Peter van den Bossche. 1989. Venture Capital in the U.S.A., Europe and Japan. *Management International Review* 29: 29–45.

Pagano, Marco, and Paolo F. Volpin. 2005. The Political Economy of Corporate Governance. *The American Economic Review* 95: 1005–1030.

Pandya, Sonal, and David Leblang. 2017. Risky Business: Institutions vs. Social Networks in FDI. *Economics & Politics* 29 (2): 91–117.

Roe, Mark J. 2003. *Political Determinants of Corporate Governance: Political Context, Corporate Impact*. Oxford: Oxford University Press.

Salvaj, Erica, and Juan Pablo Couyoumdjian. 2016. 'Interlocked' Business Groups and the State in Chile (1970–2010). *Business History* 58 (1): 129–148.

Schneider, Ben Ross. 2004. *Business Politics and the State in Twentieth-Century Latin America*. Cambridge University Press.

Viveiros, Ricardo. 2017. *ABVCAP: A Força Da Indústria de Participações No Desenvolvimento Do Brasil*. Sao Paolo: AzulSol Editora.

CHAPTER 6

Beyond Latin America

The core of the evidence for the book's arguments comes from Latin America. This region proved to be a good testing ground, given its common colonial origins, similar democratization and liberalization trends and comparable levels of development. The five cases analyzed exhibit common patterns that support the book's main arguments. Government-related money was channeled into private equity in each of the cases. And PE's interest groups that gave political voice to the industry were organized with significant public support, except maybe in Chile. Institutional variables, on their own, cannot fully explain the variation observed across cases. Instead, the extent and timing of public support does a better job, even after acknowledging for the many flaws government investment programs have. Within-case, across-time evidence provided key support to the argument about the central role pension funds have for the industry, most clearly in the Mexican case. As well as about the importance of public support for business associations, evident, for example, in the Argentine case.

Given its comparatively weaker bureaucratic capacities, Latin America can be thought of as a "least likely" region to make a policy-based argument. The region is marginal for the global private equity industry, maybe with the exception of Brazil, and its—private and public—capital markets are still at relatively early stages of development. Therefore, it could be

I. Puente, *Private Equity and Financial Development in Latin America*, Latin American Political Economy,
https://doi.org/10.1007/978-3-030-88983-8_6

argued that when Latin America is compared with other regions, the somewhat more active role of government has hindered private equity investment and undermined overall financial development. Or that some region-specific characteristic (e.g. its colonial origins) made state intervention necessary. In order to rule out these alternative explanations and broaden the scope of the argument, this chapter explores the US, European, and Asian cases, where the PE model is more widely adopted. Through case-specific primary and secondary sources, I asses the relevance of government-related investors for the emergence of this new player.

What appears to distinguish Latin America from other regions is not that they exhibit public support, but its extent. Rather than less government intervention, cases analyzed outside this region show a more systematic public-sector presence. Latin American less capable financial bureaucracies, and especially the lack of well-institutionalized channels that connect pension funds and domestic equity markets are arguably as relevant factors to explain the region's overall—financial—underdevelopment than its macro-level political and economic institutional environment.

This brief chapter provides evidence on the relationship between government-related institutional investors, private equity, and capital market development beyond Latin America. It adds external validity to the book's arguments by showing that in various cases outside this region, equity markets also appear to be nurtured by the state. The first section shows government-related investors had an active role during the emergence of private capital markets across a variety of contexts. The second section provides further evidence on the origin and role of private capital industry associations, and the quiet politics dynamics behind the industry's regulation.

6.1 The State as an Investor

Outside Latin America, the role of government-related financial institutions "incubating" private equity markets is quite stark. This section begins by briefly reviewing some historical highlights of the US case, where the private equity model originated and where it is more widely adopted. Then it continues with Europe, and finally addresses some key cases in Asia.

6.1.1 *United States*

The US is the archetypical liberal market economy with the worlds' most complete capital markets. There is no federal-level development bank, and the state has a hands-off approach to finance, except for a few specific markets (e.g. housing). Still, most analyses of the development of US's private capital markets identify two key elements for the growth of private equity that involve the public sector: first, the pioneering role of Small Business Investment Companies (SBICs), and, second, 1979s game-changing clarifications to ERISA's "Prudent Man Rule."

It is widely acknowledged that the creation of the SBICs as vehicles for small business financing was an important "catalyzing" step in the development of private capital in the US (Lerner 2009). SBICs were created by 1958s Small Business Investment Act. They were independently-owned investment companies funded through privately-raised capital together with government funds and dedicated to investing in small firms. Public funding, through loans, could provide up to three times the amount of capital raised from private sources (i.e. it provided cheap—subsidized—leverage to the private investors). SBICs also received a variety of tax incentives. By mid-1960, 700 SBICs controlled the majority of the venture—risk—capital invested in the US (Gompers 1994). While the program grew fast, it received a lot of criticism for its poor financial returns and the mismanagement of funds, and SBICs were gradually replaced by the partnership format without public funding as the main way of organizing private equity firms.[1] Still, these investment firms have repeatedly been recognized as the seed for current private capital (i.e. venture capital and private equity) investment firms (Cendrowski et al. 2011; Gompers 1994; Ibanez 1989; Lerner 2009). Some of them financed some of the leading emerging companies of the day, but, most importantly, SBICs helped develop an emergent ecosystem of independent professional fund managers as well as a network of specialized service providers such as accountants, lawyers, and data providers. Notwithstanding the many critics to the program back in the 70s (or the merits for its continuity), the SBIC model also influenced several governments around the world who tried to replicate it.

[1] For an interesting discussion of the competing models of organizing VC investors, see Hsu and Kenney (2005).

SBICs had an important role for the early PE industry. However, "the single most important factor accounting for the increase in money flowing into the venture capital[2] sector was the change in the 1979 amendment to ERISA's 'prudent man rule'" (Gompers 1994, 12).[3] Prior to the modification of this rule, pension funds were banned from investing substantial amounts of money in risky ventures. This modification explicitly allowed pension managers to invest in high-risk assets such as PE/VC, and therefore opened the door to massive capital resources for the—broadly defined—private equity asset class. To this day, pension funds—in particular public pension funds—are the single largest institutional investor in private equity funds in terms of their capital commitments and are therefore key players behind private equity markets in the US (Preqin 2017).

The modification to ERISA illustrates that key regulations that unleash private capital markets happen mostly in bureaucratic arenas, far, and at times at odds, from Congress and partisan politics. Notably, this game-changing amendment, that generated an "unprecedented increase in money flowing into the private equity sector" (Gompers 1994, 2), and in turn had profound consequences on how capitalism is organized in the US (G. F. Davis 2009), was passed as an administrative clarification of a Department of Labor's rule. Even if the change at that time went mostly unnoticed, it was far from unintended. The loosening of ERISA restrictions was the result of intense lobbying from the recently formed National Venture Capital Association—NVCA (Avnimelech et al. 2004, 25; Pincus 2000, 119). According to Kenney (2011, 1707), "NVCA's first goal was to loosen the ERISA restrictions to increase the flow of capital to the VC partnerships. Through intensive lobbying over the next 5 years, the VC industry convinced the Department of Labor, which was charged with enforcing ERISA, to reinterpret it to allow investment in professionally managed VC funds. The reinterpretation would have a dramatic effect."

Regarding the origin of this association, it was formed in 1973 and represented venture capital fund managers who had developed a separate identity and different regulatory concerns than SBIC operators, who were

[2] In this context, venture capital includes the three stages of private equity investments: VC, growth equity, and buyouts.

[3] Employee Retirement Income Security Act (ERISA) of 1974.

already organized in the National Association of Small Business Companies (NASBIC). SBICs were not explicitly excluded from NVCA, but only the larger ones were invited to join the new—by invitation only—association (Kenney 2011, 1707). Still, the NVCA was closely connected to the SBIC experience, showcasing the incubating role of SBICs. Just as an example of these connections: NVCA's first president and founding member, Ned Helzer, was also on the board of NASBIC, and was a member of the advisory committee of SBA, the federal agency that licensed SBICs.[4] And NVCA's first executive director, Stanley Rubel, was also intimately related to the SBA and had previously worked extensively with SBICs (e.g. Noone 1968).

6.1.2 Europe

In Europe, where the industry emerged later than in the US and following its lead, the role of policymakers is also noticeable. Europe's oldest private capital group, 3i (originally called Industrial and Commercial Finance Corporation), was founded by the UK government during the postwar. It pioneered an investment model that deployed long-term capital—often equity-based—to industrial SMEs and operated with substantial autonomy from both bureaucracy and politics. In the 60s, it also pioneered investments in high-technology (Coopey 1994). Beyond its direct impact as a capital provider, it is often highlighted that 3i helped disseminate human capital throughout the UK's emerging private equity industry, similar to the role of SBICs in the US (Ibanez 1989).[5] In other European countries, government-related financial institutions also exhibited an active involvement in the setup of pioneering private equity firms. For example, France's first risk capital firm, Soffinova, created in 1972,

[4] For further evidence see, for example, Helzer's statement in a 1977 Senate Hearings regarding taxation (United States Senate 1977, 75).

[5] 3i floated on the London Stock Market in 1994 and is still a leading mid-market private equity investor with ~ £14.5B in AUM. For a complete history of 3i, see Coopey and Clarke (1995). Interestingly, the origin of Actis Capital, one of the largest emerging market private equity funds with more than $15B AUM and a portfolio across Asia, Africa, and Latin America is also related to UK government. Actis resulted from the 2004 spinout from the Commonwealth Development Corporation (CDC) Group. For a pre-privatization history of the CDC, see McWilliam (2001).

was backed by state-owned Crédit National, the Ministry of Industry and TA Associates, one of America's pioneer PE firms.[6]

More recently, the European Investment Fund (EIF) appears as a key institution for the development of European risk capital markets.[7] Established in 1994 as a European Union decentralized agency, it aims to enhance SMEs access to finance. The EIF does not lend money or invest into companies directly. Instead, it provides finance through a network of intermediaries, among them venture capital and private equity firms. Notably, it became the largest European investor in risk capital funds: it has invested in ~700 funds and has more than €17 billion in private equity assets under management (EIB 2018). In 2018 alone, it committed around €3.5B to fund managers across Europe.[8]

EIF's pan-European approach is complemented by other national-level initiatives that combine capital from governments, and from other semi-public institutions such as pension funds and European Union's resources. Table 6.1 provides a non-exhaustive overview of some of the contemporary policy programs across Europe that channel public resources into private equity. Organizationally, these national-level programs tend to operate with significant autonomy from each country's regular bureaucracy and are mostly staffed by officers with a private sector background. And while these programs exhibit a variety of investment models and target different industries, they all aim to crowd-in private sector investors and in most cases grant capital allocation decision-making to third-party private sector managers.

[6] For the origin of Soffinova, and the introduction of first PE funds in continental Europe, see Brooke and Penrice (2009, 43). Soffinova turned into two sister organizations, Soffinova Ventures and Soffinova Partners, focused in the US and Europe, respectively, that have raised ~$4B since their inception, and invest mostly in the life sciences and technology sectors. Brooke, the founder of Advent, one of the pioneer international PE firms, also highlights the importance of some European families, as sponsors of pioneer PE firms in the region.

[7] The EIF is part of the EIB Group (the European Investment Bank) and is owned 60% by the EIB, 28% by the European Union through the European Commission (EC), and 12% by 30 public and private financial institutions. For a review of EIF from an development perspective, see Griffith-Jones and Tyson (2013).

[8] See Kraemer-Eis, Signore, and Prencipe (2016) for a summary of EIF role in Europe's risk capital market and its performance. As an FT analysis suggest (Financial Times, "Does the EIF have good returns?", May 11, 2017), it exhibits adequate financial returns in the period between 1997 and 2013, "compared to European private equity generally [that notably include large buy-out funds outside the scope of EIF], this isn't a great performance, but it's not catastrophically bad either."

Table 6.1 European Public Programs to Support VC/PE (as of 2019, aprox.)

Country	*Program*	*Year created*	*PE AUM (€, B)*	*Direct*
France	Bpifrance PE	2013	30.0	Yes
Regional	European Investment Fund	1994	17.3	No
Ireland	Ireland Strategic Fund	2014	4.4	Yes
UK	British Patient Capital	2017	2.5	No
Italy	*Fondo Italiano D'Investimento*	2010	2.3	Yes
Norway	Argentum	2001	1.5	No
Spain	Fond-ICO Global	2013	1.2	No
Finland	Tesi	1995	1.2	No
Denmark	Dansk Vækstkapital	2011	1.0	No
Germany	Kfw Capital	2018	0.6	No

Most of these initiatives consist of indirect investments, in which the state works as a fund of funds, and makes capital commitments to independent fund managers. For example, Argentum, the leading fund investor in Northern Europe, invests on behalf of the Norwegian state and the country's main—public and private—institutional investors. The Danish Growth Fund, a joint venture between the Danish state and Danish pension funds, also functions as a funds of funds. Similarly, Spain has arranged a €1.5B public fund of funds, FOND-ICO Global, with the goal of promoting the creation of privately-managed growth-oriented PE funds that target Spanish companies at all stages. To close the gap left by the EIF after Brexit, the UK has revamped the British Business Bank. Kfw Capital, a subsidiary of Germany's development bank, was created in 2018 to invest into equity funds investments and promote the industry, taking over two previous state-related programs aimed to promote VC markets.[9] Another example is Tesi, with €1.2 B AUM aimed to develop Finland's venture capital and private equity market.

[9] High-Tech Gründerfonds (JV between KF and large German industrial companies) that had close to 1B in AUM. And Coparion, that co-invested with private funds. Even if KFW Capital plans to make larger investments, its size is smaller than what the local industry association was lobbying for (e.g. see Roland Berger et al. 2018, 33).

In some other cases, state-related financial institutions also participate in the fund management firm (GP), or even make direct private equity investments, co-investing with private sector investors. The French state's investment bank, Bpifrance,[10] has around €30B in private equity assets under management, allocated to companies of all sizes and industries. Two-thirds of them are direct equity investments in 142 portfolio companies (in minority positions, generally co-investing with other PE firms). The rest of the capital is invested indirectly through 400 funds, managed by 150 different fund management firms (GPs). And Ireland's Strategic Investment Fund has €4.1B in direct and indirect equity investments "to support economic activity and employment in Ireland."[11] *Fondo Italiano D'Investimento*, majority-owned by *Cassa Depositi e Prestiti*, a state-controlled investment bank, also aims to "combine the objective of economic return and development of the productive system" through direct and indirect equity investments.[12] Overall, it is clear that government-related investors play a role in sponsoring private capital initiatives throughout Europe.

Central and Eastern European countries (CEE) are closer in terms of development levels to Latin America. And the emergence of private equity markets in CEE countries was also heavily sponsored by government-related investors. Earlier, during the transition from planned economies to a free-market system, these countries counted with vigorous support by a series of multilateral organizations (Klonowski 2006). Going forward, some countries developed their own national-level programs. And when joining the EU, PE funds operating in the region also received substantial support from the Union's financial institutions (Invest Europe 2018; Karsai 2018).

[10] *Banque publique d'investissement S.A* is owned by *Caisse des Dépôts et Consignations* and France's Ministry of Economics and Finance. It was founded in 2012, as the result of the merger of several state-related financial institutions: OSEO, *Fonds stratégique d'investissement* and *Caisse des dépôts et consignations's* CDC Entreprises.

[11] ISIF complements the investment programs targeted to private capital funds managed by Enterprise Ireland.

[12] There are several other examples of public initiatives that channel state-related funds through privately-managed PE funds. For example, in the infrastructure sector, Marguerite manages two PE funds that target brownfield and greenfield projects in Europe and is sponsored by the EIB together with public financial institutions from Poland, France, Italy, France, Spain, and Germany.

For example, the case of Poland, with the most developed PE market and largest stock exchange in the CEE region, appears to support the hypothesis of the market's policy-led origin. "In order to develop, the Polish private equity industry needed two critical components: a supply of viable investments projects and capital. Two igniting forces helped to spur this development: the privatization program and financial assistance from major international financial institutions and government agencies (both Western and local). It would be these forces that would ultimately transform the struggling capital market in Poland" (Klonowski 2011a, 109). In terms of funding, the European Bank for Reconstruction and Development (ERBD) together with World Bank's IFC and direct support from the US acted as the cornerstone investors of pioneer PE funds, who later attracted further private sector investments.[13] Multilateral support was followed by continuous support from the Polish government. For example, there are "about 16 major programs operated by the Polish government," (Klonowski 2011b) and the Polish Development Fund manages the largest fund of funds in the CEE region.

6.1.3 Asia

In the last couple of decades, Asia had the fastest growing capital markets (Abraham et al. 2019). And Asian companies are now the largest users of public equity financing globally, at odds with their prior bank-centric characterization (e.g. Woo-Cumings 1991). Notably, in several of these countries (e.g. China, Hong Kong, Malaysia, and Vietnam), the government is a major shareholder of public companies. In some of them the state holds, through multiple investment vehicles, close to half of the market (Carney and Child 2013; OECD 2018). In line with the overall development of Asian capital markets, private equity markets have also grown considerably, now occupying a major role in the global alternative assets industry (Preqin 2018). In PE markets, government-related investors also appear to play a key role, probably even larger than in Europe.[14]

[13] The most noted case is Enterprise Investors. Active since 1990, it has raised nine funds with total capital exceeding €2.5B, invested in 144 companies, and among its exits, it sponsored 35 IPOs.

[14] For an analysis of the government-sponsored emergence of venture capital markets in East-Asia that goes beyond the focus on investors, see Klingler-Vidra (2018).

China is by far Asia's largest private capital market (Preqin 2018). While the distinction between state and non-state capital in China is blurry (Fuller 2016), government-related money is ubiquitous throughout its financial market, and secondary sources agree on attributing the growth of the PE industry to government policy (as well as many of its perils, e.g. Fuller (2016)).[15] "The first international venture capital firms entered China in the early 1980s. The impetus for the development of the Chinese venture capital industry was government policy. Government encouraged and sponsored PE funds to invest in SOE to bring them up to world standard in terms of productivity and quality" (Ahlstrom et al. 2007, 250). National, provincial, and city governments established joint ventures with large international PE houses. But, as Leeds (2015) argues, "perhaps nothing has been more transformative in the Chinese private equity industry compared to other emerging markets countries than the 2008 decision by the National State Council to permit a select number of large, reputable state-owned saving institutions such as the National Social Security Fund (NSSF) and the Chinese Development Bank to allocate up to 10% of their assets for investments as LPs in local currency private equity funds" (p. 179).

More recently, the growth in the industry was explained mostly by the rapid increase in local currency (RMB) funds (PWC 2017), sponsored by state-related financial institutions and by "guidance funds" from different government levels (i.e. city, provincial, and national).[16] These funds are deployed through various models: special investment vehicles, co-investments alongside professional private equity groups, and as funds of funds. They target the tech sector, but also more traditional industries. The claim that guidance funds have $1.8T to deploy—a value equal to one-third of the total assets of the global private equity market—is considered an overstatement. Still, there is little doubt that the Chinese state channels massive amounts of financial resources into companies through private capital funds.[17]

[15] There are many nuances to "private equity with Chinese characteristics" (Leeds 2015, Chap. 6) I do not address in this brief paragraph. For a more complete discussion on the history and evolution of private equity in China, see Yong (2012) and EMPEA (2012). For the role of China Development Bank, see Sanderson and Forsythe (2012).

[16] See China' Money Network ranking of China's government fund ranking.

[17] International-oriented Chinese PE/VC funding has raised increased scrutiny in the US following the concern Chinese venture-capital investment in American companies

The Korean government has also made considerable efforts to develop a more vigorous private capital industry. Government-related investors play an important role in the fundraising process by making sizable capital commitments; through overlapping channels the state is still the country's largest investor in the asset class. Government also established the KOSDAQ stock market in 1996, which provided venture-capital-backed companies with the possibility of an IPO, facilitating the exit of PE investments. And indeed, listing in KOSDAQ appears to be one of the most usual forms of exit for Korean investors. In terms of the regulatory framework, the industry grew rapidly since 2004, when the government introduced regulations to foster the creation of local funds industry (see, e.g. Ko and Shin 1999; Lee 2008).

The Korean Development Bank (KDB) is among the largest direct PE investors (GPs) in the country. Indirectly (as an LP), it accounts for a sizable amount of all the investments in privately-managed domestic PE and VC funds (KDB 2016, 2018). It also partners with international funds investing in Korea. Moreover, state-owned Korea Venture Investment Corporation (KVIC) was formed in 2005 as Korea's fund of funds, investing in smaller venture-oriented funds. The National Pension Service, a public pension fund, is the other key investor who leads the Korean LP landscape, together with other government-linked pension funds (Invest Korea 2015). Acknowledging the role of the state in funding new companies, a McKinsey (2015) report on Korea states: "our in-depth conversations with more than 30 leading Korean entrepreneurs, venture capitalists and small business experts found that, within Korea's startup community, there is broad agreement that, thanks to new government policies, there is more funding available to new Korean ventures than was the case even five years ago."

Singapore and to a certain extent Malaysia are also cases worth mentioning. In addition to their British colonial legacy and its "common law" legal origins, analysts grant government-related investors a larger role in the expansion of their—private and public—capital markets.[18]

intends to give China an edge in technologies for commercial and military use (e.g. Brown and Singh 2018). While interesting, the strategic dimension of outward-oriented state-sponsored private equity is outside the scope of the book.

[18] For an early analysis of the PE/VC markets in Singapore, and comparison with Malaysia and Hong Kong cases, see (Koh and Koh 2002). In Malaysia, Gomez et al. (2018), attributes to government-linked companies the ownership of around 50% of the

The role of government-related investors was key for Singapore to become a global financial center. According to another McKinsey report on how to deepen capital markets in emerging markets (Jain et al. 2017), the government used government-related investment funds, most notably the Central Provident Fund (CPF), to allocate capital to external managers across different investment types, among them private equity, transforming the local fund management industry. It is also worth noting that Singapore's two mammoth SWF are key players in the global private equity markets. Outwards oriented, GIC is the third largest private equity allocator (LP) globally, after the Canadian Pension Plan Investment Board and Abu Dhabi's Investment Authority (Preqin 2017). And Temasek is a cornerstone investor in the largest companies of the country and continues to pursue Singapore's developmental goals, through—direct and indirect—private equity investments both inside and outside the island.

Apart from the well-known cases of GIC and Temasek, Singapore has several other government-related investment arms that, in various ways, provide equity capital to firms, usually tied to government's long-term plans (e.g. becoming a biotech and IT global hub). Temasek's venture capital arm, Vertex, has developed a proprietary global network of fund managers[19] that, as of 2020, manages assets worth over $3 billion and has equity stakes in more than 170 companies. Singapore's Economic Development Board (EDB) has its own private equity and venture capital arm, EDB Investments. With a broad scope across sectors and sizes, and in line with the EDB's priorities, it has focused on healthcare, information and communication technologies. Similarly, Infocomm Investments is an accelerator and the venture capital arm of Singapore Infocomm Media

capital markets, for example, through Khazanah Nasional, the country's SWF. Khazanah Nasional functioned mostly as a direct private equity type of investor and had a strategic focus and active involvement in its portfolio companies, at least until reforms following the 1MDB scandal (that, by the way, also illustrates in a grotesque way the corruption risks related to state-funded investment funds). Publicly-managed Employee Provident Fund, that manages the compulsory savings and retirement plans for private sector workers in Malaysia, has anchored the development of Malayan capital market (Price et al. 2018). Moreover, there are other initiatives, such as Ekuinas, a government-owned PE fund with around $1B in AUM, that deploys private equity capital both directly into companies and indirectly into funds. Together with fostering PE investments in the country, this initiative aims to promote Bumiputera's—indigenous Malays—economic participation.

[19] Vertex Ventures China, Vertex Ventures Israel, Vertex Ventures SEA & India, Vertex Ventures US, Vertex Ventures HC and Vertex Growth.

Development Authority and is focused on digital investments. As part of the Startup SG Equity program, the government also co-invests with independent, third-party investors into startups. These co-investment funds are managed by SEEDS Capital and SGInnovate. Finally, Singapore's National Research Foundation also provides capital to startups, and a majority of their portfolio is in IT. While the state is present in all stages of Singapore's dynamic venture capital ecosystem through funding, it is noteworthy that these investment programs work in tandem with other policy instruments such as R&D subsidies, grants and tax incentives to attract multinationals, and the provision of specialized infrastructure (e.g. laboratories).

Overall, even if this has not been an exhaustive compilation, it shows that government-related financing for private—and public—equity investment funds are ubiquitous (Brander et al. 2015).[20] Government-related financial institutions played a role in the emergence of private capital markets throughout regions and over time, in otherwise different financial systems. Moreover, programs channeling capital through private equity funds do not necessarily fade out after their initial incubating role, but change their investment goals. For example, the South Korean government has recently launched a $9B "start-up" investment fund. France's government has announced a €5B initiative to be channeled through French asset managers to finance late stage-investments and aims to mobilize further resources from other local institutional investors. And Europe launched what appears to be a new fund of funds, in addition to the regular activity of the EIF.

6.2 Business Associations and Regulatory Co-production

There is little doubt about the role of government-related investors such as development banks and pension funds in nurturing private equity markets. The argument about the regulatory politics is harder to assess through shadow cases. Still, I was able to gather primary and secondary sources of data to evaluate some key points. Latin American public agencies were not innovating when "seeding" fund managers' organizations,

[20] Israel's Yozma program is often mentioned as a successful example of a government initiative that helped build a domestic venture capital market, see, for example, Avnimelech (2009).

but rather following the European and Asian experiences. Outside of Latin America, private equity associations were also created with public support. Moreover, the politics behind the creation of European private equity's regulatory frameworks, as described by the few secondary sources on the topic, aligns well with this book's quiet politics argument.

The institutional process underlying the emergence of the European private capital markets exhibits a similar dynamic to the one described in Chapter 5 regarding PE in Latin America. First, a regional industry association was created with sponsorship from public authorities, in this case of the European Commission. In turn, this association played a key role "co-producing" the regulatory framework that would allow the industry to function, following a "quiet" politics approach.

In 1983, the European Commission created the Brussels-based European Venture Capital Association (EVCA, now renamed Invest Europe). As Ooghe et al. (1989, 40) describe, "from 1980 on, the European Community organized a yearly symposium concerning innovation in which one of the mains themes was venture capital. A next initiative was the creation of the European Venture Capital Association (EVCA) in November 1983. The intention of EVCA is the stimulation and coordination of the development of venture capital in an international context. EVCA received financial support and active cooperation from the European Community."[21]

On its research on the origin of new stock markets in Europe, Posner (2005, 23) argues that the actions of Brussels officials were the most important cause in a complex process of institutional change that occurred in Europe's capital market.[22] Regarding EVCA, Posner highlights how officials from the European Commission, through "seemingly innocuous interventions that drew little attention and no opposition, helped to create and then finance this political voice and interest group for European venture capitalists." In turn, he argues, the association was key to push for "seemingly small and unremarkable bureaucratic interventions accumulated over a fifteen-year period to forge new interests, catalyze

[21] For the primary documents that show the role of the European Commission founding EVCA, see European Commission's Bulletins of the European Communities: 12-1981 2.1.18, 11-1982 2.1.24, and 6-1983 2.1.46. I obtained the reference for these primary sources from Posner (2005).

[22] For the role of the European Commission driving corporate governance reform, also see Overbeek et al. (2007).

coalitions, stretch interpretations of EC laws, and frame debates" (Posner 2005, 4).[23]

The association indeed represents most of the European private equity industry. Its role is similar to the one described in Chapter 5 for the Latin American associations, albeit in a more institutionalized way. It has lobbied to create new types of investment vehicles, to obtain tax incentives, and most importantly, to open new fundraising sources.[24] Moreover, it has developed industry standards that its members have to follow. Given its European scope, it worked to harmonize regulations across countries and tried to connect national markets. And it has also served to promote and legitimize the asset class with the broader public. EVCA has also served as an umbrella institution to support national-level private capital associations.

At the national level, the institutionalization of French private equity industry, as analyzed by Benquet and Bourgeron (2020),[25] is also informative of the political dynamic behind the origin of private equity markets. The first funds were developed in the 1970s at the initiative of senior civil servants, working in public or semi-public financial institutions. Some of these pioneer managers founded a national-level private equity association—AFIC,[26] later renamed as France Invest—around the same time EVCA was founded. With leadership roles occupied by former civil servants with well-established connections with government, AFIC, in turn, played a central role in the public–private co-production of the institutional framework behind the growth of the industry. Key regulatory domains paralleled the ones analyzed in Chapter 5 for the Latin American cases: the creation of vehicles (e.g. *Fonds Communs de Placements à Risques*) and an advantageous tax framework for the industry and investors. Moreover, the article shows the PE industry grew by the opportunities opened by successive waves of privatizations. And argues private equity investments, in particular through Bpifrance, France's state-owned investment bank, became the preferred instrument of policymakers to support growth after privatizations and the decline of more traditional industrial planning programs.

[23] For the book version of this argument, see Posner (2009).

[24] See, for example, its 2014–2019 EVCA's "key policy achievements."

[25] I am grateful to Isadora Araujo Cruxên for pointing out this article.

[26] *Association Française des Investisseurs pour la Croissance* (AFIC).

Moreover, in their analysis of the institutionalization of the PE industry in France, Benquet and Bourgeron (2020) emphasize the close similarities between left and right-wing government policies directed to the sector. Using Culpepper's (2010) framework, they describe how sporadically the "private equity sector, which had built its institutional arrangement on quiet politics for three decades, briefly became an object of 'high political salience'" (p. 12). However, "only a small part of the criticism was translated into legislation," partly due to the protection from supranational legislation, but also due to the lobbying and a legitimizing campaign conducted by AFIC.

Overall, the European case appears to be in line with the arguments made in Chapter 5 about the institutionalization of private equity markets. The creation of business associations that represent the private equity industry was promoted by public agencies. In turn, these associations functioned as a policy instrument to "co-produce" the industry's regulatory framework. Most of these regulatory initiatives are restricted to bureaucratic domains, outside partisan politics and legislatures. Congress and "large" salient politics, when present, appear to have a reactive role. The game-changing modification of the ERISA rule in the US case discussed above appears to follow the same logic.

Outside these cases, the secondary evidence on the political dynamics behind the emergence of PE is more limited. Still, business associations emerged with support from governments, as part of programs to promote the asset class, except in the US. Eastern European associations, under the umbrella of the European Commission-sponsored EVCA, were founded together with the first PE firms in the region that managed mostly multilateral funds. In Asia, the Korean Venture Capital Association (KVCA) was established in 1989 as a "government-led" association to facilitate the development of the Korean venture capital industry.[27] And similarly, the Singapore Venture Capital & Private Equity Association (SVCA) was formed in 1992 under the patronage of the Economic Development Board to foster the growth of this sector.

[27] As acknowledged by KVCA's chairman Chung Sung-in in an interview with The Korea Herald (2019/05/07).

6.3 Discussion

There is a great deal of government-related resources behind capital markets outside of Latin America. These resources are deployed following different models. Equity capital is in most cases invested indirectly, through third-party fund managers. But government funds are also channeled directly into companies. Domestic fund managers are often prioritized, but some programs also engage international fund managers who invest in their home countries as well as abroad.[28] Moreover, policy initiatives are sometimes targeted to particular industries, while in other cases they are sector-agnostic and aim to develop the PE market more generally. We can observe these differences across countries, but also across programs within countries. Going forward, a more systematic approach may serve to evaluate the effectiveness of the different policy programs (Colombo et al. 2016; Da Rin et al. 2006). For example, by relating PE investments with IPOs, the role of privatizations in the growth of PE, or assessing how alternative governance and investment models of public financing crowds-in, or not, further private investments. And beyond the role of policy programs in the development of markets, the penetration of PE could also be related to country-level societal characteristics, such as investor protections and labor rights (e.g. Bedu and Montalban 2014).

While the political logic behind the emergence of private equity markets merits more research, the evidence presented above suggests the "quiet politics" dynamic followed in Latin America, as described in Chapter 5, is not just a function of the low level of development of the PE industry in this region. In most of the cases analyzed, maybe with the salient exception of the US, business associations were created through the active sponsorship of the government, and as part of broader initiatives to promote private equity and venture capital markets. The European case, as described by Posner (2005) and Benquet and Bourgeron (2020), suggests that these business associations had an important role helping write the regulations that institutionalized private capital markets. They also show that in Europe most of the politics behind

[28] Government-sponsored but externally-oriented private equity programs that are not just a function of portfolio diversification but have "developmental goals" are in themselves an interesting topic. They are much more frequent in Asia (e.g. Singapore, China and Korea). In Latin America I am not aware of any such programs.

these regulations also remain at the margins of partisan politics and Congress. Going back to the Latin American cases, these findings suggest that the dynamics described in Chapter 5 are not just a function of the region's legislatures dysfunctional policymaking capabilities, driven by the deficient technical capacities of legislative bodies, paired with weakly institutionalized party systems (Cox and Morgenstern 2001). Instead, the "quiet politics" dynamics behind private equity regulations seem to be a more common trend across political systems with different levels of institutionalization.

Beyond normative issues, these findings have theoretical implications. If the development of private equity markets is, as argued, a central components of "financial development" (i.e. external—institutional—equity capital into firms), these findings cast some doubts on the mechanisms through which democracy is a force that promotes the deepening of financial markets. And it indicates, more broadly, the need to re-think the relationship between regime type, policymaking, and financial development.

References

Abraham, Facundo, Juan Cortina, and Sergio L. Schmukler. 2019. *The Rise of Domestic Capital Markets for Corporate Financing*.

Ahlstrom, David, Garry D. Bruton, and Kuang S. Yeh. 2007. Venture Capital in China: Past, Present, and Future. *Asia Pacific Journal of Management* 24 (3): 247–268.

Avnimelech, Gil. 2009. VC Policy: Yozma Program 15-Years Perspective. *SSRN Electronic Journal*.

Avnimelech, Gil, Martin Kenney, and Morris Teubal. 2004. *Building Venture Capital Industries: Understanding the U.S. and Israeli Experiences*.

Bedu, Nicolas, and Matthieu Montalban. 2014. Analysing the Uneven Development of Private Equity in Europe: Legal Origins and Diversity of Capitalism. *Socio-Economic Review* 12 (1): 33–70.

Benquet, Marlène, and Théo Bourgeron. 2020. Building a Centre of Capital Accumulation: A Study of the Institutional Emergence of the French Private Equity Sector (from the Early 1980s to 2017). *New Political Economy* 26 (2): 1–17.

Brander, J.A., Q. Du, and T. Hellmann. 2015. The Effects of Government-Sponsored Venture Capital: International Evidence. *Review of Finance* 19 (2): 571–618.

Brooke, Peter A., and Daniel Penrice. 2009. *A Vision for Venture Capital: Realizing the Promise of Global Venture Capital and Private Equity*. Boston: New Ventures Press.

Brown, Michael, and Pavneet Singh. 2018. *China's Technology Transfer Strategy: How Chinese Investments in Emerging Technology Enable a Strategic Competitor to Access the Crown Jewels of U.S. Innovation.*

Carney, Richard W., and Travers Barclay Child. 2013. Changes to the Ownership and Control of East Asian Corporations Between 1996 and 2008: The Primacy of Politics. *Journal of Financial Economics* 107 (2): 494–513.

Cendrowski, Harry, James P. Martin, Louis W. Petro, and Adam A. Wadecki. 2011. *Private Equity History, Governance, and Operations*. Wiley.

Colombo, Massimo G., Douglas J. Cumming, and Silvio Vismara. 2016. Governmental Venture Capital for Innovative Young Firms. *Journal of Technology Transfer* 41 (1): 10–24.

Coopey, Richard. 1994. The First Venture Capitalist: Financing Development in Britain After 1945, The Case of ICFC/3i. *Business and Economic History* 23: 262–271.

Coopey, Richard, and Donald Clarke. 1995. *3i: Fifty Years Investing in Industry*. Oxford: Oxford University Press.

Cox, Gary W., and Scott Morgenstern. 2001. Latin America's Reactive Assemblies and Proactive Presidents. *Comparative Politics* 33 (2): 171–189.

Culpepper, Pepper D. 2010. *Quiet Politics and Business Power: Corporate Control in Europe and Japan*. Cambridge: Cambridge University Press.

Davis, Gerald F. 2009. *Managed by the Markets: How Finance Re-Shaped America*. Oxford: Oxford University Press.

EIB. 2018. *Facts & Figures*.

EMPEA. 2012. *The Evolution of PE in China*.

Fuller, Douglas B. 2016. *Paper Tigers, Hidden Dragons: Firms and the Political Economy of China's Technological Development*. New York: Oxford University Press.

Gomez, Edmund Terence, et al. 2018. *Minister of Finance Incorporated: Ownership and Control in Corporate Malaysia*. Singapore: Palgrave Macmillan.

Gompers, Paul A. 1994. The Rise and Fall of Venture Capital. *Business and Economic History* 23 (2): 1–24.

Griffith-Jones, Stephany, and Judith Tyson. 2013. *The European Investment Bank: Lessons for Developing Countries*.

Hsu, David H., and Martin Kenney. 2005. Organizing Venture Capital: The Rise and Demise of American Research & Development Corporation, 1946–1973. *Industrial and Corporate Change* 14 (4): 579–616.

Ibanez, Fernan. 1989. *Venture Capital and Entrepreneurial Development*. Washington, DC.

Invest Europe. 2018. *2017 Central and Eastern Europe Private Equity Statistics*.

Invest Korea. 2015. *Private Equity & Venture Capital.*

Jain, Nitin, et al. 2017. *Deepening Capital Markets in Emerging Economies.*

Karsai, Judit. 2018. Government Venture Capital in Central and Eastern Europe. *Venture Capital* 20 (1): 73–102.

KDB. 2016. *Annual Report.*

———. 2018. *KDB Annual Report 2018.*

Kenney, Martin. 2011. How Venture Capital Became a Component of the US National System of Innovation. *Industrial and Corporate Change* 20 (6): 1677–1723.

Klingler-Vidra, Robyn. 2018. *The Venture Capital State: The Silicon Valley Model in East Asia.* Ithaca: Cornell University Press.

Klonowski, Darek. 2006. Venture Capital as a Method of Financing Enterprise Development in Central and Eastern Europe. *International Journal of Emerging Markets* 1 (2): 165–175.

———. 2011a. *Private Equity in Poland: Winning Leadership in Emerging Markets.* New York: Palgrave Macmillan.

———. 2011b. Private Equity in Poland after Two Decades of Development: Evolution, Industry Drivers, and Returns. *Venture Capital* 13 (4): 295–311.

Ko, Haksoo, and Hyun Young Shin. 1999. Venture Capital in Korea? Special Law to Promote Venture Capital Companies. *American University International Law Review* 15 (2): 457–480.

Koh, Winston T.H., and Francis Koh. 2002. Venture Capital and Economic Growth: An Industry Overview and Singapore's Experience. *SSRN Electronic Journal.*

Kraemer-Eis, Helmut, Simone Signore, and Dario Prencipe. 2016. The European Venture Capital Landscape: An EIF Perspective. *EIF Research & Market Analysis* Working Paper (Volume I: The impact of EIF on the VC ecosystem).

Lee, Suil. 2008. The Development of Venture Capital Industry and the Role of Government in Korea: Venture Boom vs. Post-Boom. *KDI Journal of Economic Policy* 30 (1): 211–246.

Leeds, Roger. 2015. *Private Equity Investing in Emerging Markets: Opportunities for Value Creation.* New York: Palgrave Macmillan US.

Lerner, Josh. 2009. *Boulevard of Broken Dreams: Why Public Efforts to Boost Entrepreneurship and Venture Capital Have Failed, and What to Do About It.* Princeton: Princeton University Press.

McKinsey & Company. 2015. *The Virtuous Circle: Putting Korea's Startup Ecosystem on a Path to Sustainable Long-Run Growth.*

McWilliam, Micheal. 2001. *The Development Business: A History of the Commonwealth Development Corporation.* New York: Palgrave Macmillan.

Noone, Charles M. 1968. The 1968 Model SBIC. *The Business Lawyer* 23: 1214–1220.

OCED. 2018. *OECD Equity Market Review of Asia 2018.*

Ooghe, Herbert, Ann Bekaert, and Peter van den Bossche. 1989. Venture Capital in the U.S.A., Europe and Japan. *Management International Review* 29: 29–45.

Overbeek, Henk, Bastiaan Van Apeldoorn, and Andreas Nölke. 2007. The Transnational Politics of Corporate Governance Regulation. In *The Transnational Politics of Corporate Governance Regulation*. New York: Routledge Taylor & Francis Group.

Pincus, Lionel. 2000. Warburg Pincus. In *Done Deals. Venture Capitalists Tell Their Stories*, ed. Uduyan Gupta, 415. Boston, MA: Harvard Business School Press.

Posner, Elliot. 2005. Sources of Institutional Change: The Supranational Origins of Europe's New Stock Markets. *World Politics* 58 (01): 1–40.

Posner, Elliot. 2009. *The Origins of Europe's New Stock Markets*. Cambridge, MA: Harvard University Press.

Preqin. 2017. *The Private Equity Top 100*.

———. 2018. *Preqin Special Report: Asian Private Equity & Venture Capital*.

Price, William Joseph, et al. 2018. *Case Study on the Employee Provident Fund of Malaysia*.

PWC. 2017. *China Private Equity/ Venture Capital 2016 Review and 2017 Outlook*.

Da Rin, Marco, Giovanna Nicodano, and Alessandro Sembenelli. 2006. Public Policy and the Creation of Active Venture Capital Markets. *Journal of Public Economics* 90(8–9): 1699–1723.

Roland Berger, IEF, and BVK. 2018. *Venture Capital. Fueling Innovation and Economic Growth*.

Sanderson, Henry, and Michael Forsythe. 2012. *China's Superbank: Debt, Oil and Influence—How China Development Bank Is Rewriting the Rules of Finance*. Singapore: Wiley-Bloomberg Press.

United States Senate. 1977. Incentives for Economic Growth, Hearings Before the Subcommittee on Taxation and Debt Management Generally of the Committee on Finance.

Woo-Cumings, Meredith. 1991. *Race to the Swift: State and Finance in Korean Industrialization*. New York: Columbia University Press.

Yong, Kwek Ping. 2012. *Private Equity in China: Challenges and Opportunities*. Wiley.

CHAPTER 7

Conclusions

Thirty years ago, the idea of external financial investors buying into private companies was foreign to most economies outside the US. This is no longer the case. A financial approach to ownership and corporate governance as the one advanced by private equity investors has become part of the business landscape throughout both the developed and developing world. Institutional change is certainly slow and non-linear. The private capital model will continue to evolve and adapt to local and global market conditions and policies. Hopefully this evolution will be toward longer-term partnerships between local and international investors, fund managers, and entrepreneurs to finance firm's growth and create value through much needed productivity-enhancing initiatives.

This book's agency-based approach can help bridge context-free policy blueprints with academic arguments that highlight the historical and more structural political economy pre-conditions for financial development. From a practical perspective, it provides more clarity on the organizational pre-requisites of policies aimed at fostering the deployment of long-term capital and connecting domestic savings pools with the real economy. It brings finance back into productive development policymaking and introduces financial bureaucracies to the state capacities discussion.

I. Puente, *Private Equity and Financial Development in Latin America*, Latin American Political Economy,
https://doi.org/10.1007/978-3-030-88983-8_7

This book has descriptive value. It contributes to updating the typology of business actors in emerging economies by introducing a new "hybrid" type of investor that blends international finance with local management, deepens capital markets, and drives corporate governance modernization, as argued in Chapters 2 and 3.

But—hopefully—its contribution goes beyond describing this investment model and also helps explain its emergence, underscoring the role of policymaking in market expansion. In particular, it emphasizes the role of government-related financial institutions sponsoring—incubating—this business model both by investing in private equity (Chapter 4) and by helping the industry organize into business associations (Chapter 5).

This book makes three main contributions: (1) it introduces private equity into the development debate; (2) prompts a shift in the discussion on financial development from institutional explanations focused only on rules—democracy and investor protections—to an actor-based argument centered on institutional investors; and (3) characterizes a novel model of financial productive policymaking that forefronts financial bureaucracies and pension funds. This final chapter discusses each of these three topics, explores some of their implications, and suggests ideas for further research.

7.1 Private Equity and Development

This book is in line with a recent wave of research in political science that argues for paying more attention to business and private sector characteristics when explaining developmental outcomes (e.g. Puente and Schneider 2020). While introducing private equity, it highlights ownership models and corporate governance as consequential firm-level dimensions and emphasizes the overall centrality of finance for development.

Private equity provides firms with a distinctive source of financing that is otherwise elusive in the developing world. PE combines three characteristics: it is *risky*, *institutional* and—at least relative to other financial investors—*patient*. Private equity investors help finance firms by investing in the more risky tranches of the firm's capital structure, which usually grants them an ownership stake. PE firms channel institutional capital into firms and therefore function as an alternative to individual and family-related sources of capital. And PE exhibits longer holding periods than those of traditional asset managers focused on public securities, even though have shorter time horizons than family groups.

PE also appears at odds with prevalent corporate governance models in Latin America. Private equity investors can be described as hybrid actors in at least two ways. First, they broker domestic and international arenas by combining local embeddedness with connections to international markets. While prioritizing local management and operations, PE investors also participate in international networks of finance, technology, and management. Second, PE funds manage capital from third-party investors but act as owners. Even though they are financial investors, their role goes beyond solving capital constraints to include an active involvement in firm governance and strategic management. Crucially, PE can introduce more autonomous professional management in a context where otherwise "hierarchical" models of governance prevail.

A key assertion of this book is the connection between private equity and (financial) development. For some readers this argument may appear controversial, even provocative. The PE model is often portrayed as not more than a financial engineering exercise, more associated to value extraction than to value creation. Critics argue that the heavy use of debt and high dividend payouts, combined with aggressive restructuring plans that often involve layoffs only entail a transfer of value from firm's workers and other stakeholders to investors.

PE fund managers invest in behalf of a broad base of—mostly institutional—investors. While there is an important agency problem between managers and investors that can have large distributive implications (Phalippou 2020), ultimately the returns of PE are also the returns of their investors, among them, millions of pensioners. Instead of justifying PE's excesses, the institutional origin of its capital should point out to the levers for the increased accountability of fund managers.

Moreover, as this book defined it, private equity is a broad term that groups different "alternative assets" outside public markets. It includes buyouts, growth equity, venture capital, and infrastructure-oriented investments, among others.

Most of the criticisms are specific to—typically leveraged—buyout investors. Still, there is solid empirical evidence that shows private equity investors—including buyouts—help allocate capital more efficiently, improve management practices, drive growth, and boost productivity (e.g. Bloom et al. 2015; S. J. Davis et al. 2014, 2019; Lerner et al. 2011). Concerning the effect of private equity on employment, results indicate substantial differences across asset sub-classes. In the US, evidence indicates that "take-private" buyouts indeed have negative effects over employment rates. When PE firms acquire a listed company, they often play a restructuring role that can include substantial layoffs. Outside of these public-to-private transactions, private-to-private buyouts appear to expand employment relative to control firms (S. J. Davis et al. 2019). Beyond buyouts, the role of venture capital and growth equity investors is less disputed. These investors often enjoy a better reputation and are mostly seen as drivers of value creation, as they provide funding for firm development, growth, and innovation (Rin et al. 2013).

Some of the critiques to private equity can travel to economies with less developed financial markets, like those in Latin America. In this context, PE often also entails the extension of markets into new domains and a financial approach to corporate governance. However, most of the criticisms are less applicable in under-developed financial systems. Whatever their merits, in Latin America there are no large buyouts. Most transactions are in the equivalent of growth-oriented mid-and small-cap categories in the US. Moreover, highly-leveraged strategies are not common. As the evidence presented in Chapter 3 shows, leverage is more associated with family control than with private equity ownership. More generally, and notwithstanding the importance of reforms to discourage value extraction and promote value creation, in Latin America the low levels of external finance are arguably a preceding—and more fundamental—problem than its possible excesses.

In Latin America, beyond a few business groups and multinationals, firms are small, have concentrated ownership, and are governed through traditional structures. External sources of capital are scant, and there is no active market for corporate control. In more developed capital markets, private equity concentrates ownership as a way to discipline managers. In contrast, in Latin America, institutional private equity is an alternative to governance models organized around families and individuals. In a context where stock markets with dispersed ownership and unchecked managers are notably absent, PE plays a different—and possibly more developmental—role. It upgrades capital markets, modernizes firm ownership, and professionalizes corporate governance.

Moreover, in the path toward a more complete financial system, there is no alternative for an active equity market. The traditional dichotomy in comparative political economy between capital markets and bank-based financial systems does not seem applicable any longer. Bank loans are less of a substitute and more of a complement to equity financing. In any case, banks in the region are not a major source of patient capital since they are mostly oriented toward consumer lending. In environments with developed stock markets, PE indeed may compete with public equity markets. In contrast, in emerging economies PE is arguably a necessary condition for their expansion. As shown, PE is an important driver of stock market listings. And among the companies that list in the stock market, those backed by PE investors have a more dispersed shareholder structure and fewer kinship ties within their leadership positions, illustrating how PE drives business modernization.

Overall, this book contributes to a business-centered approach to development by characterizing a distinctive actor: private equity. By doing so, it forefronts finance and corporate governance as key dimensions in the development debate. Going forward with this agenda calls for further evaluations of the implications of alternative ownership and governance models such as PE. While there is a growing empirical literature on the economic effects of PE, it is mostly focused on developed countries. And open questions remain around how PE engages politics.

7.2 Institutions: Rules and Investors

That finance is an important driver of economic development is hardly controversial. There is solid evidence that shows that the development of a country's financial markets is causally associated with its long-term economic growth and the material well-being of its population. This book argues that the development of private equity markets, as a key source of arms-length equity financing, is an important component of a developed financial system. And regarding the political economy behind the development of financial markets, it proposes an actor-based argument that can complement longer-term rules-based hypotheses focused on economic and political institutions.

The book takes a more concrete approach and focuses directly on the role of investors. While necessary, an institutional environment that guarantees adequate investor protections does not appear enough to unleash equity markets. Instead, the case studies indicate that government-related institutional investors, in particular development banks and pension funds, are also drivers of private equity markets. Domestic and multilateral development financial institutions have an "incubating" role during the early stages of the industry, followed by pension funds. While shareholder legal rights are certainly relevant for the development of financial markets, they are insufficient to explain the path toward more complete capital markets. In order for these rights to be exercised, equity markets have to be nurtured by institutional investors.

Focusing on specific economic institutions, PE is arguably less sensible to within-firm minority shareholder rights. Given their concentrated stakes, PE investors have the incentives and the capacity to monitor management and other shareholders. Thus, they may be better able to operate in less institutionalized environments, where agency costs make stock markets unfeasible. Moreover, up to certain extent the industry's regulatory framework appears to be endogenous to the emergence of its players, who help shape their rules.

The institutionalization of the private capital industry seems to follow a "quiet politics" dynamics. The regulatory reforms that enable the industry to operate more smoothly (e.g. the creation of new investment vehicles and the rules that grant access to pension fund resources) are made mostly outside of Congress and partisan politics. Asset-specific industry associations that push for these reforms purposefully avoid these essentially "democratic" domains and, instead, act in less salient bureaucratic arenas. This dynamic is not specific to Latin America. Cases outside of the region appear to follow a similar logic, reinforcing the evidence from the case studies. This finding suggests that the quiet politics dynamics is not just a function of Latin America's under-developed PE markets or less institutionalized parties and legislatures, but a more general characteristic of this type of regulation.

Consequently, this research calls into question the literature's macro-level relationship between political institutions and the development of financial markets. The reforms that foster private capital markets do not seem to follow the mechanisms implicit in arguments that relate democracy with financial development. Although government expropriation doubtlessly jeopardize markets, equity markets do not simply unleash with more constrained executive powers. And reforms do not appear to be pushed by popular support either. The case of private capital markets suggests a review of the specific mechanisms through which democracy drives financial development. And more broadly, encourages a deeper assessment of the channels through which political regimes impact policymaking in other areas (Simison 2019), especially in those related to the expansion of markets.

From an organizational perspective, public agencies—both multilateral and domestic—help industry participants organize. The public sponsorship of business associations is surprisingly consistent across Latin America as well as in other regions. Public agencies promote business collective action, who then help "co-produce" the industry's regulatory framework. For those with an interest on interest group politics, this example of "micro-level corporatism" is in itself intriguing. And suggests possible inquiries into other industries and policy areas.

The quiet politics logic underlying the emergence of the private capital industry can raise a normative concern about democratic accountability. It also signals the practical limits of quiet politics as a strategy to promote the industry. While this approach may be successful at the micro-level, broader more structural change probably requires appealing to larger audiences beyond regulators and financial bureaucracies, limiting the feasibility of a quiet politics strategy.

The quiet politics explanation also exposes the scope of the arguments advanced in this book. The evidence from the empirical cases suggests some skepticism toward the rather linear relationship between democratic political institutions, property rights, and the expansion of markets, as portrayed in the literature. This book directs the attention to the role of government-related institutional investors, whose origin is not market-based and therefore not just intermediate steps in a longer causal chain that connect institutions and financial outcomes. Still, it leaves mostly unanswered the deeper question about the political economy origins of capable and autonomous institutional investors and their push for business modernization.

7.3 Financial Productive Policymaking: The State and Pension Funds

This work also characterizes a novel model of "financial" productive policymaking. And as part of its actor-based approach, it emphasizes a specific type of financial bureaucracies as well as the fundamental role of pension funds in developing more complete equity markets.

The book documents the extensive use of private equity as a policy instrument in otherwise market-oriented economies. States promote private equity with the "horizontal" purpose of building more robust capital markets and increasing firm's access to equity capital, otherwise elusive. Many initiatives also channel public resources through privately-managed equity funds in a more targeted way, with a focus on specific sectors. This novel policymaking model seems to be part of a paradigm shift in the way states intervene in markets: it has finance at its core and prioritizes the private sector as the main driver of development.

New "industrial" policy models have focused on policies promoting cost discovery activities and facilitating coordination among firms (e.g. Hausmann and Rodrik 2003; Rodrik 2004; Sabel et al. 2012). For the most part, they overlooked the financial side of new ventures, as well as its corporate governance. This research can help complement this literature. I call this model "financial" productive policymaking because it has finance at its core and privileges the investment channel above other policy instruments (e.g. trade regulations, R&D subsidies, tax exemptions, local content requirements, etc.). Through these policy initiatives, the state intends to "crowd-in" private investors. To do so, it often outsources capital allocation decisions to private fund managers. By acting as intermediaries between governments and target companies, PE firms can help relax some major agency issues. At the expense of losing some control, policymakers can expect to achieve better governance schemes and improve their screening and monitoring capacities. And by maintaining an arms-length relationship with firms, they can discourage rent-seeking behavior.

The cases of states investing in private equity and "outsourcing" policy-making through private fund managers have multiplied across the globe, particularly in Asia and Europe. Similar policy designs diffused across regions, as policymakers learn from the experiences of other countries. Multilateral development institutions appear to be one of the key vectors for the diffusion of these policies. They not only participate as investors, but also promote and advise in the design of policy interventions and regulatory frameworks. This diffusion effect is noteworthy, for example, in the promotion of asset-specific industry associations as well as in the creation of government-sponsored fund of funds.

Diffusion dynamics also appear to be behind arguably misplaced policies that sometimes reproduce a one-size-fits-all "Silicon Valley Consensus" (Armstrong 2016; Piore 2017) in environments where they are unlikely to succeed. For example, high-tech digital start-ups are promoted without consideration of the suitability of this model with local realities. These policies are probably as ineffective, and certainly more expensive, as sanctioning laws protecting minority shareholder rights and just waiting for capital markets to emerge. Policies that work have to adapt the model to make it "contextually rational" (Klingler-Vidra 2018). The capacity to overcome blunt isomorphism is, ultimately, one of the key indicators of state capacities (Guillén and Capron 2016).

Regarding state capacities, this book emphasizes the role of government-affiliated investors who exhibit autonomy from politicians and bureaucracies and have extensive linkages to the private sector, in line with the idea of embedded autonomy (Evans 1995; Fukuyama 2013). This novel type of financial bureaucracies is typically structured as separate entities from the rest of the state administration. In many cases, they also operate with some independence from the development institutions they are part of; some of them even have private shareholders. This enhanced autonomy enables them to operate with similar standards to those of the private sector, pay competitive salaries and build a reputation that allows them to attract talent. And arguably, it also grants them with the flexibility to better interact with the private sector and avoid pervasive adverse selection when partnering with fund managers.

Close interaction with the private sector appears as necessary condition for the successful implementation of government-sponsored investment programs. Rather than disciplining business, the key challenge is to attract and partner with external investors. In terms of outcomes, the "sweet spot" of government-funded private capital initiatives appears to be when government funds are paired with third-party sources of capital, and the state is able to effectively crowd-in other local and international private investors (Brander et al. 2015; Fuller 2016; Lerner 2009). The obstacles to this close interaction are not just technical, but also political. Particularly in contexts where business legitimacy is low, combining public and private money is politically very challenging (Di Tella et al. 2016).

The case studies also suggest that the participation of pension funds is a key step toward the viability of private capital markets. Government programs that invest in private equity usually intend to leverage local pension funds. Gaining access to pension fund resources is also the number one priority in the agenda of private capital industry associations. The main policy challenge is to create the channels that connect large pools of institutional capital—such as resources from pension funds—with long-term productive investments. And doing it in a way that prevents financial repression and expropriations and does not jeopardize the sustainability and financial returns of the pension system. As this book has hopefully pointed out, the creation of these "channels" is not automatic. It requires specific pieces of regulation, as well as the emergence of multiple specialized intermediaries including asset-specific fund managers and various service providers. Ultimately, the creation of these channels derives from extensive private-public collaboration.

Beyond its focus on private equity, this book raises the awareness of the role of pension funds in financial markets. As part of an actor-centered approach to financial development, its findings suggest a broader political economy agenda around the role of pension funds in capital markets.

Pension funds accumulate massive amounts of long-term capital as a result of compulsory saving schemes. The way these funds are invested has major political economy implications and significant potential to affect firm ownership structures and corporate governance practices. Through its narrow focus on private equity, this book only began to explore this extensive topic.

There is considerable variation in how pension funds are structured and regulated across the world. While defined contribution plans gained popularity in the last couple of decades, defined-benefit plans are still common. Publicly-run schemes co-exist with privately-managed systems. There is also a great deal of variation in how pension funds allocate their capital.[1] Beyond the exposure to "alternative" assets like private equity, there are differences in the composition of their investment portfolios across multiple dimensions. For example, the extent to which pension funds are used as captive investors to finance the public sector, how much of the capital is invested outside domestic markets, the proportion of equity vs. debt, or whether they outsource to third-party asset managers or build in-house investment teams. And even more broadly, the extent to which pension funds play an activist corporate role as investors and make use of their "voice" on issues as varied as gender relations in the workplace, environmental sustainability, executive pay and share buy-backs (e.g. Henderson et al. 2020). Variation observed across countries does not appear to reconcile with traditional political economy frameworks, such as varieties of capitalism, and has not been explored through a development lens. A systematic understanding of the causes and consequences of these variations is an exciting—and promising—research agenda.

[1] For a description of how pension funds are organized across different countries, and the extent to which their regulatory framework as well as their portfolio allocations varies, see PWC (2020) report.

References

Armstrong, Ben. 2016. Unraveling the Silicon Valley Consensus. *Boston Review*.

Bloom, Nicholas, Raffaella Sadun, and John Van Reenen. 2015. Do Private Equity Owned Firms Have Better Management Practices? *American Economic Review* 105 (5): 442–446.

Brander, J.A., Q. Du, and T. Hellmann. 2015. The Effects of Government-Sponsored Venture Capital: International Evidence. *Review of Finance* 19 (2): 571–618.

Davis, Steven J., et al. 2014. Private Equity, Jobs, and Productivity. *The American Economic Review* 104: 3956–3990.

Davis, Steven J. et al. 2019. *The Economic Effects of Private Equity Buyouts*.

Di Tella, Rafael, Juan Dubra, and Alejandro Luis Lagomarsino. 2016. *Meet the Oligarchs: Business Legitimacy, State Capacity and Taxation*. Cambridge, MA.

Evans, Peter B. 1995. *Embedded Autonomy: States and Industrial Transformation*. Princeton: Princeton University Press.

Fukuyama, Francis. 2013. What Is Governance? *Governance* 26 (3): 347–368.

Fuller, Douglas B. 2016. *Paper Tigers, Hidden Dragons: Firms and the Political Economy of China's Technological Development*. New York: Oxford University Press.

Guillén, Mauro F., and Laurence Capron. 2016. State Capacity, Minority Shareholder Protections, and Stock Market Development. *Administrative Science Quarterly* 61 (1): 125–160.

Hausmann, Ricardo, and Dani Rodrik. 2003. Economic Development as Self-Discovery. *Journal of Development Economics* 72 (2): 603–633.

Henderson, Rebecca, George Serafeim, Josh Lerner, and Naoko Jinjo. 2020. HBS Case *Should a Pension Fund Try to Change the World? Inside GPIF's Embrace of ESG*.

Klingler-Vidra, Robyn. 2018. *The Venture Capital State: The Silicon Valley Model in East Asia*. Ithaca: Cornell University Press.

Lerner, Josh. 2009. *Boulevard of Broken Dreams: Why Public Efforts to Boost Entrepreneurship and Venture Capital Have Failed, and What to Do About It*. Princeton: Princeton University Press.

Lerner, Josh, Morten Sorensen, and Per Strömberg. 2011. Private Equity and Long-Run Investment: The Case of Innovation. *The Journal of Finance* 66 (2): 445–477.

Phalippou, Ludovic. 2020. *An Inconvenient Fact: Private Equity Returns & The Billionaire Factory*.

Piore, Micheal. 2017. *Economic Policy in the Time of Reactionary Populism*.

Puente, Ignacio, and Ben Ross Schneider. 2020. Business and Development: How Organization, Ownership and Networks Matter. *Review of International Political Economy*: 1–25.

PWC. 2020. *Beyond Their Borders: Evolution of Foreign Investments by Pension Funds*.

Rin, Marco da, Thomas Hellmann, and Manju Puri. 2013. A Survey of Venture Capital Research. In *Handbook of the Economics of Finance*, 573–648. Amsterdam: Elsevier B.V.

Rodrik, Dani. 2004. Industrial Policy for the Twenty-First Century.

Sabel, Charles F., et al. 2012. *Export Pioneers in Latin America*. Washington, DC: Inter-American Development Bank.

Simison, Emilia. 2019. *Democracies, Dictatorships, and Policy Change*.

References

Abiad, Abdul, Enrica Detragiache, and Thierry Tressel. 2010. A New Database of Financial Reforms. *IMF Staff Papers* 57 (2): 281–302.

Abraham, Facundo, Juan Cortina, and Sergio L. Schmukler. 2019. *The Rise of Domestic Capital Markets for Corporate Financing.*

ABRAPP. 2014. *The Brazilian Pension System.*

ACAFI. 2018. *Reporte Venture Capital & Private Equity 2016–2017.*

Acemoglu, Daron, Simon Johnson, and James A. Robinson. 2001. The Colonial Origins of Comparative Development: An Empirical Investigation. *American Economic Review* 91 (5): 1369–1401.

———. 2005. Institutions as a Fundamental Cause of Long-Run Growth. In *Handbook of Economic Growth*, ed. Philippe Aghion and Steven Durlauf, 385–472. Amsterdam: North-Holland.

Acharya, Viral V., Oliver F. Gottschalg, Moritz Hahn, and Conor Kehoe. 2013. Corporate Governance and Value Creation: Evidence from Private Equity. *The Review of Financial Studies* 26 (2): 368–402.

Aggarwal, Reena, Isil Erel, Miguel Ferreira, and Pedro Matos. 2011. Does Governance Travel Around the World? Evidence from Institutional Investors. *Journal of Financial Economics* 100 (1): 154–181.

Agrawal, Ashwini, and Prasanna Tambe. 2016. Private Equity and Workers' Career Paths: The Role of Technological Change. *Review of Financial Studies* 29 (9): 2455–2489.

Aguilera, Ruth V., and Rafel Crespi-Cladera. 2016. Global Corporate Governance: On the Relevance of Firms' Ownership Structure. *Journal of World Business* 51 (1): 50–57.

I. Puente, *Private Equity and Financial Development in Latin America*, Latin American Political Economy,
https://doi.org/10.1007/978-3-030-88983-8

Aguilera, Ruth V., and Gregory Jackson. 2010. Comparative and International Corporate Governance. *Academy of Management Annals* 4 (1): 485–556.

Aguilera, Ruth V., Ricardo L. Kabbach De Castro, Jun Ho Lee, and Jihae You. 2012. Corporate Governance in Emerging Markets. In *Capitalisms and Capitalism in the Twenty-First Century*, ed. Glenn Morgan and Richard Whitley. Oxford: Oxford University Press.

Ahlstrom, David, Garry D. Bruton, and Kuang S. Yeh. 2007. Venture Capital in China: Past, Present, and Future. *Asia Pacific Journal of Management* 24 (3): 247–268.

Aldunate, Felipe, Felipe Gonzaalez, Mounu Prem, and Francisco Urzua. 2020. *Privatization and Business Groups: Evidence from the Chicago Boys in Chile.*

Alfaro, Laura. 2017. Gains from Foreign Direct Investment: Macro and Micro Approaches. *The World Bank Economic Review* 30: S2–15.

Aminadav, Gur, and Elias Papaioannou. 2020. Corporate Control Around the World. *The Journal of Finance* 75 (3): 1191–1246.

Anzia, Sarah F., and Terry M. Moe. 2019. Interest Groups on the Inside: The Governance of Public Pension Funds. *Perspectives on Politics* 17 (4): 1059–1078.

Appelbaum, Eileen, and Rosemary Batt. 2014. *Private Equity at Work: When Wall Street Manages Main Street*. New York: Russell Sage Foundation.

Armstrong, Ben. 2016. Unraveling the Silicon Valley Consensus. *Boston Review*.

Avnimelech, Gil. 2009. VC Policy: Yozma Program 15-Years Perspective. *SSRN Electronic Journal*.

Avnimelech, Gil, Martin Kenney, and Morris Teubal. 2004. *Building Venture Capital Industries: Understanding the U.S. and Israeli Experiences.*

Ayyagari, Meghana, Pedro Juarros, Maria Soledad Martinez Peria, and Sandeep Singh. 2021. Access to Finance and Job Growth: Firm-Level Evidence Across Developing Countries. *Review of Finance* 25 (5): 1473–1496.

Bain & Company. 2020. *Global Private Equity Report 2020.*

Balan, Pablo, Juan Dodyk, and Ignacio Puente. 2021. *The Political Behavior of Family Firms: Evidence From Brazil.*

Baltin, Matthias, and Philipp Bell. 2001. Venture Capital in South America: Unlocking the Potential for Venture Creation in an Emerging Market. WHU.

Bancoldex. 2015. *Informe de La Junta Directiva y Del Presidente a La Asamblea General de Accionistas.*

———. 2016. *Informe de La Junta Directiva y Del Presidente a La Asamblea General de Accionistas.*

———. 2017. *Informe de La Junta Directiva y Del Presidente a La Asamblea General de Accionistas.*

Barker, Roger, and David Rueda. 2007. SSRN Electronic Journal *The Labor Market Determinants of Corporate Governance Reform.* Elsevier BV.

Bebchuk, Lucian A., and Michael S. Weisbach. 2010. The State of Corporate Governance Research. *Review of Financial Studies* 23 (3): 939–961.

Bebchuk, Lucian A., Alma Cohen, and Scott Hirst. 2017. The Agency Problems of Institutional Investors. *Journal of Economic Perspectives* 31 (3): 89–112.

Beck, Thorsten. 2016. *Long-Term Finance in Latin America.*

Beck, Thorsten, and Ross Levine. 2004. Stock Markets, Banks, and Growth: Panel Evidence. *Journal of Banking and Finance* 28 (3): 423–442.

Beck, Thorsten, and Maria Soledad Martinez Peria. 2008. *Foreign Bank Acquisitions and Outreach: Evidence from Mexico.*

Beck, Thorsten, Berrak Büyükkarabacak, Felix K. Rioja, and Neven T. Valev. 2012. Who Gets the Credit? And Does It Matter? Household vs. Firm Lending Across Countries. *B.E. Journal of Macroeconomics* 12 (1): 1–46.

Beck, Thorsten, Asli Demirguc-Kunt, Luc Laeven, and Ross Levine. 2008. Finance, Firm Size, and Growth. *Journal of Money, Credit and Banking* 40 (7): 1379–1405.

Beck, Thorsten, Vasso Ioannidou, and Larissa Schäfer. 2018. Foreigners vs. Natives: Bank Lending Technologies and Loan Pricing. *Management Science* 64 (8): 3792–3820.

Bedu, Nicolas, and Matthieu Montalban. 2014. Analysing the Uneven Development of Private Equity in Europe: Legal Origins and Diversity of Capitalism. *Socio-Economic Review* 12 (1): 33–70.

Benquet, Marlène, and Théo Bourgeron. 2020. Building a Centre of Capital Accumulation: A Study of the Institutional Emergence of the French Private Equity Sector (from the Early 1980s to 2017). *New Political Economy* 26 (2): 1–17.

Berger, Allen N., and Gregory F. Udell. 1998. The Economics of Small Business Finance: The Roles of Private Equity and Debt Markets in the Financial Growth Cycle. *Journal of Banking & Finance* 22 (6–8): 613–673.

Berle, Adolf, and Gardiner Means. 1932. *The Modern Corporate and Private Property.*

Bernstein, Shai, and Albert Sheen. 2016. The Operational Consequences of Private Equity Buyouts: Evidence from the Restaurant Industry. *Review of Financial Studies* 29 (9): 2387–2418.

Bernstein, Shai, Josh Lerner, and Filippo Mezzanotti. 2019. Private Equity and Financial Fragility During the Crisis. *The Review of Financial Studies* 32 (4): 1309–1373.

Bernstein, Shai, Josh Lerner, and Antoinette Schoar. 2013. The Investment Strategies of Sovereign Wealth Funds. *Journal of Economic Perspectives* 27 (2): 219–238.

Bernstein, Shai, Josh Lerner, Morten Sorensen, and Per Strömberg. 2017. Private Equity and Industry Performance. *Management Science* 63 (4): 1198–1213.

Bertrand, Marianne, and Antoinette Schoar. 2006. The Role of Family in Family Firms. *Journal of Economic Perspectives* 20 (2): 73–96.

Bloom, Nicholas, and J. Van Reenen. 2007. Measuring and Explaining Management Practices Across Firms and Countries. *The Quarterly Journal of Economics* 122 (4): 1351–1408.

Bloom, Nicholas, and John Van Reenen. 2010. Why Do Management Practices Differ Across Firms and Countries? *Journal of Economic Perspectives* 24 (1): 203–224.

Bloom, Nicholas, et al. 2013. Does Management Matter? Evidence from India. *The Quarterly Journal of Economics* 128 (1): 1–51.

Bloom, Nicholas, Raffaella Sadun, and John Van Reenen. 2015. Do Private Equity Owned Firms Have Better Management Practices? *American Economic Review* 105 (5): 442–446.

Borsato da Silva, Filipe, and Fabio Luiz Biagini. 2016. *Capital de Risco e o Desenvolvimento de Empresas de Base Tecnológica No Brasil – a Experiência Dos Fundos Criatec e Perspectivas.*

Boucly, Quentin, David Sraer, and David Thesmar. 2011. Growth LBOs. *Journal of Financial Economics* 102 (2): 432–453.

Brander, J.A., Q. Du, and T. Hellmann. 2015. The Effects of Government-Sponsored Venture Capital: International Evidence. *Review of Finance* 19 (2): 571–618.

Braunstein, Juergen. 2019. *Capital Choice: Sectoral Politics and the Variation of Sovereign Wealth Funds*. Ann Arbor, MI: University of Michigan Press.

Bril-Mascarenhas, Tomás. 2016. *How States Shape Markets in Latin America.* PhD dissertation, University of California, Berkeley.

Bril-Mascarenhas, Tomás, and Aldo Madariaga. 2019. Business Power and the Minimal State: The Defeat of Industrial Policy in Chile. *The Journal of Development Studies* 55 (6): 1047–1066.

Bril-Mascarenhas, Tomás, and Antoine Maillet. 2019. How to Build and Wield Business Power: The Political Economy of Pension Regulation in Chile, 1990–2018. *Latin American Politics and Society* 61 (1): 101–125.

Brooke, Peter A., and Daniel Penrice. 2009. *A Vision for Venture Capital: Realizing the Promise of Global Venture Capital and Private Equity*. Boston: New Ventures Press.

Brown, Gregory W., et al. 2015. What Do Different Commercial Data Sets Tell Us About Private Equity Performance? *SSRN Electronic Journal.*

Brown, Michael, and Pavneet Singh. 2018. *China's Technology Transfer Strategy: How Chinese Investments in Emerging Technology Enable a Strategic Competitor to Access the Crown Jewels of U.S. Innovation.*

Bruhn, Miriam, and Inessa Love. 2014. The Real Impact of Improved Access to Finance: Evidence from Mexico. *Journal of Finance* 69 (3): 1347–1376.

Bruhn, Miriam, Dean Karlan, and Antoinette Schoar. 2010. What Capital Is Missing in Developing Countries? *American Economic Review* 100 (2): 629–633.

Campello, Daniela. 2015. *The Politics of Market Discipline in Latin America: Globalization and Democracy*. Cambridge: Cambridge University Press.

Carney, Richard W., and Travers Barclay Child. 2013. Changes to the Ownership and Control of East Asian Corporations Between 1996 and 2008: The Primacy of Politics. *Journal of Financial Economics* 107 (2): 494–513.

Caselli, Francesco. 2014. *The Latin American Efficiency Gap*.

Catão, Luis A.V., Carmen Pagés, and María Fernanda Rosales. 2009. *Financial Dependence, Formal Credit and Informal Jobs: New Evidence from Brazilian Household Data*.

Çelik, Serdar, and Mats Isaksson. 2013. *Institutional Investors as Owners: Who Are They and What Do They Do?*

Cendrowski, Harry, James P. Martin, Louis W. Petro, and Adam A. Wadecki. 2011. *Private Equity History, Governance, and Operations*. Wiley.

Center for Global Development. 2019. *Making Basel III Work for Emerging Markets and Developing Economies*.

Chandler, Alfred Dupont. 1977. *The Visible Hand: The Managerial Revolution in American Business*. Cambridge: Belknap Press.

Charvel, Roberto, and Juan Carlos de Yeregui. 2002. Private Equity in Latin America: The Mexican Case. *The Journal of Private Equity*: 1–12.

Cheibub, José Antonio, Jennifer Gandhi, and James Raymond Vreeland. 2010. Democracy and Dictatorship Revisited. *Public Choice* 143 (1): 67–101.

Chemmanur, Thomas J., Karthik Krishnan, and Debarshi K. Nandy. 2011. How Does Venture Capital Financing Improve Efficiency in Private Firms? A Look Beneath the Surface. *Review of Financial Studies* 24 (12): 4037–4090.

Chong, Alberto, and Florencio Lopez-de-Silanes. 2007. *Investor Protection and Corporate Governance: Firm-Level Evidence Across Latin America*. Stanford: Inter-American Development Bank/Stanford University Press.

Cihak, Martin, Asli Demirguc-Kunt, Erik Feyen, and Ross Levine. 2012. Benchmarking Financial Systems Around the World, 1–58.

Cioffi, John W., and Martin Höpner. 2006. The Political Paradox of Finance Capitalism: Interests, Preferences, and Center-Left Party Politics in Corporate Governance Reform. *Politics & Society* 34 (4): 463–502.

Claessens, Stijn, and Neeltje Van Horen. 2014. Foreign Banks: Trends and Impact. *Journal of Money, Credit and Banking* 46 (s1): 295–326.

Coffee, John C. 1999. The Future as History: The Prospects for Global Convergence in Corporate Governance and Its Implications. *Northwestern University Law Review* 93 (3): 641–707.

Cohen, Stephen D. 2007. *Multinational Corporations and Foreign Direct Investment: Avoiding Simplicity, Embracing Complexity*. Oxford: Oxford University Press.

Cohn, Jonathan, and Erin Towery. 2013. *The Determinants and Consequences of Private Equity Buyouts of Private Firms: Evidence from U.S. Corporate Tax Returns*.

Cohn, Jonathan B., Nicole Nestoriak, and Malcolm Wardlaw. 2019. *Private Equity Buyouts and Workplace Safety*.

Colombo, Massimo G., Douglas J. Cumming, and Silvio Vismara. 2016. Governmental Venture Capital for Innovative Young Firms. *Journal of Technology Transfer* 41 (1): 10–24.

Colpan, Asli M., and Takashi Hikino. 2018. *Business Groups in the West: Origins, Evolution, and Resilience*. Oxford: Oxford University Press.

Coopey, Richard. 1994. The First Venture Capitalist: Financing Development in Britain After 1945, The Case of ICFC/3i. *Business and Economic History* 23: 262–271.

Coopey, Richard, and Donald Clarke. 1995. *3i: Fifty Years Investing in Industry*. Oxford: Oxford University Press.

Coppedge, Michael, et al. 2019. V-Dem [Country-Year/Country-Date] Dataset V9. *Varieties of Democracy (V-Dem)*.

CORFO. 2018. *Informe Publico de Capital de Riesgo*.

Cornelius, Peter. 2011. *International Investments in Private Equity: Asset Allocation, Markets, and Industry Structure*. Amsterdam: Academic Press.

Cox, Gary W., and Scott Morgenstern. 2001. Latin America's Reactive Assemblies and Proactive Presidents. *Comparative Politics* 33 (2): 171–189.

Cox, Gary W., and Barry R. Weingast. 2018. Executive Constraint, Political Stability, and Economic Growth. *Comparative Political Studies* 51 (3): 279–303.

CPI Fundos de Pensao - Relatorio Final. 2016. Brasilia.

Culpepper, Pepper D. 2010. *Quiet Politics and Business Power: Corporate Control in Europe and Japan*. Cambridge: Cambridge University Press.

Da, Zhi, Borja Larrain, Clemens Sialm, and José Tessada. 2018. Destabilizing Financial Advice: Evidence from Pension Fund Reallocations. *The Review of Financial Studies* 31 (10): 3720–3755.

Datz, Giselle. 2012. The Inextricable Link Between Sovereign Debt and Pensions in Argentina, 1993–2010. *Latin American Politics and Society* 54 (01): 101–126.

Davis, Gerald F. 2009. *Managed by the Markets: How Finance Re-Shaped America*. Oxford: Oxford University Press.

Davis, Gerald F., and Suntae Kim. 2015. Financialization of the Economy. *Annual Review of Sociology* 41 (1): 203–221.

Davis, Steven J., et al. 2014. Private Equity, Jobs, and Productivity. *The American Economic Review* 104: 3956–3990.

———. 2019. *The Economic Effects of Private Equity Buyouts.*

Deeg, Richard, and Iain Hardie. 2016. What Is Patient Capital and Who Supplies It? *Socio-Economic Review* 14 (4): 627–645.

Dell, Melissa. 2010. The Persistent Effects of Peru's Mining Mita. *Econometrica* 78 (6): 1863–1903.

Demekas, Dimitri, and Anica Nerlich. 2020. *Creating Domestic Capital Markets in Developing Countries: Perspectives from Market Participants.*

Dieguez, Consuelo. 2009. Sergio Rosa e o Mundo Dos Fundos. *Piaui.*

Doidge, Craig, G. Andrew Karolyi, and René M. Stulz. 2017. The U.S. Listing Gap. *Journal of Financial Economics* 123 (3): 464–487.

Donelli, Marcelo, Borja Larrain, and I. Francisco Urzúa. 2013. Ownership Dynamics with Large Shareholders: An Empirical Analysis. *Journal of Financial and Quantitative Analysis* 48 (2): 579–609.

Durand, Francisco, and Eduardo Silva. 1998. *Organized Business, Economic Change, and Democracy in Latin America.* Coral Gables: North-South Center Press.

Dyck, Alexander, and Luigi Zingales. 2004. Private Benefits of Control: An International Comparison. *The Journal of Finance* 59 (2): 537–600.

Eaton, Charlie, Sabrina T. Howell, and Constantine Yannelis. 2019. When Investor Incentives and Consumer Interests Diverge: Private Equity in Higher Education. *The Review of Financial Studies* 33 (9): 4024–4060.

EIB. 2018. *Facts & Figures.*

EMPEA. 2012. *The Evolution of PE in China.*

———. 2016. *Special Report: Private Equity in Mexico.*

van Essen, Marc, J. (Hans) van Oosterhout, and Pursey P.M.A.R. Heugens. 2013. Competition and Cooperation in Corporate Governance: The Effects of Labor Institutions on Blockholder Effectiveness in 23 European Countries. *Organization Science* 24 (2): 530–551.

Etchemendy, Sebastián. 2011. *Models of Economic Liberalization: Business, Workers, and Compensation in Latin America, Spain, and Portugal.* Cambridge: Cambridge University Press.

Etchemendy, Sebastián, and Ignacio Puente. 2017. Power and Crisis: Explaining Varieties of Commercial Banking Systems in Argentina, Brazil and Mexico. *Journal of Politics in Latin America* 9 (1).

Evans, Peter B. 1995. *Embedded Autonomy: States and Industrial Transformation.* Princeton: Princeton University Press.

Ewens, Michael, and Joan Farre-Mensa. 2019. *The Deregulation of the Private Equity Markets and the Decline in IPOs By.*

EY. 2015. *Estudio Sobre La Industria de Capital Emprendedor En Mexico.*

Faccio, Mara, and Hung-Chia. Hsu. 2017. Politically Connected Private Equity and Employment. *The Journal of Finance* 72 (2): 539–574.

Fairfield, Tasha. 2015. *Private Wealth and Public Revenue in Latin America: Business Power and Tax Politics*. New York: Cambridge University Press.

Fernández-Arias, Eduardo, Charles F. Sabel, Ernesto Stein, and Alberto Trejos. 2016. *Two to Tango: Public-Private Collaboration for Productive Development Policies*. Washington, DC: Inter-American Development Bank.

Fracassi, Cesare, Alessandro Previtero, and Albert Sheen. 2020. *Barbarians at the Store? Private Equity, Products, and Consumers.*

Fukuyama, Francis. 2013. What Is Governance? *Governance* 26 (3): 347–368.

———. 2014. *Political Order and Political Decay*. New York: Straus and Giroux Farrar.

Fuller, Douglas B. 2016. *Paper Tigers, Hidden Dragons: Firms and the Political Economy of China's Technological Development*. New York: Oxford University Press.

Gerschenkron, Alexander. 1962. *Economic Backwardness in Historical Perspective: A Book of Essays*. Cambridge: Harvard University Press.

Girma, S., and A. Shortland. 2007. The Political Economy of Financial Development. *Oxford Economic Papers* 60 (4): 567–596.

Goldsmith, Raymond. 1969. *Financial Structure and Development*. New Haven: Yale University Press.

Gomes Schapiro, Mario. 2013. Rediscovering the Developmental Path? Development Bank, Law, and Innovation Financing in the Brazilian Economy. In *Law and the New Developmental State: The Brazilian Experience in Latin American Context*, ed. David M. Trubek, Helena Alviar Garcia, Diogo R. Coutinho, and Alvaro Santos. Cambridge: Cambridge University Press.

Gomez, Edmund Terence, et al. 2018. *Minister of Finance Incorporated: Ownership and Control in Corporate Malaysia*. Singapore: Palgrave Macmillan.

Gompers, Paul A. 1994. The Rise and Fall of Venture Capital. *Business and Economic History* 23 (2): 1–24.

Gormley, Todd A. 2010. The Impact of Foreign Bank Entry in Emerging Markets: Evidence from India. *Journal of Financial Intermediation* 19 (1): 26–51.

Gourevitch, Peter, and James Shinn. 2005. *Political Power and Corporate Control: The New Global Politics of Corporate Governance*. Princeton: Princeton University Press.

Goyer, Michel. 2011. *Contingent Capital Short-Term Investors and the Evolution of Corporate Governance in France and Germany*. Oxford: Oxford University Press.

Griffith-Jones, Stephany, and José Antonio Ocampo, eds. 2018. *The Future of National Development Banks*. Oxford: Oxford University Press.

Griffith-Jones, Stephany, and Judith Tyson. 2013. *The European Investment Bank: Lessons for Developing Countries.*

Guillén, Mauro F., and Laurence Capron. 2016. State Capacity, Minority Shareholder Protections, and Stock Market Development. *Administrative Science Quarterly* 61 (1): 125–160.

Guiso, Luigi, Paola Sapienza, and Luigi Zingales. 2004. The Role of Social Capital in Financial Development. *American Economic Review* 94 (3): 526–556.

Haber, Stephen H., Douglass C. North, and Barry R. Weingast. 2008. *Political Institutions and Financial Development*. Stanford: Stanford University Press.

Haggard, Stephan, and Robert R. Kaufman. 2008. *Development, Democracy, and Welfare States: Latin America, East Asia, and Eastern Europe*. Princeton: Princeton University Press.

Haggard, Stephen, and Sylvia Maxfield. 1996. The Political Economy of Financial Internationalization in the Developing World. *International Organization* 50 (01): 35.

Haggard, Stephan, Andrew MacIntyre, and Lydia Tiede. 2008. The Rule of Law and Economic Development. *Annual Review of Political Science* 11 (1): 205–234.

Hall, Peter A., and David W. Soskice. 2001. *Varieties of Capitalism: The Institutional Foundations of Comparative Advantage*. Oxford: Oxford University Press.

Hardie, Iain, David Howarth, Sylvia Maxfield, and Amy Verdun. 2013. Banks and the False Dichotomy in the Comparative Political Economy of Finance. *World Politics* 65 (04): 691–728.

Harris, Robert S., Tim Jenkinson, and Steven N. Kaplan. 2014. Private Equity Performance: What Do We Know? *The Journal of Finance* 69 (5): 1851–1882.

Hausmann, Ricardo, and Dani Rodrik. 2003. Economic Development as Self-Discovery. *Journal of Development Economics* 72 (2): 603–633.

Hellmann, Thomas, and Manju Puri. 2002. Venture Capital and the Professionalization of Start-Up Firms: Empirical Evidence. *The Journal of Finance* 57 (1): 169–197.

Henderson, Rebecca, George Serafeim, Josh Lerner, and Naoko Jinjo. 2020. HBS Case *Should a Pension Fund Try to Change the World? Inside GPIF's Embrace of ESG.*

Heng, Dyna, et al. 2016. *Advancing Financial Development in Latin America and the Caribbean.*

Herrera, Ana Maria, and Eduardo Lora. 2005. Why So Small? Explaining the Size of Firms in Latin America. *The World Economy* 28 (7): 1005–1028.

Hirschman, Albert O. 1970. *Exit, Voice, and Loyalty: Responses to Decline in Firms, Organizations, and States*. Cambridge: Harvard University Press.

Hochstetler, Kathryn, and Alfred P. Montero. 2013. The Renewed Developmental State: The National Development Bank and the Brazil Model. *Journal of Development Studies* 49 (11): 1484–1499.

Hotchkiss, Edie, David C. Smith, and Per Strömberg. 2010. *Private Equity and the Resolution of Financial Distress*. National Bureau of Economic Research, Inc.

Hsu, David H., and Martin Kenney. 2005. Organizing Venture Capital: The Rise and Demise of American Research & Development Corporation, 1946–1973. *Industrial and Corporate Change* 14 (4): 579–616.

Huang, Yongfu. 2010. Political Institutions and Financial Development: An Empirical Study. *World Development* 38 (12): 1667–1677.

Ibanez, Fernan. 1989. *Venture Capital and Entrepreneurial Development*. Washington, DC.

IDB/IIC. 2017. *Comparative Study of Equity Investing in Development Finance Institutions*. Washington, DC.

Inoue, Carlos F.K.V., Sergio G. Lazzarini, and Aldo Musacchio. 2013. Leviathan as a Minority Shareholder: Firm-Level Implications of State Equity Purchases. *Academy of Management Journal* 56 (6): 1775–1801.

Invest Europe. 2018. *2017 Central and Eastern Europe Private Equity Statistics*.

Invest Korea. 2015. *Private Equity & Venture Capital*.

Ivashina, Victoria, and Anna Kovner. 2011. The Private Equity Advantage: Leveraged Buyout Firms and Relationship Banking. *The Review of Financial Studies* 24 (7): 2462–2498.

Ivashina, Victoria, and Joshua Lerner. 2019. *Patient Capital: The Challenges and Promises of Long-Term Investing*. Princeton: Princeton University Press.

Jain, Nitin, et al. 2017. *Deepening Capital Markets in Emerging Economies*.

Jeng, Leslie, and Josh Lerner. 2016. Making Private Data Accessible in an Opaque Industry: The Experience of the Private Capital Research Institute. *American Economic Review* 106 (5): 157–160.

Jeng, Leslie A., and Philippe C. Wells. 2000. The Determinants of Venture Capital Funding: Evidence Across Countries. *Journal of Corporate Finance* 6 (3): 241–289.

Jensen, Michael Cole. 1989. The Eclipse of the Public Corporation. *Harvard Business Review*, September.

Jensen, Michael C., and William H. Meckling. 1976. Theory of the Firm: Managerial Behavior, Agency Costs and Ownership Structure. *Journal of Financial Economics* 3 (4): 305–360.

Jiang, Wei, Kai Li, and Pei Shao. 2010. When Shareholders Are Creditors: Effects of the Simultaneous Holding of Equity and Debt by Non-Commercial Banking Institutions. *The Review of Financial Studies* 23 (10): 3595–3637.

Johnston-Ross, Emily, Song Ma, and Manju Puri. 2020. *Private Equity and Financial Stability: Evidence from Failed Bank Resolution in the Crisis*.

Jones Luong, Pauline, and Erika Weinthal. 2010. *Oil Is Not a Curse: Ownership Structure and Institutions in Soviet Successor States*. Cambridge: Cambridge University Press.

Kaplan, Steven N. 1989. The Effects of Management Buyouts on Operating Performance and Value. *Journal of Financial Economics* 24 (2): 217–254.

Kaplan, Steven N., and Josh Lerner. 2010. It Ain't Broke: The Past, Present, and Future of Venture Capital. *Journal of Applied Corporate Finance* 22 (2): 36–47.

Kaplan, Steven N., and Per Strömberg. 2001. Venture Capitalists as Principals: Contracting, Screening, and Monitoring. *The American Economic Review* 91: 426–430.

———. 2009. Leveraged Buyouts and Private Equity. *Journal of Economic Perspectives* 23 (1): 121–146.

Karsai, Judit. 2018. Government Venture Capital in Central and Eastern Europe. *Venture Capital* 20 (1): 73–102.

Kayo, Eduardo K., et al. 2018. Capital Structure Adjustment in Brazilian Family Firms. *Revista de Administração Contemporânea* 22 (1): 92–114.

KDB. 2016. *Annual Report*.

———. 2018. *KDB Annual Report 2018*.

Kenney, Martin. 2011. How Venture Capital Became a Component of the US National System of Innovation. *Industrial and Corporate Change* 20 (6): 1677–1723.

Kerner, Andrew. 2014. What We Talk About When We Talk About Foreign Direct Investment. *International Studies Quarterly* 58 (4): 804–815.

———. 2018. Pension Returns and Popular Support for Neoliberalism in Post-Pension Reform Latin America. *British Journal of Political Science* 50 (2): 1–36.

Khanna, Tarun, and Yishay Yafeh. 2007. Business Groups in Emerging Markets: Paragons or Parasites? *Journal of Economic Literature* 45 (2): 331–372.

Khoury, Theodore A., Marc Junkunc, and Santiago Mingo. 2015. Navigating Political Hazard Risks and Legal System Quality. *Journal of Management* 41 (3): 808–840.

King, R.G., and R. Levine. 1993. Finance and Growth: Schumpeter Might Be Right. *The Quarterly Journal of Economics* 108 (3): 717–737.

Klingler-Vidra, Robyn. 2018. *The Venture Capital State: The Silicon Valley Model in East Asia*. Ithaca: Cornell University Press.

Klonowski, Darek. 2006. Venture Capital as a Method of Financing Enterprise Development in Central and Eastern Europe. *International Journal of Emerging Markets* 1 (2): 165–175.

———. 2011a. *Private Equity in Poland: Winning Leadership in Emerging Markets*. New York: Palgrave Macmillan.

———. 2011b. Private Equity in Poland after Two Decades of Development: Evolution, Industry Drivers, and Returns. *Venture Capital* 13 (4): 295–311.

———. 2013. Private Equity in Emerging Markets: The New Frontiers of International Finance. *Journal of Private Equity* 16 (2): 20–37.

Ko, Haksoo, and Hyun Young Shin. 1999. Venture Capital in Korea? Special Law to Promote Venture Capital Companies. *American University International Law Review* 15 (2): 457–480.

Kochan, Thomas A. 2013. The American Jobs Crisis and Its Implication for the Future of Employment Policy: A Call for a New Jobs Compact. *ILR Review* 66 (2): 291–314.

Koh, Winston T.H., and Francis Koh. 2002. Venture Capital and Economic Growth: An Industry Overview and Singapore's Experience. *SSRN Electronic Journal*.

KPMG-ABVCAP. 2016. Consolidação de Dados. Indústria de Private Equity e Venture Capital No Brasil—2016.

Kraemer-Eis, Helmut, Simone Signore, and Dario Prencipe. 2016. The European Venture Capital Landscape: An EIF Perspective. *EIF Research & Market Analysis* Working Paper (Volume I: The impact of EIF on the VC ecosystem).

De La Cruz, A., A. Medina, and Y. Tang. 2019. *Owners of the World's Listed Companies*. OECD Capital Market Series, Paris.

Laeven, Luc. 2014. *The Development of Local Capital Markets: Rationale and Challenges*.

Larrain, Borja, and Urzúa I. Francisco. 2016. Do Business Groups Change with Market Development? *Journal of Economics & Management Strategy* 25 (3): 750–784.

Latini, Estevão Teixeira., Joaquim Rubens Fontes-Filho, and Eric L. Chambers. 2014. Private Equity and Corporate Governance: Managing Brazilian SMEs. *Corporate Governance* 14 (2): 220–237.

Lavelle, Kathryn C. 1999. International Financial Institutions and Emerging Capital Markets in Africa. *Review of International Political Economy* 6 (2): 200–224.

Lazonick, William, and Mary O'Sullivan. 2000. Maximizing Shareholder Value: A New Ideology for Corporate Governance. *Economy and Society* 29 (1): 13–35.

Lazzarini, Sérgio. G. 2010. *Capitalismo de Laços*. Elsevier.

Lazzarini, Sérgio. G., Aldo Musacchio, Rodrigo Bandeira-de-Mello, and Rosilene Marcon. 2015. What Do State-Owned Development Banks Do? Evidence from BNDES, 2002–09. *World Development* 66: 237–253.

Leal, Antonio Martinez, and Pino Del Sesto. 2013. *Private Equity in Mexico: Primed for Significant Growth*.

Leamon, Ann, and Josh Lerner. 2012. *Creating a Venture Ecosystem in Brazil: FINEP's INOVAR Project*.

Lee, Suil. 2008. The Development of Venture Capital Industry and the Role of Government in Korea: Venture Boom vs. Post-Boom. *KDI Journal of Economic Policy* 30 (1): 211–246.

Leeds, Roger. 2015. *Private Equity Investing in Emerging Markets: Opportunities for Value Creation*. New York: Palgrave Macmillan US.

Lemos, Renata, and Daniela Scur. 2012. *Management Practices, Firm Ownership, and Productivity in Latin America*.

Lerner, Josh. 2009. *Boulevard of Broken Dreams: Why Public Efforts to Boost Entrepreneurship and Venture Capital Have Failed, and What to Do About It*. Princeton: Princeton University Press.

Lerner, Josh, and Alberto Ballve. 2001. The Exxel Group. *HBS Case Collection*.

Lerner, Josh, and Antoinette Schoar. 2005. Does Legal Enforcement Affect Financial Transactions? The Contractual Channel in Private Equity. *The Quarterly Journal of Economics* 120 (1): 223–246.

Lerner, Josh, Alex Hoye, and Gonzalo Pacanins. 1997. The Exxel Group.

Lerner, Josh, Morten Sorensen, and Per Strömberg. 2011. Private Equity and Long-Run Investment: The Case of Innovation. *The Journal of Finance* 66 (2): 445–477.

Leslie, Armijo. 2017. The Public Bank Trilemma: Brazil's New Developmentalism and the BNDES. In *Democratic Brazil Divided*, ed. Peter R. Kingstone and Thimoty J. Power. Pittsburgh: University of Pittsburgh Press.

Leslie, Phillip, and Paul Oyer. 2008. Managerial Incentives and Strategic Change: Evidence from Private Equity. *National Bureau of Economic Research*.

Levine, Ross. 2005. Finance and Growth: Theory and Evidence. In *Handbook of Economic Growth*, ed. Philippe Aghion and Steven Durlauf, 865–934. Amsterdam: Elsevier.

Levine, Ross, and Sara Zervos. 1998. Stock Markets, Banks, and Economic Growth. *American Economic Review* 88 (3): 537–558.

Levine, Ross, Norman Loayza, and Thorsten Beck. 2000. Financial Intermediation and Growth: Causality and Causes. *Journal of Monetary Economics* 46 (1): 31–77.

Li, Quan, and Adam Resnick. 2003. Reversal of Fortunes: Democratic Institutions and Foreign Direct Investment Inflows to Developing Countries. *International Organization* 57 (1): 175–211.

Little, Bruce. 2008. *Fixing the Future: How Canada's Usually Fractious Governments Worked Together to Rescue the Canada Pension Plan*. Toronto: University of Toronto Press.

Mahoney, James. 2010. *Colonialism and Postcolonial Development: Spanish America in Comparative Perspective*. Cambridge: Cambridge University Press.

Márquez, Luis Antonio, and Fernando Sandoval-Arzaga. 2017. Myths and Realities of Family Offices in Mexico from an Investment Perspective. *Family Capital*.

Mauboussin, Michael J., and Dan Callahan. 2020. *Public to Private Equity in the United States: A Long-Term Look.*

Mazzucato, Mariana. 2018. Mission-Oriented Innovation Policies: Challenges and Opportunities. *Industrial and Corporate Change* 27 (5): 803–15. https://academic.oup.com/icc/article/27/5/803/5127692 (May 30, 2021).

Mazzucato, Mariana, and Caetano C.R. Penna. 2016. Beyond Market Failures: The Market Creating and Shaping Roles of State Investment Banks. *Journal of Economic Policy Reform* 19 (4): 305–326.

McCarthy, Michael A. 2014. Turning Labor into Capital: Pension Funds and the Corporate Control of Finance. *Politics & Society* 42 (4): 455–487.

McKinsey & Company. 2015. *The Virtuous Circle: Putting Korea's Startup Ecosystem on a Path to Sustainable Long-Run Growth.*

———. 2019. *Private Markets Come of Age: McKinsey Global Private Markets Review 2019.*

McWilliam, Micheal. 2001. *The Development Business: A History of the Commonwealth Development Corporation.* New York: Palgrave Macmillan.

Menaldo, Victor. 2016. The Fiscal Roots of Financial Underdevelopment. *American Journal of Political Science* 60 (2): 456–471.

Menaldo, Victor, and Daniel Yoo. 2015. Democracy, Elite Bias, and Financial Development in Latin America. *World Politics* 67 (04): 726–759.

Mian, Atif. 2006. Distance Constraints: The Limits of Foreign Lending in Poor Economies. *The Journal of Finance* 61 (3): 1465–1505.

Michelitsch, Roland, et al. 2017. *Comparative Study of Equity Investing in Development Finance Institutions.*

Minardi, Andrea Maria Accioly Fonseca, and Rafael Honório Bassani. 2016. *Investimentos Em Private Equity Feitos Por Fundos de Pensao Brasileiros.*

Minardi, Andrea Maria, Guilherme Lopes Ferrari, and Pedro Carvalho Araújo-Tavares. 2013. Performances of Brazilian IPOs Backed by Private Equity. *Journal of Business Research* 66 (3): 448–455.

Minardi, Andrea Maria Accioly Fonseca, Ricardo Vinicius Kanitz, and Rafael Honório Bassani. 2014. Private Equity and Venture Capital Industry Performance in Brazil: 1990–2013. *The Journal of Private Equity* 17: 48–58.

Moguillansky, Graciela, Rogerio Studart, and Sebastián Vergara. 2004. Foreign Banks in Latin America: A Paradoxical Result. *Cepal Review* 82: 19–35.

Monteiro Ramalho, Caio Cesar. 2013. An Essay on Private Equity: The History and Fundamentals of Fundraising in Brazil. FGV-EPGE.

Morck, Randall. 2005. *A History of Corporate Governance around the World: Family Business Groups to Professional Managers*, ed. Morck Randall. Chicago: University of Chicago Press.

Morck, Randall, and Bernard Yeung. 2004. Family Control and the Rent-Seeking Society. *Entrepreneurship Theory and Practice* 28 (4): 391–409.

Mosley, Layna. 2003. *Global Capital and National Governments*. Cambridge: Cambridge University Press.

Mueller, Holger M., and Thomas Philippon. 2011. Family Firms and Labor Relations. *American Economic Journal: Macroeconomics* 3 (2): 218–245.

Musacchio, Aldo. 2009. *Experiments in Financial Democracy*. Cambridge: Cambridge University Press.

Musacchio, Aldo, and Sérgio G. Lazzarini. 2014. *Reinventing State Capitalism: Leviathan in Business, Brazil and Beyond*. Cambridge: Harvard University Press.

Musacchio, Aldo, Sérgio. G. Lazzarini, and Ruth V. Aguilera. 2015. New Varieties of State Capitalism: Strategic and Governance Implications. *Academy of Management Perspectives* 29 (1): 115–131.

Musacchio, Aldo, Sérgio G. Lazzarini, Pedro Makhoul, and Emily Simmons. 2017. *The Role and Impact of Development Banks: A Review of Their Founding, Focus, and Influence*.

Naishtat, Silvia, and Pablo Maas. 2000. *El Cazador: La Historia Secreta de Los Negocios de Juan Navarro y El Grupo Exxel*. Planeta.

Nenova, Tatiana. 2003. The Value of Corporate Voting Rights and Control: A Cross-Country Analysis. *Journal of Financial Economics* 68 (3): 325–351.

———. 2006. Control Values and Changes in Corporate Law in Brazil. *Latin American Business Review* 6 (3): 1–37.

Noone, Charles M. 1968. The 1968 Model SBIC. *The Business Lawyer* 23: 1214–1220.

OECD. 2008. *OECD Benchmark Definition of Foreign Direct Investmen—4th Edition*.

———. 2018. *OECD Equity Market Review of Asia 2018*.

Ooghe, Herbert, Ann Bekaert, and Peter van den Bossche. 1989. Venture Capital in the U.S.A., Europe and Japan. *Management International Review* 29: 29–45.

Opazo, Luis, Claudio Raddatz, and Sergio L. Schmukler. 2014. *Institutional Investors and Long-Term Investment: Evidence from Chile*. The World Bank.

Overbeek, Henk, Bastiaan Van Apeldoorn, and Andreas Nölke. 2007. The Transnational Politics of Corporate Governance Regulation. In *The Transnational Politics of Corporate Governance Regulation*. New York: Routledge Taylor & Francis Group.

Pagano, Marco, and Paolo F. Volpin. 2005. The Political Economy of Corporate Governance. *The American Economic Review* 95: 1005–1030.

Pagés, Carmen. 2010. Big Questions About Small Firms. In *The Age of Productivity*, ed. Carmen Pagés, 207–222. New York: Palgrave Macmillan US.

Pandya, Sonal, and David Leblang. 2017. Risky Business: Institutions vs. Social Networks in FDI. *Economics & Politics* 29 (2): 91–117.

Panizza, Ugo, and Barry Borensztein, Eduardo Eichengreen. 2006. *Debt Instruments and Policies in the New Millennium: New Markets and New Opportunities*.

Parise, Gianpaolo, Fabrizio Leone, and Carlo Sommavilla. 2018. *Family First? Nepotism and Corporate Investment*.

Pereiro, Luis E. 2001. Tango and Cash: Entrepreneurial Finance and Venture Capital in Argentina. *Venture Capital* 3 (4): 291–308.

Perotti, Enrico C., and Ernst-Ludwig von Thadden. 2006. The Political Economy of Corporate Control and Labor Rents. *Journal of Political Economy* 114 (1): 145–175.

Phalippou, Ludovic. 2020. *An Inconvenient Fact: Private Equity Returns & The Billionaire Factory*.

Phalippou, Ludovic, Christian Rauch, and Marc Umber. 2018. Private Equity Portfolio Company Fees. *Journal of Financial Economics* 129 (3): 559–585.

Philippon, Thomas. 2015. Has the US Finance Industry Become Less Efficient? On the Theory and Measurement of Financial Intermediation. *American Economic Review* 105 (4): 1408–1438.

Pincus, Lionel. 2000. Warburg Pincus. In *Done Deals. Venture Capitalists Tell Their Stories*, ed. Uduyan Gupta, 415. Boston, MA: Harvard Business School Press.

Pinto, Pablo M., Stephen Weymouth, and Peter Gourevitch. 2010. The Politics of Stock Market Development. *Review of International Political Economy* 17 (2): 378–409.

Piore, Micheal. 2017. *Economic Policy in the Time of Reactionary Populism*.

Polanyi, Karl. 1944. *The Great Transformation: The Political and Economic Origins of Our Time*. Boston, MA: Beacon Press.

La Porta, Rafael, Florencio Lopez-de-Silanes, Andrei Shleifer, and Robert W. Vishny. 1998. Law and Finance. *Journal of Political Economy* 106 (6): 1113–1155.

La Porta, Rafael, et al. 2002. Investor Protection and Corporate Governance: Origins, Consequences, Reform. *Journal of Financial Economics* 58 (1–2): 3–27.

Posner, Elliot. 2005. Sources of Institutional Change: The Supranational Origins of Europe's New Stock Markets. *World Politics* 58 (01): 1–40.

———. 2009. *The Origins of Europe's New Stock Markets*. Cambridge, MA: Harvard University Press.

Post, Alison E. 2014. *Foreign and Domestic Investment in Argentina: The Politics of Privatized Infrastructure*. Cambridge University Press.

Preqin. 2017. *The Private Equity Top 100*.

———. 2018. *Preqin Special Report: Asian Private Equity & Venture Capital*.

Price, William Joseph, et al. 2018. *Case Study on the Employee Provident Fund of Malaysia*.

Puente, Ignacio, and Ben Ross Schneider. 2020. Business and Development: How Organization, Ownership and Networks Matter. *Review of International Political Economy*: 1–25.

Puri, Manju, and Rebecca Zarutskie. 2012. On the Life Cycle Dynamics of Venture-Capital- and Non-Venture-Capital-Financed Firms. *The Journal of Finance* 67 (6): 2247–2293.

PWC. 2017. *China Private Equity/Venture Capital 2016 Review and 2017 Outlook.*

———. 2020. *Beyond Their Borders: Evolution of Foreign Investments by Pension Funds.*

Rajan, Raghuram G., and Luigi Zingales. 1998. Financial Dependence and Growth. *The American Economic Review* 88: 559–586.

———. 2003. The Great Reversals: The Politics of Financial Development in the Twentieth Century. *Journal of Financial Economics* 69 (1): 5–50.

Remes, Jaana, et al. 2019. *Latin America's Missing Middle.*

Da Rin, Marco, and Ludovic Phalippou. 2017. The Importance of Size in Private Equity: Evidence from a Survey of Limited Partners. *Journal of Financial Intermediation* 31: 64–76.

Da Rin, Marco, Thomas Hellmann, and Manju Puri. 2013. A Survey of Venture Capital Research. In *Handbook of the Economics of Finance*, 573–648. Amsterdam: Elsevier B.V.

Da Rin, Marco, Giovanna Nicodano, and Alessandro Sembenelli. 2006. Public Policy and the Creation of Active Venture Capital Markets. *Journal of Public Economics* 90 (8–9): 1699–1723.

Rivas, Gonzalo. 2012. *La Experiencia de Corfo y La Transformación Productiva de Chile.*

Rodríguez Guzmán, Guillermo, Juan Carlos Elorza, and Diana Mejia. 2015. *Private Equity y Venture Capital En America Latina.*

Rodrik, Dani. 2004. Industrial Policy for the Twenty-First Century.

Roe, Mark J. 2003. *Political Determinants of Corporate Governance: Political Context, Corporate Impact*. Oxford: Oxford University Press.

Roe, Mark J., and Jordan I. Siegel. 2009. Finance and Politics: A Review Essay. *Journal of Economic Literature* 47 (3): 781–800.

———. 2011. Political Instability: Effects on Financial Development, Roots in the Severity of Economic Inequality. *Journal of Comparative Economics* 39 (3): 279–309.

Roe, Mark J., and Massimiliano Vatiero. 2015. Corporate Governance and Its Political Economy. In *Oxford Handbook of Corporate Governance*, ed. Jeffrey N. Gordon and Wolf-Georg Ringe. New York: Oxford University Press.

Roland Berger, IEF, and BVK. 2018. *Venture Capital. Fueling Innovation and Economic Growth.*

Sabel, Charles F., et al. 2012. *Export Pioneers in Latin America*. Washington, DC: Inter-American Development Bank.

Salvaj, Erica, and Juan Pablo Couyoumdjian. 2016. 'Interlocked' Business Groups and the State in Chile (1970–2010). *Business History* 58 (1): 129–148.

Samila, Sampsa, and Olav Sorenson. 2011. Venture Capital, Entrepreneurship, and Economic Growth. *Review of Economics and Statistics* 93 (1): 338–349.

Sanderson, Henry, and Michael Forsythe. 2012. *China's Superbank: Debt, Oil and Influence—How China Development Bank Is Rewriting the Rules of Finance*. Singapore: Wiley-Bloomberg Press.

Scharfstein, David. 2018. Presidential Address: Pension Policy and the Financial System. *The Journal of Finance* 73 (4): 1463–1512.

Schmukler, Sergio L., Juan Carlos Gozzi, and Augusto De la Torre. 2007. Capital Market Development: Whither Latin America?

Schneider, Ben Ross. 2004. *Business Politics and the State in Twentieth-Century Latin America*. Cambridge University Press.

———. 2008. Economic Liberalization and Corporate Governance: The Resilience of Business Groups in Latin America. *Comparative Politics* 40: 379–397.

———. 2009. A Comparative Political Economy of Diversified Business Groups, or How States Organize Big Business. *Review of International Political Economy* 16: 178–201.

———. 2013. *Hierarchical Capitalism in Latin America: Business, Labor, and the Challenges of Equitable Development*. Cambridge: Cambridge University Press.

———. 2014. Studying Political Economy in Latin America: Gaps and Methods. *Latin American Politics and Society* 56: 20–23.

———. 2015. *Designing Industrial Policy in Latin America: Business-State Relations and the New Developmentalism*. New York: Palgrave Macmillan US.

Schrank, Andrew. 2007. Asian Industrialization in Latin American Perspective: The Limits to Institutional Analysis. *Latin American Politics and Society* 49 (2): 183–200.

Settel, Daniel, Abu Chowdhury, and Ryan Orr. 2009. The Rise of MDFI Investments in Private Equity Funds. *The Journal of Private Equity Spring* 200: 60–76.

Shirley, Mary M. 2005. Institutions and Development. In *Handbook of New Economic Institutionalism*, ed. Mary M. Shirley and Claude Menard. Boston: Springer.

Sierra, Jazmin. 2017. *Global Champions Are Made At Home: The Brazilian Development Bank and Domestic MNCs*.

Simison, Emilia. 2019. *Democracies, Dictatorships, and Policy Change*.

Stallings, Barbara, and Rogelio Studart. 2006. *Finance for Development: Latin America in Comparative Perspective*. Washington, DC: Brookings Institutions Press.

Storm, Servaas. 2018. Financialization and Economic Development: A Debate on the Social Efficiency of Modern Finance. *Development and Change* 49 (2): 302–329.

Stulz, René M., and Rohan Williamson. 2003. Culture, Openness, and Finance. *Journal of Financial Economics* 70 (3): 313–349.

Taylor, March Zachary. 2016. *The Politics of Innovation: Why Some Countries Are Better than Others in Science & Technology*. New York: Oxford University Press.

Di Tella, Rafael, Juan Dubra, and Alejandro Luis Lagomarsino. 2016. *Meet the Oligarchs: Business Legitimacy, State Capacity and Taxation*. Cambridge, MA.

Torres, Ernani, and Rodrigo Zeidan. 2016. The Life-Cycle of National Development Banks: The Experience of Brazil's BNDES. *The Quarterly Review of Economics and Finance* 62: 97–104.

United States Senate. 1977. Incentives for Economic Growth, Hearings Before the Subcommittee on Taxation and Debt Management Generally of the Committee on Finance.

Viveiros, Ricardo. 2017. *ABVCAP: A Força Da Indústria de Participações No Desenvolvimento Do Brasil*. Sao Paolo: AzulSol Editora.

Wang, Yuhua. 2015. *Tying the Autocrat's Hands: The Rise of the Rule of Law in China*. New York: Cambridge University Press.

Wellhausen, Rachel L. 2014. *The Shield of Nationality*. New York: Cambridge University Press.

Weyland, Kurt. 2005. Theories of Policy Diffusion Lessons from Latin American Pension Reform. *World Politics* 57 (2): 262–295.

Wilhelmus, Jakob, and Willian Lee. 2019. *Private Equity IPOs. Generating Faster Job Growth and More Investment*.

Woo-Cumings, Meredith. 1991. *Race to the Swift: State and Finance in Korean Industrialization*. New York: Columbia University Press.

World Bank. 1996. *Investment Funds in Emerging Markets*. Washington, DC.

———. 2017. *The Evolution of the Canadian Pension Model: Practical Lessons for Building World-Class Pension Organizations*.

Yadav, Vineeta, and Bumba Mukherjee. 2016. *The Politics of Corruption in Dictatorships*. Cambridge: Cambridge University Press.

Yang, Benhua. 2011. Does Democracy Foster Financial Development? An Empirical Analysis. *Economics Letters* 112 (3): 262–265.

Yeyati, Eduardo Levy, Alejandro Micco, and Ugo Panizza. 2007. A Reappraisal of State-Owned Banks. *Economía* 7: 209–259.

Yong, Kwek Ping. 2012. *Private Equity in China: Challenges and Opportunities*. Wiley.

Young, Michael N., et al. 2008. Corporate Governance in Emerging Economies: A Review of the Principal-Principal Perspective. *Journal of Management Studies* 45 (1): 196–220.

Zysman, John. 1983. *Governments, Markets and Growth: Financial Systems and the Politics of Industrial Change*. Ithaca: Cornell University Press.

Index

I. Puente, *Private Equity and Financial Development in Latin America*, Latin American Political Economy,
https://doi.org/10.1007/978-3-030-88983-8

The manufacturer's authorised representative in the EU is Springer
Nature Customer Service Centre GmbH, Europaplatz 3, 69115 Heidelberg,
Germany. If you have any concerns regarding our products, please
contact ProductSafety@springernature.com

Printed and bound by CPI Group (UK) Ltd, Croydon, CR0 4YY
30/09/2026
02225499-0010